BERLITZ®

DISCOVER
SWITZERLAND

Edited and Designed by
D & N Publishing,
Lambourn, Berkshire.

Cartography by
Hardlines, Charlbury, Oxfordshire.

All photographs by the author except:
page 59 (top and bottom), Paul Sterry,
Nature Photographers Ltd.

Cover photographs by the author:

Phototypeset by Wyvern Typesetting,
Bristol.

Printed in the USA by Ringier
America, New York.

*Although we have made every effort to
ensure the accuracy of all the information in this book, changes occur
incessantly. We cannot therefore take
responsibility for facts, addresses and
circumstances in general that are constantly subject to alteration.*

Acknowledgements

The author would like to thank the
following people for their helpful assistance during his research for this
book: Heidi Reisz at the Swiss National Tourist Office in London, and
Leslie Ralph at Swissair. In addition,
he is grateful to the staff at the local
tourist offices in Basel, Interlaken,
Lugano, Verbier, Bern and Zurich.

 The Berlitz tick is used to
indicate places or events of
particular interest.

BERLITZ®

DISCOVER
SWITZERLAND

Neil Ray

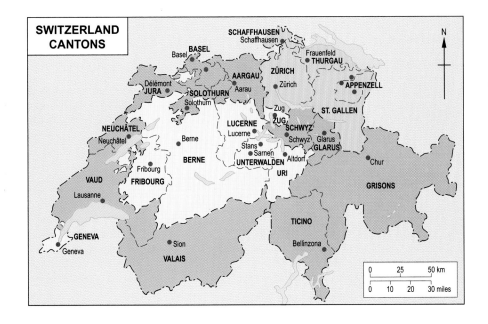

Contents

From the Appenzell to the Jungfrau, Switzerland is a Superb Destination

At the very centre of Europe, Switzerland attracts visitors from all corners of the globe: business people, diplomats, skiers, walkers and mountain gazers congregate here throughout the year. Each have their preconceptions of what the country is about, but is there more to this mountainous country than watches, banks and chocolate?

It can offer peace and quiet, or a week of crazy stunts on the mountains. The choice is endless, with the added benefit of the best tourist organization in the world.

Everyone has their own ideas on Switzerland: it is expensive, lacking in character, it is mountainous, they have nice cows and they produce some of the best chocolate and the most expensive watches around. These are the preconceptions of a country which is so full of anomalies that it is difficult to say with certainty what Switzerland *is*. It's a country so diverse in charac-ter, landscape and language that it seems unfair to categorize it, as much as it would be to say similar things about America or Australia. What is peculiar about Switzerland is that it is all these things, and more, but they are packed into an area a fraction the size of most countries. Its people, probably because of the country's size, have become fiercely defensive, and in my travels throughout the country, the vast majority of the people I have met have been self-critical, but supportive of their nation.

Switzerland remains outside the European Community (EC), confident of its ability to look after its own affairs. Switzerland will not change its ways because of other nations, leaving visitors to the country, even other

The summit of Mt Fort, near Verbier. From here you can explore the four valleys of Bagnes, on skis, cable car or by foot.

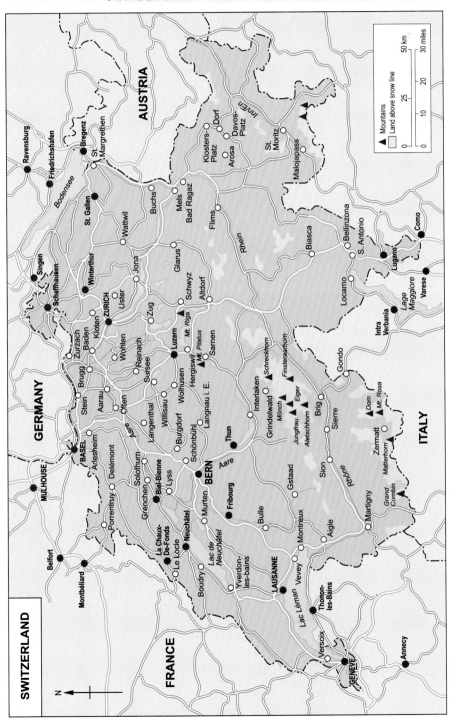

Europeans, still needing their travel documents. The country is less expensive than it used to be, and this will be confirmed in later pages. There are parts of Switzerland that are seriously businesslike, as there are in most countries. There are also parts which have all the character of neighbouring France and Italy. Despite the country having been used as an international thoroughfare for 50 years, the scenery remains outstanding, From the rolling hills of the Appenzell to the icy peaks of the Matterhorn and Jungfrau, Switzerland is an outstanding holiday destination. But there is more to this country, and some of its less-known aspects are featured in this book: Basel's three-day non-stop festival; the open-air parliament in the mountains; and horse racing on ice are some of the events that point to a country that not only makes the finest watches, but also has a new image to portray. But it still has very nice cows!

Getting There

Situated almost in the very heart of Europe, Switzerland is serviced by just about every form of transport. This, despite the jokes about the Swiss Navy, includes arriving in the country by boat.

By Air
The options for air travel are based mainly around Zurich and Geneva.

From Britain
Swissair   London Heathrow to Zurich, Geneva and Basel; Manchester to Geneva and Zurich; Birmingham to Zurich; Bristol to Zurich (Crossair).
British Airways   London Heathrow to Zurich, Geneva and Basel.
Dan Air   London Gatwick to Zurich and Bern.

*G*eneral map of Switzerland (opposite).

A view down into the Lauterbrunnen Valley, where the river, the road and the railway follow the same course (right).

The Swissair and British Airways flights operate every day, with up to 10 departures in each direction on each day. Dan Air's service to Bern is less frequent, with flights on Monday, Wednesday, Friday, Saturday and Sunday. Their service to Zurich is daily.

Other European Cities

Flights from other European cities are operated by Swissair and the respective national airlines, with regular flights into Zurich and/or Geneva from:

Amsterdam, Brussels, Paris, Turin, Rome, Venice, Berlin, Cologne/Bonn, Munich, Stuttgart, Frankfurt, Dusseldorf, Copenhagen, Stockholm, Oslo, Helsinki, Warsaw, Vienna, Prague, Zagreb, Budapest, Belgrade, Bucharest, Sofia, Istanbul, Athens, Salonika, Malta, Barcelona, Valencia, Malaga, Madrid, Bilbao, Lisbon and Oporto.

In addition, smaller European cities are covered by Switzerland's internal air system *Crossair*, which also operates a network of routes between the major cities in Switzerland (including Lugano). Their international routes include:

Luxembourg, Strasbourg, Bremen, Munster/Osnabruck, Nurnberg, Linz, Graz, Klagenfurt, Innsbruck, Ljubljana, Florence, Genova, Nice, Marseilles, Lyons and Bordeaux, Jersey and Guernsey.

Detailed information is available from the Swiss National Tourist Offices, or from Crossair at:

Crossair
CH-4030 Basel-Flughafen, Basel.
Tel: (061) 325 25 25
Fax: (061) 325 32 68.

Further Afield

There are regular transcontinental flights, mainly into Zurich.

From the USA Anchorage, Atlanta, Boston, Chicago, Denver (via Chicago), Detroit (via Boston), Houston (via Atlanta), Los Angeles, Miami (via Boston or Atlanta), New York, Philadelphia, San Francisco (via Chicago), Washington (via Boston).

From Canada Montreal, Toronto, Vancouver (via Toronto or Los Angeles).

From South America Buenos Aires, Caracas, Mexico City (via New York or Atlanta), Rio de Janeiro, Santiago de Chile (via Rio or Buenos Aires), Sao Paulo.

From Australia and the Far East Bangkok, Beijing, Bombay, Hong Kong, Jakarta, Karachi, Singapore, Seoul, Sydney (via Bangkok), Tokyo.

Airports

The airports at Zurich and Geneva are some of the best designed and "user friendly" in the world. No clamouring through crowds of arrival and departure passengers here; no stumbling over luggage with the probability of having a trolley bashed into your heel.

Zurich

The local underground and the national network trains are below the airport terminals. There are two sets of elevators to go down to reach the platforms, with the ticket offices situated at the first level. The left luggage lockers are on this level—called the Airport Plaza—as well as police and banks. Also at this level are shops including a pharmacy, grocer's, photographic

supplies, sports goods and a bakery. You can take your luggage trolley on the elevator, and although at first it would seem that your bags are about to board the train before you, the cleverly designed system *does* work. If you are in doubt there are illustrated boards alongside the elevators to show you how they operate.

Geneva

Geneva is equally straightforward, but here the rail system is next to the terminal. It is a smaller airport than Zurich, so you can come straight out into the arrivals hall, turn left past the car hire counters, and carry straight on to the automatic doors. You are then in the railway station and the ticket offices are on the same level (right-hand side). The platforms are down one flight of escalators.

Oberried on the shores of Brienzer See. The narrow promenade is bedecked with flowers in summer, and it is from here that many of the lake fishermen work.

Bern

This must be the only capital city in the world with the country's smallest airport. Belp, the airport for Bern, is everything that Geneva and Zurich are not, which can be an advantage. Quite why Belp has never been developed as a large international airport is something of a mystery, but, since it has not yet been selected for greater things, it is hardly likely to change now.

Dan Air operate a twice-weekly service from Gatwick to Belp. If your destination is Interlaken, or any of the central Swiss towns, then this service is very useful. It is also good to have an alternative to the bigger airlines, who will use only the larger airports. There are no lengthy walks from satellite gates to baggage reclaims where you have to wait at least ten minutes. At Belp a 50 m conversion walk across the tarmac takes you to a rather temporary-looking building to collect your bags: this building also houses the passport control and customs. There is a strong possibility that the same person does all three jobs.

The major car hire firms have representatives at the airport, but they usually come in from their downtown offices. If no one is there, you can use the free telephones to contact them. The car will be brought out to the airport for you.

If you are using public transport, maybe using your Swiss Pass, then the bus outside takes you directly to the railway station at the centre of Bern. From here, you are at the very heart of the Swiss rail network. For those going to Interlaken there is a direct coach link which meets the Dan Air flights, taking about an hour to reach the resort.

Departure from Belp is an equally leisurely affair, and the only choice you need to make is whether you leave from gate one or two. The ancient custom of baggage identification is unlikely at Bern, due mainly to its low level of traffic, but it is sometimes necessary even here. Crossair also use Bern a lot for their connections to the other major cities of the country, and if time were a problem, and your budget allowed for such a luxury, then you could connect up with a Crossair flight to Lugano.

Car Hire

All the car hire firms are represented at all of the major airports, so if you are travelling using a hire car the airport is the best place to collect it. Some hire firms will collect a car from a different departure point, but this is usually quite expensive.

Internal Flights

Air travel within Switzerland is using Crossair. It is hardly worth the expense of flying in such a small country, but routes such as Basel to Lugano are useful if you are really short of time. Also, by travelling in this way you treat yourself to a dramatic view of the Alps from a 34-seat Saab aircraft.

By Rail

Due to its position in Europe, rail travel to Switzerland is full of choices. Travellers coming from any of the other European countries can find a train from the major cities. Visitors from Britain favour the Calais and Paris routes, but direct connections can be made from Amsterdam, Ostend and Hamburg. Many trains to Switzerland are actually going on to Eastern European countries, such as Hungary and Yugoslavia, as well as Italy and Austria.

The days of Europe's rich and famous boarding the Simplon Express for Zurich and Istanbul are long gone, but there is still a certain magic about being on a platform waiting for a train which has come from Vienna and is on its way to Paris. If the traditions of luxury rail travel appeal you could take the Trans-Europe Express trains (TEE), which are first class only, with a supplement payable on top. TEE trains to Switzerland are *The Rheingold* (Amsterdam to Basel) and *The Gottardo* (Zurich to Milan).

Many of the other fast European routes are now intercity, with both first and second class. They offer connections from:

Calais to Basel (11 hours overnight);
Paris to Zurich (9 hours overnight);
Amsterdam to Basel (9 hours);
Ostend to Basel (12 hours);
Hamburg to Basel and Geneva (12 hours).

For many train enthusiasts Switzerland, and Basel in particular, is a crossroads of activity, but for the traveller who is intent on using the rail system just to get there the best route is very much the SNCF-operated Paris to Lausanne and Geneva route. These are the fast TGV trains linking Paris directly with central Europe.

Example Journey Times

Leaving Paris Lyon at 12.25p.m. will get you into Lausanne at 4.06p.m. (*The Cisalpin* TGV23), or leaving Paris Lyon at 10.36p.m., you can be in Geneva at 2.05p.m. (*The Voltaire* TGV 923). The midday trains are the best to use, since there is a supplement payable on the early departures, but there are five departures a day to both Lausanne and Geneva from around 7.00a.m. to 6.00p.m. On board there is buffet catering and, in first class, a restaurant. These trains may not be decorated with chintz curtains and mahogany, relying more on modern plastics, but they are fast, and the idea of being in Switzerland within four hours of leaving Paris is impressive.

Generally, the European rail network works like clockwork, despite using rolling stock from many different countries, so if the time factor is not that important and you want to see something of Europe, the train is a good way to go. In terms of cost there is little to choose between air and rail, but of the two rail is probably the more relaxing.

By Road

The routes by road into Switzerland follow the same passes as the rail system, except for a few very minor country lanes. Coming from Britain the best way is across France from Calais or Boulogne although this is also the most expensive because of the French motorway tolls. Dunkerque (from Ramsgate) is another possibility, going on to Lille and Liège, to then travel down the Rhine motorway through Boppard (beautiful in summer), and into Switzerland at Basel.

For motorists coming to Switzerland, apart from the usual documents necessary for European travel you will also need to buy a Swiss road tax disc. The cost is 30 SFr, and you can either buy it in advance at a Swiss tourist office, or at a border control point. The Swiss frontier guards are quite keen, so they will ask you questions about your luggage etc. Once in Switzerland the roads vary between good fast motorways, especially between the major cities (Zurich, Basel, Bern and Geneva), and mountain roads which need some careful driving. It is as well to ensure that if you are planning to arrive at a high mountain resort (such as Verbier or Crans Montana) late in the evening you are not too tired to

negotiate the likely hairpin bends on the road to the village. Plan your trip so that you arrive, either after a rest or the next day. What may appear on the map as an 8 km (5 miles) drive can also mean a 2,000 m (7,000 ft) climb through 14 hairpins—not something you want to try in the dark after a 14-hour journey. In the winter, fewer people travel to Switzerland by car, but if you are taking a skiing holiday using you own car, you will certainly have to fit it out with snow chains or studded tyres for the last leg of your journey.

Ferries and the Channel Tunnel
Currently the only way to take your car over to mainland Europe from Britain is by way of the ferries operated by the likes of P&O, Sealink, Sally Line and Hoverspeed. The biggest drawback to this is the time it takes, not only on the ship but also in getting your car on and off at the terminals. The opening of the Channel Tunnel in 1993 may well see the change that many travellers have been looking for. The terminal at the English side will be at Folkestone, and you will emerge in France at Coquelles, not far from Calais. Car drivers and their passengers will drive straight onto a "shuttle" train after going through toll, frontier and security checks. The traveller is then free to drive straight out onto the roads of either France or England. You will have to stay in your vehicle for the duration of the trip,

which will be, platform to platform, about 35 minutes. Motorcyclists will have lounges to sit in, and each shuttle wagon will have its own toilet facilities. The real bonus will be in the speed of the operation which will eliminate the need for reservations, delays, queues and cancellations. Operating every 15 minutes, 24 hours a day will be a great benefit to those who don't enjoy the sea breezes of the English Channel. For those that do, and regard sailing to France as part of the holiday, undoubtedly the various operators will be trying hard to keep that custom.

Some ideas of the distances involved in a drive to Switzerland are:

Calais–Geneva   734 km (456 miles);
Dunkerque–Basel   833 km (518 miles);
Ostend–Basel   714 km (444 miles).

By Boat
The final route into Switzerland can be made using the mighty Rhine. Many people are surprised to find that Switzerland has as much water, and as many vessels, as most countries. With its many lakes and rivers it has a substantial number of ferries and pleasure boats, but the only actual city-to-city service operates from Rotterdam and Amsterdam, through Germany to Basel. The service runs from April to October, and is ideal for people who want to see Europe at a leisurely pace. Passengers booking a trip straight through will have priority over those using only a portion of the service, but if you are going to Switzerland by boat, the chances are that you will want to see all of the sights. The voyage takes six days from Rotterdam,

The Bagnes Valley and Le Châble. It is from this town that the cable car to Verbier operates.

A bridge across the mighty Rhine, near Schaffhausen, before it runs into the Bodensee.

calling at Dusseldorf, Cologne, Koblenz, Strasbourg and Basel. The Amsterdam route uses a bus service to the embarkation point at Nijmegen, and this trip takes five days.

Getting Around

By Road

Although it is a small country, journeys in Switzerland can take longer than expected, especially by road. Mountain passes such as the Furka, 2,431 m (7,975 ft) or the Simplon,

2,005 m (6,578 ft), add many an hour to a journey.

By the time you have stopped half a dozen times to take in the view, visited the glaciers and had a coffee in the ubiquitous Swiss mountain hotel, a day has gone by. This in itself is not a bad thing, but if you are planning to race across Switzerland from side-to side-and top-to-bottom then you may be in for a longer stay than you had anticipated.

Car Hire

If you choose to hire a car in Switzerland you will have the obvious advantage of driving on the left side of the car—something which can be quite handy when going up the mountain roads.

The major car hire companies have offices in the airports and the cities:

Avis Basel, Bern, Geneva, Zurich, Lugano, Lausanne;
Budget Basel, Bern, Geneva, Zurich, Lugano, Lausanne, Lucerne, Montreux;
Eurorent Basel, Zurich;
Europcar Basel, Geneva, Zurich, Lugano, Lausanne;
Hertz Basel, Bern, Geneva, Zurich, Lugano, Lausanne.

The roads of Switzerland offer stunningly beautiful tours, through some of the finest scenery in Europe. There are few places where the engineering brilliance of the Swiss has not been able to put a road or a railway track, so in summer you can spend your entire holiday visiting small villages high in the mountains or valleys tucked away in the heart of the Alps.

Because of this ability to run a pass over, or build a tunnel through, a mountain, Switzerland is an ideal

country to make three- or four-day motoring tours.

A Few Suggested Routes

Starting in **Bern** take the N12 to **Fribourg** and then on to **Gruyères**, where the famous cheese is made. On then to **Chateau D'oex** and **Gstaad**, and south to **Martigny** and **Sion**. In this region you can go to many of the high mountain villages, such as **Nandez, Crans, Zermatt** and **Saas Fee**.

If you wanted to take a short cut to **Interlaken**, there is a car-rail service over the **Lotschenpass** from **Steg** to **Kandersteg**. This service also stops just

The long and winding road up into Verbier. It's only 8 km (5 miles) but it takes in more than a dozen hairpin bends and rises 670 m—over 2,000 ft.

a few kilometres from Steg at **Goppenstein**, where a road runs into the **Lötschental Valley**, one of the most remote valleys of Europe. Surrounded by glaciers, this valley saw its first motor traffic as late as 1950. (More detailed information about Lötschental is given on page 220). The main tour continues over the **Furka Pass** and the **Susten Pass** to **Interlaken**, alongside the **Thuner See**, through **Thun** and back to Bern.

Other interesting motor tours can be made from **Basel** through the **Jura mountains**, taking in **La Chaux de Fonds**, **Neuchâtel**, the **Joux Valley**, **Lausanne**, **Geneva**, **Montreux**, and back to Basel via **Estavayer**, **Murten** and **Solothurn**.

From **Zurich**, another tour goes north to **Schaffhausen**, along the Rhine to **Stein am Rhein** and south to **St Gallen**. Carrying on south through the **Appenzell** district and **Liechtenstein**, and then west to **Lucerne**. Around Lake Lucerne to **Zug** and then back up to Zurich.

The fourth and most southerly tour goes from **Chur** and takes in **Dabs** and the **Grison** area. On this trip you will pass through **St Moritz**, see the Italian lakes at **Lugano** and **Locarno**, and travel over the **St Gothard Pass**, to turn east again along the **Disentis** valley, **Flims** and back to Chur.

Each of the tours mentioned above takes in a particular influence of Switzerland (Italian, French, or German), although you will never be in any doubt as to the fact that you are in Switzerland. This is a country in which you can sample the finest Italian pizzas one day and the best French croissants the next.

By Rail

Driving around Switzerland is interesting and exciting, but where there is a road, there is nearly always a rail line. The Swiss have made rail travel something of an art, and one of the most astonishing aspects of the network is its age. It not only looks brand new, but the trains operating are so smooth that you cannot believe that the tracks were often laid at the beginning of the century.

In Switzerland you will benefit from the best rail network in the world, travelling on clean trains which run on time. The old cliché of setting your watch by the Swiss train departure is still largely true: if you arrive one minute early you will have to wait; if you're one minute late look for another form of transport! It is encouraging to see, however, that even the famous Swiss rail system can be tied in knots. When about 2,000 flag-waving schoolchildren descended on Lucerne's otherwise orderly platforms, I witnessed the absolute horror on the faces of station staff desperately trying to despatch trains on schedule and failing miserably. Cheers and applause rang out around the station as engines departed with their chaotic loads up to 20 minutes late.

The Swiss Pass

To get the best out of the rail system in Switzerland a Swiss Pass is essential. It has to be purchased outside Switzerland, and is available in all other European countries. With this pass you can use all the SBB (state-run) trains, get discounts on the privately operated trains, and travel on the urban tram and bus services of most cities, lake steamers and post-bus services. The private rail systems are usually on the mountain routes such as Interlaken to Jungfrau, and Montreux to Gstaad. Many visitors to Switzerland are disappointed to find that their Swiss Pass is not valid for many of these routes, so it's worth checking a detailed map of the country which will give you all the valid routes, and finding out which private lines offer discounts etc. This map is included with the pass. You should sign the pass and write your passport number in it. Passes are available for 8-, 15- and 30-day periods. As a holder of this pass, the country is yours to

explore. Leave the train where you choose. You can make a detailed plan of exactly where you want to stop or you can make it up as you go along. Apart from the bigger cities, and that really only totals four, most of the towns and villages can be easily explored from the railway station.

The Swiss Pass is excellent, but you may find a tendency to ensure you get your money's worth out of it. The fact that you can go anywhere by any route may mean you spend a holiday in a railway carriage, eating ham rolls, and gazing at the scenery over the top of your latest timetable. To use the service to see the country is the idea, so perhaps the alternative—the **Swiss Flexi Pass**—is better. This gives you a choice of travel on any three days in a frame of 15. It is less expensive than the unlimited version, and gives you the opportunity to have a few days out to see a city or another side of Switzerland, so that you don't spend a lot of your valuable time standing on railway platforms.

Special Deals
There is a multitude of special deals, not so much on individual fares but more on block arrangements. There are day cards, half-fare cards, transfer tickets (for your onward journey from an airport), family tickets and regional passes. The Swiss National Tourist

Le Châble is a typical smart railway station. The connections go from here up to Verbier and through the valley to Martigny.

Office produces a booklet called *Travel Tips in Switzerland* which is updated each year and will give you the latest fares. On the high mountain railways, which can be very expensive for a single trip, you can often find deals or round trips which include the cost of the mountain train, saving quite a lot.

Railway Information

The Swiss produce a phenomenal amount of information regarding rail routes, connections and times. In each station you will find booklets which will give you most of the main services from that station. The smaller regional train services are shown in a light script while the main city-to-city routes are in bold. On the intercity trains there is usually a mini-bar, and if you travel first class (not too expensive on a rail pass), there may well be a restaurant car. Sadly, many of the journey times are too short to enjoy the delights of eating your lunch as the train meanders through the Alpine scenery.

Where the system becomes complicated is in the crossover from state trains to private lines, but only in the matter of buying tickets. The two

merge into one large system, and you can only admire the operation as trains from various companies nestle into the timetable of the national network, making even the most remote mountain villages accessible. The areas of complication appear on mountains such as the Jungfrau, where part of the journey can be made on the Swiss Pass, while the rest comes into a discounted private system—more information is included in the section on Interlaken.

Luggage

A final point on the rail system relates to that dreadful luggage you inevitably have to carry around with you, which is an even less attractive proposition on the homeward journey. If you don't mind paying—it costs around 10 SFr per item—the rail or bus service will take your luggage through to your departure airport, where it will be checked through to your final destination. In other words you can leave your resort—say Verbier—and spend a day in Geneva before leaving for London, without having to do battle with either your bags or a stubborn left-luggage locker. There are some security questions at the airport, and they will check with the baggage controllers that your luggage is going through, but the advantage is that the next time you will see your luggage will be at the carousel in London. It's well worth it!

The Post Bus

Where the train cannot take you the bus will. The yellow buses with the horn emblem on the side service the villages not reached by rail, and are fully integrated into the rail network timetables. (The Swiss Pass and its relatives can be used on the post-bus services as well.) The system works with uncanny accuracy, making a journey by rail and bus a leisurely affair. The main point to watch is the times of the last buses, which can often be quite early, especially if their route is to one of the high mountain villages.

By Boat

The last piece of the travel system jigsaw in Switzerland is the boat. On lakes such as Lucerne the choice between a train journey, a bus journey or a trip over the lake is easy. The lake steamers are relaxing, the views are superb and you will reach a village on the opposite shores just as quickly as by train or bus. Steamers operate on Lac Léman (Geneva), Lucerne, Neuchâtel, Interlaken, Zürichsee, Bodensee, and the Italian lakes from Locarno and Lugano. There can be no doubting the value of these services to the local people who use them as an integral part of the network. However, on some of the lakes—the Thuner See at Interlaken for instance—many of the sailings only operate in the summer, so it is as well to check with the information office before planning a trip.

At Ouchy landing stage, the old paddle steamers are constantly coming and going en route to Geneva and Montreaux.

Walking and Cycling

For many visitors, Switzerland is a place where you leave your home comforts behind—the car or the train are not required—for this is a walker's country and more recently a cyclist's. Cyclists have always come to Switzerland but the upsurge in popularity of the mountain bike has meant more cyclists visit every year. Add to this the fact that cycles of several types can be hired at any railway station and you have a very popular way of travelling in Switzerland.

Walking can be quite easy three- or four-hour strolls or day-long, fairly strenuous affairs to the base of great mountains. Paths and signposts are

*T*he smaller
wanderweg *signs give time and distance, but this type are pointers to the cable cars and skiing routes (above).*

*M*ain footpaths of the *Valais region (opposite).*

very clearly marked with bright yellow pointers, and the estimated time for each walk given. Remember, however, that these are for Swiss walkers, who

22

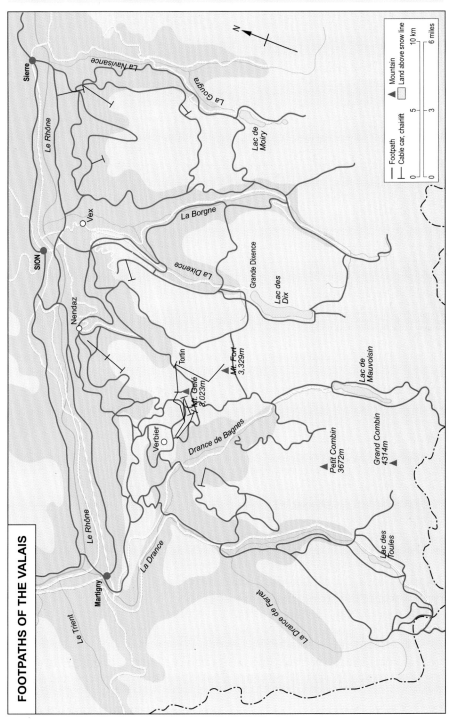

FOOTPATHS OF THE VALAIS

probably don't stop much to admire the view, so if your time doesn't match the one given on the signpost, don't worry. They do give you an opportunity to decide whether you care to walk for that length of time, or indeed if you feel fit enough.

Precautions

Walking and cycling through Alpine countryside is one of the delights still left in the world today. The air is pure, it's usually quiet, and on the higher routes it is still possible to get that "away from it all" feeling. However, you should remember that the Alps are high mountains, so sunglasses and a good sun screen should go with you, as well as a variety of clothing to cover those areas which may suffer from excess exposure to the sun. The weather in the mountains can change very rapidly, so if you plan a long walk let someone know where you are going. All precautions should be observed when walking in potentially dangerous areas, like around glaciers or on ridges.

Finally, it is an offence to collect rare Alpine flowers, so it is best to simply admire the beauty of such things without disturbing them, and the same goes for other forms of wildlife The saying in the mountains is "Bring only yourselves, take only photographs, leave only footprints".

Details of walks can be found in later chapters, but going your own way is what Swiss Alpine walking is all about, and there are hundreds of kilometres of walking country. Most tourist offices can supply walking and cycling maps, so at the first opportunity buy one—the Swiss countryside is then yours to explore.

When to Go

Switzerland is a country for all seasons, summer offering the beauty of lakes and mountains, walking, cycling, sailing, swimming and all manner of summer sports. Winter in Switzerland is still regarded as the ideal in terms of ski facilities, weather and scenery. In between, the spring and autumn, although quieter, give something of a taste of winter and summer. More often than not the mountains are still well covered with the winter snow in May, and in October the warmth of summer is still there.

Many winter resorts, however, do use the June period to carry out maintenance work on equipment such as lift systems and swimming pools. It is important to check with the information office if you travel in Switzerland at this time of the year, especially if you have set your sights on a day trip to one of the high peaks.

The busiest summer months are July to September, with February and March the favourite times in the winter season, although the less expensive January is also popular, if a little colder. Whichever season you choose to go, there will be plenty to see and do, mainly because the Swiss are possibly the most well-organized nation in the world when it comes to catering for visitors.

Accommodation

Despite having a reputation for being very expensive, Switzerland can provide just as wide a range of facilities as any other country. If you want to pay a lot of money, it's easy; there are hotels in this country which are the envy of the world. Some of the greatest chefs of recent times have been Swiss, and their catering prowess is well known. But there is a good choice of accommodation and, with the exception of a few major cities, reasonably priced accommodation can be found without difficulty. There are good sites for camping and caravanning, and more recently the Farmers' Association have got together to form a farmhouse accommodation list. Possibly the most popular way of staying in Switzerland, especially in the winter, is to hire a chalet, and there is an abundance of types and sizes of these available. One company which specializes in self-catering accommodation is:

Interhome
383 Richmond Road
Twickenham
Middlesex
TW1 2EF
Tel: 081 891 1294.

The red shuttered chalets of Switzerland are world famous and this one near Vers l'Eglise is typical, with a good stockpile of wood for the winter.

Their lists for Switzerland are good, since they are a Swiss company. They are also efficient, and you will get a good quality apartment or chalet from them. Early booking is advised though, because you are competing for accommodation with visitors from all over Europe.

Hotels

The hotels in Switzerland, no matter what the price, are clean, sometimes a little spartan, but generally good value for money. In the cities it is a little more difficult to obtain cheaper rooms, but in the country a room (for one or two people) can cost as little as 30 SFr. On a tour of Switzerland it is interesting to see where the dialects of France, Germany and Italy meet. Asking for a room in Switzerland is excellent practice for a course in European languages! Booking in advance is advisable in the busy seasons, but there

are tourist offices in most towns through which you can book accommodation. If the tourist office is closed when you arrive—by an evening train for example—there are telephone lines direct to the hotels at the major stations. There should be signs for the service; at Interlaken it is to the left of platform 1 and in Lucerne it is at the first lower level. The boards show photographs of most of the hotels, and include rates for various rooms, whether accommodation is available, and a telephone number. At the side of the board is a telephone. Nothing could be easier, and it is a pleasure to say that I have yet to see one vandalized.

Farm Holidays

Swiss Farm Holidays is a relatively recent idea, presented by the Swiss Farmers' Association. Switzerland is an agricultural land, not a mass finance house, and it was once known as a nation of farmers. If you want to stay on a real farm and watch or help the farmers at work, then there is a booklet which will give you a list of farms, region by region. Most of the accommodation is in apartments, so you have some independence from the family. The information given in the booklet leaves you in no doubt as to what to expect at your farm. It gives the usual details like price—and this can vary from 20 SFr to 60 SFr per apartment per night—and which facilities are available, but it also gives an idea

Much of Switzerland is agricultural land, a scene which has remained unchanged for centuries.

of the type of animals on the farm, and whether it is suitable for children. Possibly the most useful feature of the booklet is one which can make or break a family holiday: it tells you if there are any other children on the farm, and gives the year of each birth. You can thus work out, say, that there are two children aged six and nine living on the farm.

On the last few pages there are the *Maiensaess*—mountain huts used by

A dairy farm in the centre of Switzerland, between Lucerne and Bern. The farm buildings almost make up a small village of their own.

farmers for the period between spring and summer. These rustic, simple huts are available, again through the Swiss Farmers' Association, at a very low cost—10–40 SFr per night. The altitude of each hut is given, and whether access is possible by car.

Camping and Caravanning

Camping in Switzerland is quite an organized affair. This may put many people off, since the idea of camping is that you are left to find your own way, be adventurous and explore the country without the ties of set accommodation. Having said that, the campsites provided by the Society of Swiss Camping Site Owners are in outstandingly beautiful areas, around lakes and in mountain valleys.

The sites are clean, well run and are graded from simple one-star sites with basic amenities to luxury five-star establishments that offer every facility, especially in the area of sports. This is where many of the lakeside sites excel; you can stay right on the lakeshores, and practise or be taught any number of water-based sports. The book which lists all the sites of the SOSCSO and gives all the details by area is well worth studying. The explanation of symbols is exhaustive: at my last count there were 136 symbols grouped from A–D. It's quite a list, but it does give you absolutely every piece of information imaginable, including the availability of foot baths on site and whether there is a car wash. Is this really camping?

Despite the tendency of some continental sites to veer towards the luxury end of the market, there are enough simple campsites in Switzerland to satisfy most campers. Look for the one-star or non-classified sites if you don't want to be in with the motor-homes and caravans.

For those campers who simply cannot abide the idea of being on a site, there is a possibility of "wild camping", as the Swiss put it. There are regulations as to where you can put up a tent, and if you are in a well-populated area you may have problems. However, each canton treats "wild camping" differently, so check with the local tourist office for information. At the very least, you will have to get the landowner's permission to camp.

If you own a motorhome or caravan, then the bigger sites are for you, and you will probably find none better than the four- and five-star sites of Switzerland.

Each area has its own pamphlet, which ties in with the national guide available from the Swiss National Tourist Office. Each area is numbered, from 1 (the Grisons in eastern Switzerland) to 11 (the Berner Hinterland). If you have a specific area in mind the SNTO will be able to supply a smaller guide to that area. To complete the information package there is a national map which marks out all the campsites in Switzerland—unfortunately, they have chosen a dark purple colour for the sites, so you have to look quite hard to see the tent symbol.

*S*aturday mornings are a favourite time for the open-air markets all over Switzerland.

Youth Hostels

Youth Hostel accommodation in Switzerland is available for visitors up to the age of 25 years. Those over 25 are admitted only if there is room, and all hostellers must hold a valid membership card from their national organization, which will be affiliated to the International Youth Hostelling Federation.

All the major cities have youth hostels, and in the map provided by the SNTO there are 84 listed, in town and country. The useful practical information contained in this map includes the distance from the railway station, and which tram or bus to catch to get to the hostel. As usual the information generally is comprehensive, so the youth hosteller should have no difficulty in finding his or her way round.

The Less Able Visitor

As a mountainous country, you would expect Switzerland to have some difficulty in providing for the disabled visitor. In fact this is not the case, and although difficulties can arise, as in any country, Switzerland does more than most to assist. One of the gratifying points is that those glorious views from the summits of mountains can be enjoyed by anybody. The Swiss have conquered most of the Alpine peaks with a restaurant or a café, with a railway to get you up there, so the problems often encountered by visitors with a disability are minimized. Also, many of the campsites and youth hostels cater for the disabled, as do most of the hotels. The leaflets and brochures from the SNTO all declare their facilities, but if further information is required, then contact RADAR for detailed advice:

RADAR
25 Mortimer Street
London W1N
Tel: 071 637 5400.

Money Matters

Currency

The currency in Switzerland is the Swiss Franc—100 Centimes = 1 SFr. It is probably one of the most stable currencies in the world, and the Swiss monetary system never suffers from many ups and downs. In areas close to the French, Italian and German borders you may find that the currencies of those countries will also be accepted. The coins are 5, 10, 20 centimes and ½, 1, 2 and 5 SFr. The ½ SFr coin is particularly elusive, due to its small size, but it is worth a reasonable amount.

Quite a lot of the telephone boxes only take ½, 1 and 5 SFr pieces.

Credit Cards

All the major cards (Visa, American Express, Diners Card, and Mastercard) are accepted. Most shops will accept these cards, but relatively few garages will take credit cards as payment for petrol, so check before filling up.

Cheques

Travellers cheques in any of the main currencies can be exchanged at the

Swiss Banks

The Swiss bank has something of a reputation, due largely to the excessive imaginations of novelists over the past 30 years. However, unless you are arranging a particularly unusual deal, then the banks of Switzerland are the same as those of any other country. There are a few banks, particularly in the larger cities, which probably would not change your travellers cheques, but then you may not even be allowed through the front door!

Opening Hours: Monday–Friday 8.30a.m. to 6.30p.m.

banks. An alternative is to buy Swiss Bankers Travellers Cheques from a branch of a Swiss bank in your own country or any major bank. These cheques can be exchanged in Switzerland at their face value without any deductions. It is also possible to cash a personal cheque at the larger SBB railway stations using an American Express card. The officials are not that keen on this, since it involves extra paperwork but if you want to use this facility insist, and it will be done.

Security

Compared with many countries, Switzerland has a low crime rate. In the mountain villages you have the feeling of total security, both for your personal belongings and for yourself. However, there have been thefts from hotels and it is in your own interest to have insurance cover, just in case. The Swiss cities are not as idyllic as they were, and like many big towns there are some less than pleasant people around. This is particularly noticeable at events like the Basel *Fasnacht*, which

attracts people from all over Europe, so take care to protect your bags and personal belongings.

Gratuities

Tipping in Switzerland is not really expected. In hotels and restaurants, and even in some taxis and hairdressers, a service charge is added to the bill anyway, so there would seem little point in paying twice.

Health

Switzerland does not have a national health service, and everything in the medical line has to be paid for. It is not a member of the European Community, so any reciprocal arrangements between EC countries will not apply here.

It is an unfortunate fact of life in Switzerland that in the case of an accident your ability to pay will be checked very quickly. This clearly requires you to have good insurance cover, and in the case of winter sports, insurance which covers any skiing accidents. On the positive side, you will be treated to some of the finest health care in Europe, in extremely clean hospitals.

Pharmacists open from 8.00a.m. to 12.00p.m. and from 2.00p.m. to 5.00p.m. Notices of pharmacies open for duty outside normal hours are displayed on the door.

There are no requirements for visitors to have any inoculations or vaccinations if arriving from a country in the western hemisphere.

Travel Documents

Travellers from the UK or any other EC country require only their national passport. The new regulations regarding the travel of EC subjects throughout Europe may not apply to Switzerland since it is not a member of the European Community.

Shops

Notwithstanding a hunt for the Swiss watch and the cuckoo clock, shopping in Switzerland is not as exciting as

*T*he highest ranges of the Alps are still inaccessible, but can often be viewed from a nearby summit, such as this range in the Valais.

many other countries. Imports from the Far East have left few genuine opportunities for tourists to buy souvenirs. However, if you do want a good watch or a cuckoo clock of any size or description, then Switzerland is full of them. Some of the winter sports equipment is quite reasonably priced out of season.

Food and Drink

Restaurants

Due mainly to its geographical position, Switzerland has absorbed many of the culinary delights of its neighbours. You can sample the very best Italian, French and German meals throughout the country, but there is a tendency for the better versions to be close to the respective borders.

Actual Swiss food is rather limited, and the national dish is the cheese fondue. This is made up of Gruyère, Emmental or Vacherin cheese (or a secret mixture of all three), garlic, white wine, spices and kirsch. A good fondue will take all evening to eat, dipping your cubes of bread into the cauldron-like pot. Try not to lose your bread in the pot, since according to Swiss custom you will have to buy a bottle of wine! It is difficult to produce a good fondue, one that doesn't have a sticky layer of cheese at the bottom, so you will find good and bad fondue restaurants. Other less famous Swiss dishes are the Raclette—another cheese-based dish—sausage, *rösti*—tasty potato and sausage fry-up—and *baundner-fleisch*, an air-dried beef from the Grisons region.

Eating out is not particularly cheap in Switzerland, so if all you need is a good solid meal then often hotel restaurants or railway buffets can provide you with one. It is not by chance that most of the railway station buffets are generally quite full at lunchtime—with locals. In the main cities there are the usual fast food and burger outfits which appear with monotonous regularity throughout the world. They are no worse and no better in Switzerland than anywhere else.

If you are after a quick bite to eat, you can sometimes find a stall selling German sausages with mustard. These can make a tasty and warming snack on a winter's day.

It is particularly difficult to resist the delicious Swiss pastries. A portion of gateau, or the world-renowned *apfelstrudel* can cost about 6 or 7 SFr—expensive but worth every centime!

A selection of restaurants in the main towns is given in the information section at the end of the book.

Eating "Out"

The Swiss enjoy a picnic as much as anyone, and on a summer Sunday many families will head up to the mountain pastures for their lunch, followed by a walk. In some areas just off the main paths and near cable car stations you will find tables and benches, and even barbecue stones, ready for your picnic. The ingredients can be found in the local supermarket, and few villages do not have a store of this kind. Although you will probably find the main food shops open on a Saturday in the summer months, some may be closed. It is also worth noting that in the higher villages, fresh meats sell quickly in the morning, so you can often find that by 11.00a.m. there is little left.

Wine

You may like to finish off your meal or picnic with a bottle of Swiss wine. Unlike its German, French and Italian (and Austrian) counterparts, Swiss wine is not very famous; in fact many people are surprised to learn that there

*T*he *midway stations on the cable cars nearly all have their mountain cafés. Winter or summer, it's a pleasure to sit out here, many thousands of feet up the mountain.*

is a wine industry here of any description. The major vineyards are around Lac Léman (Geneva), Lugano, Schaffhausen, and the Valais. White vintages to look out for are Lavaux, Dezaley, Fechy and Yvorne, while some of the better reds are from Nostrano, Dole and Cortaillod.

Apart from the vineyard walks in the hills, there are plenty of similar wine-growing areas alongside the Rhine, near Schaffhausen.

Communications

Telephones
Gradually, the common phone box appears to be making an appearance across Europe. In the bad old days every instrument was different, but now it would seem that the same layout is used in all countries.

Useful Numbers
Emergency police: 117
Fire brigade: 118
Ambulance: 144
Avalanche bulletin: 187
Weather report: 162
Traffic report: 163
Tourist information: 120
Time: 161
Telegrams: 110

To Dial Out

Calls from Switzerland to Britain are prefixed 0044. Omit the first 0 of the British number: 071 123 4567 will become 0044 71 123 4567 from Switzerland.

Postage

The Swiss post box is bright yellow, with a bugle emblem on the side.

Opening Times

Post offices in the large towns are open Monday to Friday at the following times: 7.30a.m. to 12.00p.m. and 1.45p.m. to 6.30p.m. Except for the large ones in major cities, post offices close at 11a.m. on Saturdays.

The Stamp of Diplomacy

Helvetia, the name which appears on all Swiss postage stamps, is an old Roman name. This was the name given to the Celtic tribe who, in 200 BC, settled on the shores of Lac Léman. Some 150 years later in 58 BC, many of the Helvitii, who were also living in the Jura mountains and along the River Rhine, tried to migrate to Gaul (France). They were stopped and defeated by the troops of Julius Caeser, and returned to their homeland. So much for Helvetia, but why does it still appear as the name for Switzerland on their stamps? In 1850, the first adhesive stamps were introduced to the country, and, not surprisingly, no-one could decide which language to use: French, German, Italian or Romansch. The end result was that none of them were used, thus upsetting no one, and the old name of Helvetia, the land of the Helvetii, was printed on the stamps.

Electricity

Voltage in Switzerland is 220 volts a.c. requiring continental plugs or a recommended adaptor.

Children's Switzerland

Children of all ages will enjoy Switzerland, from the young toddler seeing those wide-eyed cows, to the teenager tackling the slopes of Crans Montana. It has a wealth of opportunities for all ages, and there can be few countries that offer such practical geographical and geological lessons as Switzerland. The people, especially in the country areas, will welcome younger travellers openly, without the gushing emotionalism of the Latin countries.

Facilities

Before most places even thought about it, Switzerland was way ahead with babycare amenities at service stations, railway stations and all the public buildings such as museums. Certainly, most have changing rooms as part of their amenities. There is a great emphasis on children's playgrounds, and these are found in some unlikely locations. At places such as midpoint cable car stations you are more than likely to find swings, slides and a younger children's area. Even at the very top of some of the mountains there are areas set aside for kids.

Accommodation

Accommodation is usually priced per room, and a great number of double rooms have an extra bed, to make up a family room at no extra cost so you can make a saving—that is, if you don't mind trying to sleep with the gang. More recently, the rise in popularity of chalets and self-catering accommodation has solved this problem, and I think that most families tend to choose this option.

One area where Switzerland can be difficult is in the restaurant or café. Unlike many countries, there is seldom a children's menu. If you don't mind eating at the fast food places, then there is less of a problem, but if you would like your children to enjoy some real pasta dishes or some good French cooking, then it can be tricky. I will never forget the sight of my five-year-old faced with an adult-sized portion of spaghetti bolognese (I had to help him finish it!).

Theme Parks

Switzerland relies to a great extent on its natural resources to attract visitors. It does not have to build theme parks and the like, as in Spain or France. The natural beauty of the country, its history and its sports should be enough to attract the tourists. However, there

*T*oboganning is still a popular pastime for Swiss children, and here on the lower slopes of Mt Pilatus it is better than the skiing.

T he ski schools take in pupils from four-year-olds upwards with a strong emphasis on the best safety equipment. This school on the high slopes above St Moritz ensures good snow and bright sunshine.

are a few of these parks appearing. The biggest is probably the Alpa Mare at **Zürichsee**, near Pfaffikon, at the very end of the lake. This features water slides, swimming pools and all the usual facilities of the tropical theme park. The need for this type of attraction is debatable, since so many of the resort swimming arenas have water slides, cafés and such like: go to any public swimming pool and you will find at the very least a superb complex, which is clean and a pleasure to use. The facilities do vary, but often (for example at Morat or Verbier) there are indoor and outdoor pools, saunas, whirlpools and water slides. Also, at some of the larger towns (Geneva, Lugano and Lucerne) there are large parks next to the lake. Of these the one at Geneva, the Lido, is

four-year-old to don a crash helmet and a pair of skis and skid down a hillside, then they will provide a children's play area. Younger children are often catered for by a crèche, or playgroup, supervised by a qualified nursery teacher. However, it is always as well to check out the arrangements beforehand, since even Switzerland can sometimes get it wrong. The minimum age for learning to ski in Switzerland is usually four years.

Museums
The favourite museum for children is undoubtedly the Transport Museum at Lucerne, although some of the cheese-making demonstrations at Gruyères and Emmental may be interesting to older children.

Sports
Sport is one area which children, especially the older ones, can enjoy to the full in Switzerland. You may feel some reluctance to let them go bridge jumping or hydrorafting, but there are opportunities at almost every level. Mountain biking is becoming a great favourite, and at most resorts you can hire a bike for a day. Rafting is very popular in the Alpine rivers at Laax and Chateau d'Oex, and all the necessary safety equipment is provided. For the very adventurous, there are full weeks of activity sports, and the one at Interlaken—Crazy Week—takes the prize for the most inventive programme.

Add all this to the more ordinary sports of tennis, golf, swimming, windsurfing and just plain old walking, and you have a country hard to match in the sports arena.

very good, with pools of all sizes and for all ages.

Zoos
Each of the main towns has a zoo, but Basel is regarded as the best. Zurich, Bern, Geneva and Lausanne also have zoos, and there is a tropical butterfly park—the Papiliorama—at Marin, near Lausanne.

Skiing
All the ski schools will have facilities for children. If they cannot persuade you that it's perfectly all right for your

39

"To last, if God will, for ever..."

Switzerland has had its ups and downs over the past 700 years, and to a certain extent this is there for all to see: the historical documents in Schwyz, the battle grounds at Morat and Grandson, and the modern history showing a development which has in some cases gone beyond normal boundaries. In amongst it all the Swiss people have remained true to their country. They can be critical if necessary, but are quick to defend their homeland.

When the foresters of Schwyz, Unterwalden and Uri met in 1291 to form a small group to counter the appointment of the Austrian Hapsburg dynasty as bailiffs, they were forming a pact which would continue for centuries. These were the origins of the Helvetic Confederation, a union of people from the hills and valleys around Lucerne. They were not too pleased at the appointment of an Austrian landlord who would interfere and possibly take over the distribution of land, pastures and flocks. Their agreement "to last, if God will, for

T *he cradle of Switzerland from the top of Mt Pilatus. To the right of the lake (Lucerne) is Weggis, and in the far distance the Rossberg range.*

ever" has remained true. With the passage of 700 years, there seems little change in the determination of Switzerland and its people to remain its own country.

Over those 700 years there have been setbacks to the confederation, and many would say that the true birth date of the nation was 1848, following the fall of the Napoleonic empire. However, states gradually joined this confederation, starting with Lucerne in 1332, followed by Zurich in 1351, Glarus and Zug in 1352 and Bern in 1353. This allegiance grew, century by century, forming the strong bond that remains today. Despite its relatively peaceful reputation Switzerland has had to fight hard for its peace.

Its greatest test came when Napoleon made Switzerland part of his empire. The country was, for the first

The symbol of the United Nations—the globe—is alongside a footpath to the right of the main building in Geneva.

Rutli Field: Birthplace of a Nation?

This clearing in the forest, as Rutli means, has become a place of some sanctity, although there is no firm evidence that the place was used as originally believed, to sign the confederative charter. It was certainly used in 1940 by General Guisan to address his officers. He suggested at the time that it would be from this central point of the country that they would defend Switzerland, if they had to, rather than at its frontiers.

But its real place in the history books goes back to that date of 1 August 1291, when the three states of Uri, Nidwalden and Schwyz met to form their pact. No documentary evidence is available to confirm the Rutli Field as the meeting point, but there is an idea that it was used either in 1307 or 1315 for much the same purposes. Whichever is true, the field has certainly become a much visited site, either by way of the path from Seeliberg or, more popularly, by boat.

time in centuries, unable to exercise its independence, and even Napoleon saw that his ruling did not work, due partly to the continual internal disorder. In 1803 he imposed an Act of Mediation, where the federative nature of the state was recognized, but with a three-tiered structure of towns, villages and cantons. Fortunately for Switzerland Napoleon's empire fell, leaving the country to continue along its confederative path. Gradually, the list of cantons grew to 22.

The constitution was formed in 1848 and has had two subsequent revisions, in 1874 and 1978. Switzerland today is a confederation of 26 cantons, each very distinct from the others.

A Neutral Country

Switzerland has retained its right of neutrality since the Congress of Vienna declared it as international law in 1815. This has led to it being the centre for all humanitarian causes; yet with all the international bodies centred in Switzerland, it is not itself a member of the United Nations. It has one of the strongest currencies in the world, but is not a member of the European Community. This determination to be involved with, but remain outside of, international events has led to a country unique in the modern world.

There is no doubt that the world needs a Switzerland: a country where warring factions can meet, disagreements and causes can be viewed dispassionately, without fear of involvement by the host country. Since the right to neutrality was granted to Switzerland, most of the major international bodies—the United Nations, the International Red Cross, the Council for Nuclear Research—have established headquarters here, which shows that Switzerland, and particularly Geneva, has an ever more demanding rôle to play in international affairs.

The International Red Cross was formed by Henri Dunant in 1863, after the death and injury to thousands of soldiers in several wars across Europe. His concern was that there was no provision for treatment or the basic human rights of soldiers, and he immediately began to establish an organization for this. Switzerland has since provided that sanctuary, and cares not only for the world's soldiers, but also for its poorer communities and countries.

A Financial Centre

Alongside Switzerland's development as a centre of neutrality came another strength. Its financial acumen, though largely misunderstood, has led to a stable, secure and rich country. The Swiss bank has a reputation for dealing with unsavoury characters and the finances of the less scrupulous governments of the world. Much of this reputation is due to the excessive imagination of 20th-century novelists, but the fact is that the Swiss bank does not cast moral judgements on its clients or ask many questions. The Swiss banking secrecy laws were made to protect individuals from the persecution of Nazi Germany, but since those laws still remain, it is difficult to probe into the finances of a Swiss bank account. The result is that the Swiss bank has provided a home for the millions acquired by some of the world's notorious dictators. It is an anomaly that a dictator stores a personal fortune in Switzerland, probably gained through the misfortune of its population, while the Swiss Red Cross is trying to bring comfort to the people being oppressed.

Despite its development as a country of international standing, Switzerland was known as a nation of farmers. There is in some respects little difference in the attitudes and character of the people of the forest states today from those of the originators of the confederation. The people of Switzerland do not follow their government blindly, and many Swiss are very critical of policy. They are keen to discuss politics, and have no hesitation in making their views known. But they are fiercely defensive of their country, and their right to independence. There is a saying in Switzerland which runs "we will defeat Switzerland tomorrow". Hitler never even made the attempt; partly because of the natural barrier of the Alps, but also because he knew that every Swiss would be armed and ready to repel him.

Today the possibly outdated requirement for every male aged between 20 and 50 to have a rifle and ammunition at home, ready to defend his country, is a point of contention and has been the subject of several referendums.

The Swiss Army

Military service has become one of the most contentious issues in Switzerland. The arguments have raged for many years, and every so often the country has a referendum on the subject. The vote never seems to come up with a definite decision, so the requirement for men to continue their service and top-up courses continues. There are three groups of servicemen, split into age bands. The elite are the youngest at 20 to 32, then come the middle band of 32 to 43 year olds, who are the *Landwehr*. Finally, the old guard of 43 to 50 year olds is the *Landsturm*.

Many men obviously resent having to spend 20 days every two years playing soldiers, although many will privately admit that it is good to keep up the fitness. Target practice is also of great importance, and even when not on a course, the part-time defenders of the country have to keep up their marksmanship. This is checked in a points scoring book, so there is no escaping it. In fact, the army is never that far away from the life of the Swiss male, who fortunately will probably never have to use his weapons in earnest. But, they best be ready just in case.

This determination to defend the Swiss boundaries is typical of the solid nature of the Swiss people. They are cautious, and there can be no doubt that their reputation has suffered because of this. They are indeed so cautious that women had no right to vote in federal elections until 1971.

Swiss Politics: Democracy in Action

A federal vote is a national affair, but much of Swiss politics is local. Before cantonal authority is brought in, communities make their own decisions. The 3,020 communes have the right to self-administration, but will refer to the cantonal body in the case of an appeal. In some of the older cantons, such as Appenzell and Glarus, ceremonial *Landsgemeide* meetings are held in the village square. This annual gathering of active citizens of the canton is real democracy in action. On the various proposals and applications affecting the community a show of hands decides the issue. There can be few better opportunities to watch the democratic process amongst the people than there is at the *Landsgemeide*. They are held on the last Sunday in April in Appenzell and on the first Sunday in May at Glarus.

Despite its conservative ways, the Swiss democracy arguably has the oldest form of direct popular vote still in existence. Particularly in the mountain communities, the people feel a need to be involved with local politics and, presumably, there are also financial benefits for keeping local control on the development of a village.

Cantonal politics are a serious affair, bringing in villagers and country folk from the whole region. In Glarus, the atmosphere is less formal than Appenzell.

The Effects of Tourism

The tourist industry has meant a lot to the high villages of the alpine regions. Most have retained their character as small communities while expanding ski areas, cable car systems and rail routes to attract the winter sports enthusiast. Nowhere has the development been better managed than in the old villages of the Engadine and the Valais. Some villages, like Verbier, have made a new resort further up the mountain, partly to cater for the needs of the winter tourists, but also to take the main traffic away from the old village. In a few places, such as Crans Montana and St Moritz, the modern development is more obvious, with larger hotels and chalet-style buildings built. Generally, though, the needs of the modern tourist have been integrated without causing undue harm or unsightly additions to the surrounding countryside.

Switzerland's need for a vibrant tourist industry was recognized very early in its history. The natural scenic beauty made it an obvious choice for the affluent traveller of the 1800s. Thomas Cook started the idea of tours to Switzerland in 1843, and its response to the needs of its visitors are now legendary. There are few countries where visitors can rely on such a high standard of accommodation, transport and service as in Switzerland. It is not by chance that in Himalayan regions the Swiss Bus Service is so named in an attempt to use the reputation gained by that country for quality and comfort. (Unfortunately, those standards are not quite met on the Nepalese buses!)

As a land-locked country Switzerland has had to rely on its rail system and, more recently, its airline to bring visitors into the country. In the early days of tourism the stylish European trains would transport the richer people of Europe to their alpine retreats, so that Switzerland gradually gained the reputation as a playground of the rich. Places like St Moritz, Gstaad, Klosters and Montreux became synonymous with the wealthy. This was not a holiday place for the ordinary person, but a place you couldn't afford. Switzerland remained psychologically out of bounds to many tourists even up to the 1950s and 1960s. Austria, Germany, France and Italy probably attracted most people who enjoyed the mountains, and competition from the Spanish resorts could not be ignored. Even today, when Switzerland is mentioned, the natural assumption is that you must be reasonably well-off, just to go there. Is it really so expensive?

The famous names of St Moritz and Gstaad still attract their share of wealthy people, and some "stars" have opted to live there. Prince Charles always skis at Klosters and on the average winter's day you will probably see someone famous out on the slopes or in one of the hotels. However, the actual cost of a trip to Switzerland has come down considerably over the past ten years. As Europe has become more integrated, so the difference in commodities has levelled off, and the cup of coffee you pay for in Britain will not cost that much more in Germany, Austria or Switzerland. Self-catering in the many chalets and apartments of the mountain villages has meant that families can keep their costs to a minimum. Shopping at the local Swiss supermarket will not cost much more than that at home, and the costs of hiring these chalets has also levelled off to compete with the surrounding countries. To a great degree the decision as to whether there is extra expense in a trip to Switzerland has to do with value for money. It does cost a little more for a holiday here, but that is balanced by the quality of the facilities available. Rooms in hotels, including the one- and two-star establishments, provide good accommodation often in historic buildings. The chalets tend to be larger, they are clean and invariably in superb locations. The food is fresh, and in the cafés and restaurants the standards of service, the quality (and

quantity) of the food is excellent. The facilities on the mountains, if you are keen on winter sports, are the best in the world, and if you come in the summer, then the walking, route marking, and transport is second to none. Measure that against the facilities provided by many other countries and you will realize why Switzerland has retained and expanded its visitor base for a century or more.

*N*ot a chalet for rent, but this old mountain hut in the hills above Verbier could be used by farmers in the summer.

Switzerland's Airline

A major factor in the success of Switzerland in more recent years has been the associated success of its national airline, Swissair. The airline was founded in 1931, with a total of 13 aircraft. Only operating in fair weather, they were also limited to flying between March and October. Since then the network has grown to a staggering 340,000 km with more than 100 destinations. As an introduction to the country, Swissair is a good pointer—to my knowledge, it is the only airline whose in-flight magazine is distributed personally before each flight. It is therefore in perfect condition. The staff are courteous without being gushing, and the food is reasonable, certainly compared with the normal standards of airline catering.

Over the years Swissair has gained a reputation as a solid, efficient and good quality airline, and has won numerous awards for service amongst the business community. The success of Swissair is directly related to the success of its national tourist industry, which in turn is related to the general economy of the country, so it is clear that the airline has a major role to play in the future. Balancing this against the increased awareness of the need to protect the environment has meant that

T imber is another of Switzerland's major industries, especially in the central part of the country.

Swissair have changed many of their aircraft for quieter, more fuel-efficient models. The MD-81, the Airbus and the Fokker 100 are recent additions to the fleet which serves Basel, Zurich and Geneva.

It is one of the unfortunate facts of modern life that to be successful in the tourist field sacrifices have to be made in other areas. Swissair have tried to lessen the effect on local communities of increased numbers visiting their country, by using these low-noise planes and installing all manner of noise-reduction systems at their testing grounds. So once again, the national trait of the careful, solid character comes through. But is the typical Swiss person as stolid, cold thinking and calculating as reputation would suggest?

Industries

Much of Swiss success has been due to that careful thinking approach to problems. Apart from the tourist industry the Swiss have gained a reputation on many other industrial fronts. Although an agricultural land, with dairy farming as one of its major sources of employment and income, the country rightfully claims to have some of the finest engineering brains in the world. The early development of engineering brilliance can be easily seen in the design and construction of many of the mountain railways—bear in mind that most of these tracks were laid in the early part of the century, and you begin to realize that only the carefully thought-out approach could have succeeded in taking those tracks to the mountain tops.

Swiss Exports

The world is very familiar with the Swiss army penknife and the Swiss precision watch. There have been tablets from Basel and cheese from Gruyères. But what else has Switzerland produced for the world. There is nothing to suggest that this was the first shoe shop, but Carl Franz Bally brought back to his home country in 1851 the idea of stocking shoes. As everyone knows, Bally shoes have not done too badly since! Toblerone chocolate is still synonomous with the mountains of Switzerland, if only for its shape. 80 tons of it is consumed every day. Another odd export, and probably one familiar mainly to those in the aircraft industry, is the Pilatus Porter. This dated-looking aircraft is made in the town of Stans, Nidwalden, and has the ability to land on just about any surface—water, rocks or desert. Finally, that mixture of roughage eaten for breakfast the world over does not have Alpine pictures on it for effect. The mixture of oats, honey, nuts and fruit was concocted by a Zurich doctor, Dr Maximillian Bircherbenner, in the 1930s.

Apply this engineering acumen to a penknife and you have the famous Swiss Army Pocket Knife with up to 29 features, including scissors, wire cutters, can opener and a toothpick.

The Swiss watch comes in so many forms, shapes, sizes and materials that it would be impossible to mention them all, except to say that all Swiss watches, from the hideously bejewelled one-offs to the colourful plastic production-line models, have one common factor: they are uncannily accurate; and 15 per cent of the world's watches originate in Switzerland.

Not-so-famous accounts include the world's first surviving newspaper, dating back to 1597, the *Rorschacher Monatsschrift*, printed on the shores of Lake Constance. Valium was first produced in Basel, and Superglue was also invented here. For such a small country Switzerland can claim quite remarkable achievements. But is it all down to a careful, dour national character? Who are the real Swiss? Are they the monocled watchmakers of the Jura, the high-flying skiers of the Valais, or perhaps the careful Zurich bankers or the creative Swiss chefs? In a country so diverse, so the people will follow that diversity.

The Swiss Character

As with all races it is impossible to produce a "typical" Swiss person. In Switzerland it is more difficult because of the influences from other regions. The most Swiss parts of Switzerland are the Romansch regions of the Engadine and Glarus regions. This is old Switzerland, populated by whose lives have remained closely tied to their farms and pastures for centuries. Go across to Lausanne and you will find a sophisticated, cosmopolitan people whose closeness to the style and lives of the French is clear. Then travel to Lugano, and sample the orderly chaos

*T*he huge waterwheel at the papermill in Basel is just outside the main exhibition area where the whole paper-making process is explained.

which brings a delightful mixture of Italy and Switzerland to its people. Finally, if you spend some time in the vineyards around Schaffhausen, you would swear you were in Germany. It is impossible to talk about the Swiss as a people because they are such a diverse mixture of cultures that the "typical" Swiss does not exist. The mixture of these nationalities has led to many of the younger Swiss people becoming what should be the typical "European": the person that can speak four languages, can understand the thoroughness of Germany, the style of France and the character of Italy. To suggest that a Swiss is unexciting is not only untrue but also insulting. A visitor to the *Fasnacht* in Basel would see another side of the Swiss, and to see them perform on skis or a bobsleigh proves that the "cautious" nature is often thrown to the winds.

For all their success in engineering, tourism, and the sciences, the Swiss have cleverly merged the 20th-century world with a traditional past.

The Blend of Old and New

On a walk around the large cities of Switzerland, the visitor cannot escape noticing the blend of modern and old. High-technology devices have been operating in the country for some time, with car park payment, cash machines, and fuel supply at garages automated. You can also keep an eye on the current stocks and shares at a number of visual display units outside banks. But this use of modern technology is well balanced with a keen appreciation of

The inner courtyard of the Rathaus—the town hall—in Basel has frescoes dating back to the 1600s.

the traditional. Christmas in Switzerland has none of the commercialism of Britain or USA. It is a quiet, religious, occasion with few mass shopping expeditions.

There are several indications of how seriously the Swiss take their past in the way they attend to the upkeep of their historical buildings and in the list of festivals held throughout the country. The parades are often religious by nature, but they also include some odd celebrations involving dressing up in quite outlandish costumes. The Swiss National Tourist Office produces a booklet listing these festivals, their historical significance, location and dates. You will find that almost every month some village or other will be performing a parade. Examples of

these customs are the *Nuninchlinger* at Zeifen where bachelors of the village parade in hats up to 2 m (6 ft) tall, and the *Kalausjagen* at Kussnacht where the locals wear huge bishops' mitres on the eve of St Nicholas. The *Achetringele*, held in the Bernese village of Laupen at New Year, strictly means "the downhill rattling and ringing of the bells". The custom here is for three groups of bell ringers, broom men and bladder men to parade through the streets, stopping occasionally to bid farewell to the old year and to welcome in the new. At the end, the broom and bladder men proceed to beat onlookers over the head with inflated pigs' bladders! This is not as violent as it may sound since pigs' bladders are more like light balloons; nevertheless it is an odd custom.

Probably the biggest, yet least publicized, carnival, is held in Basel on the first Monday after Ash Wednesday. About 15,000 of the local inhabitants take part in the Basel *Fasnacht*, and it

52

Traditional Switzerland

History and things traditional have a large part to play in the life of the Swiss. In the parades and ceremonies around the country it is quite clear that the ways of the past are not to be left in the history books. This is particularly noticeable in the dress of certain areas. In the Appenzell, on the day of the *Langesmeide*, you will still see the women wearing their traditional costume featuring lace headgear, and men carrying their swords. In the Gruyères the herdsmen still wear their *brezon*, and the velvet jackets are still popular in the Bernese Oberland. But, up until the 18th century, the land workers, or peasants, were disqualified from wearing any form of elaborate dress under the Sumptuary laws. Under this, anyone earning less than 1,000 guilders was not allowed to have metalwork on the belt, and no silk borders on bodices. Even the material for waistcoats and breeches was defined, in that sleeves had to be made of cloth or wool according to the class of the wearer. The reason for these apparently strict rules was that the lords and masters of the time did not want the lesser folk to be wasting their money on such niceties as clothes. But was that really the reason?

is a most unlikely festival, found in a city more famous for its business life than for parades around the streets in strange costumes, playing piccolos for a full 72 hours. This particular display of an odd side of Swiss life is balanced by a strong religious connection with most folklore and culture. Most of the parades and festivals take place in the Christmas period. Christianity is as strong in Switzerland as in any country in Europe, and there is a lot

of fine religious architecture to be seen throughout the country. A trip down the valleys around the Engadine shows a great variety of styles of churches.

Basel, Bern, Zurich, Lausanne and, to a lesser extent, Geneva, all feature a remarkable collection of ancient buildings. The unusual feature about many of these buildings is that they do not look very old. The Swiss have been carrying out conservation programmes for almost their entire history. Basel Cathedral is a good example: a building which dates back to 1019, in a city whose beginnings go back as far as the Romans and Julius Caesar. Yet, standing in the Markplatz, in the centre of Basel, the visitor is struck not only by the cleanliness of the street, but also by the condition of its buildings. Bern is another example of a city which has not neglected its heritage, but has used it to attract visitors for over a century. UNESCO has declared the city a World Cultural Landmark. The centre of Bern is full of the most exquisite architecture, including one of the oldest (and longest) shopping arcades in the world. The only depreciation of the sights are the tramwires in almost every street. It's a great pity that some other form of transport was not used in the area. However, one of the more unusual architectural sights to be found is in the underground concourse at the main railway station. Whilst excavating for the foundations of the new station, the remains of one of the old city walls was uncovered. Instead of simply concreting over it, Bern left it in the middle of the concourse where, along with the bars, cafés and flower shops, it now serves as a meeting point and feature of the station.

*T*he Engadine house is unique in Switzerland, with huge
doors and heraldic figures. This one is in the small village of Zuoz.

Swiss Housing

There is a concern over the conservation of their architecture in the country. The people of the Alps have kept to traditional styles of house building, even if the materials they use have changed. Apart from the odd indiscretion, such as Interlaken's Hotel Metropole, most new hotels, chalets and homes have an Alpine feel to them.

This upholding of the tried and tested is not for the sake of sentiment but out of respect for the landscape; a practical as well as emotional attitude. The need for buildings which work for the people who live under the towering peaks is of paramount importance, but instead of searching for new ways of protecting the family, the crops and the livestock against the harsh winters, the Alpine Swiss have kept to the old ways—with variations. From the stone cottage-style farms of the Ticino to high-roofed wooden houses of the Valais, the peasant workers of Switzerland have always made their homes dual purpose. The most typical house or chalet in Switzerland is one with ornate wooden carvings, the overhanging eaves and brightly coloured window shutters. This is the house of the Bernese Oberland, and you will find that the mountain folk of the Oberland are extremely proud of their carved pillars and beams. But if you travel to the Lucerne area, you will find an entirely different structure, with steep-sided roofs, and a ground floor which is reached by an outside staircase. Another type of Bernese house has a barn within its structure, with the roof reaching almost to the floor, but in most instances it is only two storeys high. To make up for the lack of height, the house is very wide, which sometimes allows for a huge timber arch to be made in place of the front, triangular part, of the roof.

Possibly the most unusual, and in some ways least typical, Swiss house is in the Engadine. This, the oldest and most "Swiss" part of the country, has an aspect unique amongst the regions: the Engadine house resembles some of those found in the Austrian Tyrol while also drawing on some Italian influences. The huge grey masonry structure is decorated with *sgraffito* of floral, geometric and heraldic designs. In another style some of the houses also have oriel windows, similar to those found in the Germanic towns of Schaffhausen and Stein am Rhein. The structure is big enough to house two families, and probably the best examples of the true Engadine house are to be found in Zuoz and Guarda.

Swiss Scenery

The heritage of Switzerland has been faithfully upheld, but probably the most popular reason for visiting the country is its mountains. Some people want to climb them, some want to ski down them, and others simply want to admire them as scenery.

That "scenery" has clearly been Switzerland's biggest asset. It has provided a natural barrier against would-be aggressors, it has kept communities together, upholding the traditional family life, and it has provided the country with one of its major industries—tourism. Over half (60 per cent) of the confederation is Alpine, and

High Spots in The Alps

Apart from Austria, Switzerland has the largest portion of the Alps, and in amongst that portion are the highest points in the chain. In all, the Swiss Alps have no less than 14 peaks over the 4,000 m (13,100 ft) mark. At the centre of the range is Mt Rosa, which stands at 4,634 m (15,203 ft). After that there is little to choose between the next 13 mountains with a mere 503 m (1,650 ft) separating them.

Of them all, the Jungfrau is the most likely one for a visit, since its railway will take you up to within a few hundred metres of the summit. Alternatively, for those looking to walk to their mountain, the pathways out of Zermatt offer a whole range of routes to the Matterhorn. Some of these should only be tackled by experienced climbers and walkers with good equipment.

has 14 mountains over 4,000 m (13,123 ft) high. The centre of this collection of peaks, valleys and glaciers is Mount Rosa, 4,634 m (15,203 ft). The formation of this natural attribute dates back to the Miocene period (26 million years ago) when the African plate ground against the Eurasian plate. This event formed the Mediterranean, pushed up the Alps into a craggy chain of mountains, and even gave formation to the Himalayas. The Alpine peaks are still rising today. For a good idea of the nature and geology of the Alps, a visit to the research station on the Jungfrau is useful.

This station is permanently monitoring the Jungfrau glacier, its movement along the mountain being of particular interest. In the exhibition area you can see how the glaciers of the Alps have been formed, and the work that has been carried out over the last 30 years. There is a permanent exhibition situated within the rock, in the underground tunnels. The display is now showing signs of age, but gives information on the geology of the Alps, the effects on the body of living at height, and aspects of meteorology. One of the more fascinating facts in the exhibition is that a piece of rock has moved from position 5.8 m on the glacier (measured in 1926) to position 12.3 m (in 1959), a movement of 6.5 m (18 ft 4 inches) over a period of 33 years; proof indeed that the glaciers are on the move.

The Jungfrau is one of many glaciers in Switzerland, another favourite being the large deposit of ice at the top of the Furka Pass, the Rhône Glacier. However, these sometimes threatening masses are not to everyone's taste, and they may not be regarded as picturesque. If it is pure scenery that appeals, there are some wonderful vantage points from where the views are simply stunning. Mt Pilatus commands an almost central position in the country, so views of the Alps and the Jura can be seen. Most of the mountains of the Valais, such as Mt Fort and Tortin, and the resorts to the east at Zermatt and Saas Fee have railways or cable systems to take you to the heights of the roof of Europe. The Matterhorn is probably the finest vantage point in the Alps, but to reach it you will need the assistance of an expert guide, and be a good climber yourself.

It cannot be totally guaranteed, but if you are looking for a holiday based on clean mountain air, with the possibility of getting away from it all, Switzerland is hard to beat.

Flowers, Birds and Beasts

Switzerland has always been renowned for having some of the most beautiful Alpine flowers. In May and June the hills of the *Valais* are covered in the yellows, blues and violets of hundreds of small plants, the commoners in the world of Alpines. Further up though are some of the rarities, the precious few survivors of an unlikely climate, surviving despite massive variations in temperature. They grow in cracks and crevices which hardly seem capable of supporting life.

For the casual visitor, it is enough to see the display of Alpines on the way up the mountain on the chair lift. For some the temptation to decorate the rented chalet with a bunch of Alpines is too great. This is one practice which the Swiss would dearly like to put a stop to, but they simply make a polite request, "do not pick the flowers". More than this, perhaps the biggest threat to the Alpine ecology is from the thunderous trucks which use Switzerland as a highway between Germany and Italy. Being located between these two high-output industrial nations is fine for the economy and commercial enterprise, but what of the lower-level tree-line? The concern is now so great that there are attempts to reduce the numbers of lorries using the autoroutes through Switzerland. This may appear like bolting the stable door after the horse has gone, but something will have to be done soon. The whole structure of the Alpine forests is in danger of being seriously eroded, and if that happened, then the consequences would go beyond Switzerland's boundaries.

At the same time the European Community is making suggestions that the commercial traffic between Italy and Germany is increased. Switzerland believes that the only answer is to put those lorries on trains, and transport them across the country by rail. There is no doubt a commercial angle to this suggestion, since the Swiss Government would probably also charge a hefty amount for the ride. Who will win this argument is difficult to say, but there may come a time when the Swiss just refuse to allow a certain tonnage over its borders.

Rare Plants

High up in the mountains, there is less concern with lorries or flower arrangers, and fortunately this is where many of the rare species of plant can be found. Rarities of Switzerland include the Round-Leaved Pennycress, which is peculiar to the country. On the Jura there is the Alpine Butterbur and in the eastern Alps there are the Glacier Pink and the Least Primrose. In the Titless region, one rare flower is located on a single mountain, the Mount Cenis Bellflower, but for most tourists the sight of the Edelweiss, the buttercups and pansies is enough to enjoy.

One area which seems to excel in wild flowers is around the Valais Alps. By an oddity the villages and mountain stations tend to have a low season in May and June. This is at the very time when the Alpines are at their best, so for those with a particular interest in the subject, be prepared to do some steep walking since the chair lifts will often be closed at this time.

To see the real rarities of the mountains, there are botanical gardens which

The truly wild flowers are best seen in the early months of summer. This field of colour is in the hills above Verbier.

Switzerland's Fauna

For those keen on the more mobile natural history of Switzerland, there are some interesting differences between Switzerland and the rest of Europe. The species which always springs to mind, and indeed is a speciality of this region, is the Ibex. This graceful high-mountain animal, related to sheep and goats, was almost extinct, and even today there are only a few small protected herds living in Switzerland. The Ibex was revered by the Romans, who believed its horns held miraculous healing powers. The place to see these rare animals in a natural habitat is in the National Park near Zernez.

A less rare species is the Chamois, which looks like a cross between a goat and a deer with hook-shaped horns. It can be seen on the mountains, although it is very wary of visitors. There are areas above Verbier for instance where the Chamois can be seen in summer, feeding on herbs and flowers. The best way to see them is to find a mountain guide with local knowledge of where to look. In the forest regions of Switzerland Roe Deer will be active.

While most of these rather shy animals keep a watchful eye on anything that moves, the Marmots seem to invite scrutiny. In the summer, it is a common sight to see these squirrel-like rodents pop out of their burrows, have a quick look around and run off to another hole. Obviously it is better to be quiet and inconspicuous, and often you will see more from the cable car (or gondola) *en route* to a mountain top.

For ornithologists, there are several species to be found in the high mountains which can be seen in few other places in Europe. The Alpine Chough, a

have such displays. This may not be as exciting as finding a rare Alpine on the side of a rock face at 4,000 m (13,100 ft), but then not that many of us have such opportunities, and botanical gardens are a good substitute.

The National Park in the Grisons is one area where the flora and fauna have been well protected. Motor vehicles are not allowed into the park. At Villars, at Pont de Nant, there is an Alpine garden which has over 2,000 species of mountain plants. It can be reached on the main road from Montreaux to Martigny, at Bex. The winding road to Gryon passes the turn off to Pont de Nant, which is just a short distance up the hill.

handsome Jackdaw-sized bird with a yellow curved beak and red legs, can be seen at most of the high-level chair-lift stations. Here too you might be lucky enough to see the sparrow-like Alpine Accentor and the attractive Snow Finch. It is always worth scanning the skies for birds of prey as the Golden Eagle hunts in the mountains. Kites may also be seen, and around Lac Léman in particular Black Kites should be found. Kites are easily recognized by their broad, fingered wings and their forked tail. The Black Redstart can be seen in the regions around Zermatt in early April, and there are legions of ducks and grebes on Lac Léman in the winter months, including Red-crested Pochard and Black-necked Grebe.

These species apart, you will also see most of the common birds of Europe, as Switzerland is the favoutite haunt of many species. The way to make sure you do have success with your bird-watching is to speak to the locals. They always know the best areas to look.

Above: the Alpine Marmot, a squirrel-like rodent that can be seen in higher ground.

Below: an Alpine Chough. This bird, although a rarity elsewhere in Europe, is found at most of the high-level chair-lift stations.

Switzerland's Cantons, Towns and Villages

Cantonal pride accounts for a lot in Switzerland, even though there is a strong national unity. Each canton has equal power in the politics of the country and, in cases where the people feel strongly about a matter, the cantons can, if the joint opinion is strong enough, bring about national referenda. There are some oddities to the system such as Basel, which has become divided into "town" and "district". But whatever the make-up of the canton, the crest and identification letters are displayed with some pride. A list of the cantons with their respective identification letters is given in the table below.

Geographically, the cantons can be grouped into five areas, and this is the division adopted for the rest of the book:

North-West: Basel, Jura, Solothurn and Aargau.
North-East: Zurich, Schaffhausen, Thurgau, St Gallen and Appenzell.
South-East: Glarus, Grisons and Ticino.
South-West: Valais, Vaud, Geneva, Fribourg and Neuchatel.
Central: Bern, Lucerne, Unterwalden, Uri, Schwyz, and Zug.

The Cantons of Switzerland
Schwyz (SZ)
Uri (UR) The Forest states
Unterwalden/Obwalden (NW and OW)
Zurich (ZH)
Glarus (GL)
Lucerne (LU)
Zug (ZG)
Bern (BE)
Fribourg (FR)
Solothurn (SO)
Basel–Basel town (BS)
Basel–Basel District (BL)
Schaffhausen (SH)
Appenzell–Inner Rhoden (AI)
Appenzell–Ausser Rhoden (AR)
Aargau (AG)
Grisons (GR)
St Gallen (SG)
Thurgau (TG)
Ticino (TI)
Vaud (VD)
Jura (JU)
Geneva (GE)
Neuchâtel (NE)
Valais (VS)

A church spire in Zuoz shines out in the crisp Alpine air during the middle of winter. Zuoz is one of the villages of the Engadine.

Just the Essentials

On a first-time visit to Switzerland, you may be overwhelmed by the sheer wealth of choices you have wherever you start. The major landmarks and places to see and visit are proposed here to help you establish your priorities.

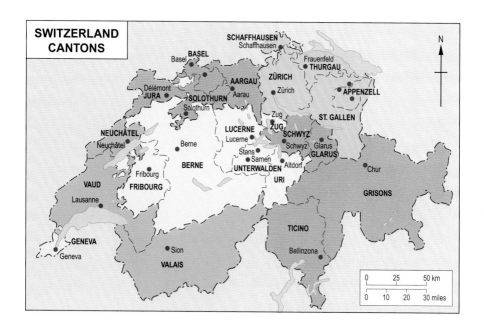

The North-west

Basel Munster and town hall (*rathaus*)
Basel Fasnacht, a pulsating 72-hour carnival
Lake Biel
St Peter's Island, Lake Biel
International Museum of Horology at La Chaux de Fonds
Ligerz, a beautiful village
Between Neuchâtel and Morat for castles and châteaux
Saut du Doubs gorge near Les Brenets

Central Switzerland

Foundations of the Christoffel Tower in Bern
Bern Cathedral
The town of Morat to the west of Bern
L'Eglise des Cordeliers, Fribourg
Cheese dairy in Gruyères
Train journey up the Jungfrau and passing through the Eiger from either Grindelwald or Wengen
Lucerne for the Kapellbrücke and a fine transport museum
Views of the cradle of Switzerland from Mt Rigi

The South-west

Geneva for its famous fountain (Jet d'Eau) and the United Nations
Lausanne Cathedral
Steamers on Lac Léman
Montreux
Picturesque Gstaad
Verbier for superb sports amenities
St Bernard Pass
Zermatt for skiing
Open rack railway to Gornergrat for views of the Matterhorn
Lötschental valley for the totally unspoilt Alps

The North-east

Zurich, Switzerland's main commercial centre
Swiss National Museum (Landsmuseum), Zurich
Zurich Cathedral
Landsgemeinde in Glarus
Liechtenstein
Appenzell for green rolling hills
St Gallen Cathedral
Stein am Rhein
Rhine Falls

The South-east

White-water rafting in the gorge of the Rein Anteriur river between Flims and Laax
Horse races on ice at St Moritz
The Engadine for unique architecture and *sgraffito*
Zuoz, a typical Engadine village
Lugano, especially the Customs House Museum
Locarno
Bellinzona for town walls and castles

Going Places with Somewhere Special in Mind

Switzerland is a land of contrasts and the following section provides a range of itineraries to help the traveller find a whole series of places of interest. The maps will help to show where each of the numbered sites can be found by reference to a more detailed map of each area.

Churches of the Ticino

Within a small area, and following two valley roads, there are some of the most "Italian" churches in Switzerland. Coming from the north, over the San Bernadino Pass, these delightful, romantic buildings hang onto precipices, or sit astride rocky outcrops.

*T*he minor roads offer
a wealth of routes to explore
away from the motorways.

1 MESOCCO
The first church on this route is at Mesocco; there is also a castle here. Inside the 15th-century Santa Maria church, there are fine murals.

There are three smaller village churches at Soazza, Santa Maria and San Vittore, before arriving at:

2 BELLINZONA
This large city has three castles, which dominate the older part of the city. The medieval section is by far the most interesting, but is often passed by.

From Bellinzona, take the north-western road out of the city for:

3 BIASCA
Here, there is the 13th-century St Peter and Paul Romanesque church, which

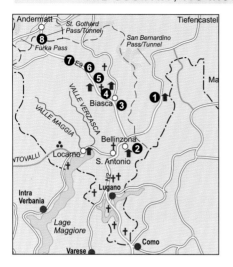

houses frescoes from the same period. If the church is not obviously open, ask for the key in the village.

4 GIORNICO
The church to look for is actually just before Giornico, and is one of the best in the region. It's another Romanesque, 12th-century church well worth a visit. Quite close to here in 1478 the Swiss army defeated the Milanese, despite being heavily outnumbered.

5 CHIRONICO
Not far north of the last stop is Chironico, with a 14th-century church, again containing frescoes from that century.

6 FAIDO
This small village has a number of typical old houses, which are of interest, and on the opposite side of the river is the town of Rossura.

7 QUINTO
This is one of the last churches to be found in the lower regions, and has a 17th-century church, with a 12th-century tower.

8 AIROLO
Heading further north, and just before the St Gothard Pass and tunnel, there is another Romanesque church at Airolo.

Schaffhausen Wine Tour

This area is tucked up into the far northern point of Switzerland. Its wines are, as is its architecture, from a Germanic background. The pleasure of a trip into this self contained region is its peaceful countryside, well away from the normal rush of Swiss tourist traffic. Each of the villages in the area has its own charm, usually based on the wine and the grape. Things to look out for are the decor in the inns and on churches, such as the grape-fingered clock at Oberhallau.

The small circular tour, beginning in the town of Schaffhausen, and the Murmot, takes the traveller to:

NEUNKIRCH

HALLAU

OBERHALLAU

HEMMENTAL

High Peaks of the Alps

With the high number of plus 4,000 m (13,100 ft) mountains in Swiss territory,

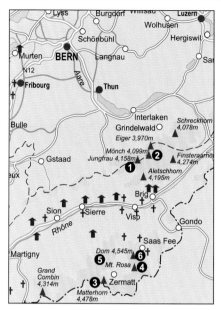

before moving on back to Interlaken, and Spiez. From Spiez the route goes through to Kandersteg, and the rail/car service through to Goppenstein, and the road to Brig.

The next range to see is at Zermatt, and at the small town of Visp, before reaching Brig, there is a small road leading to Zermatt. Again, it is best to use the rail service through to the famous mountain town, and once there the most legendary of all the Swiss mountains is in view:

3 THE MATTERHORN
4,478 m (14,691 ft).

To complete the collection of the highest Alpine mountains, take the rack railway up to Gornergrat (3,090 m; 10,138 ft), where the view takes in:

4 MONTE ROSA
The highest Swiss peak at 4,634 m (15,203 ft).

5 WEISSHORN
4,505 m (14,780 ft).

6 DOM
4,545 m (14,911 ft).

it is an easy tour to take in a few of them, especially since there is an added bonus of travelling to many of the high regions on the private rail systems.

To see seven of the highest, a good place to start is Interlaken. From here the main points of interest are:

1 THE JUNGFRAU
4,158 m (13,642 ft).
Once at the restaurant terrace, the view from here will take in:

2 THE MONCH
4,099 m (13,448 ft), with the Eiger smaller at 3970 m (13,025 ft) but no less impressive. In all, the scene from the Jungfrau also covers the Schreckhorn, and the Lauteraarhorn.

By travelling back on the opposite side to the ascent, either by Grindelwald or Wengen , there is the opportunity to see a great range of high mountains,

The Cradle of Switzerland

This is a delve into the historic part of Switzerland, using the Lucerne steamers, and rail systems.

1 LUCERNE
Having looked at the Kappellbrucke and the city ramparts, take a lake steamer to:

2 WEGGIS

The terminus for the rack railway up to:

3 RIGI

One of the most famous scenic view-points in Europe.

From Weggis, the road runs alongside the lake before the road turns inland and up to:

4 SCHWYZ

The town's museum holds the original charter of the Confederation of Switzerland.
From Schwyz return to the lakeside road to take in:

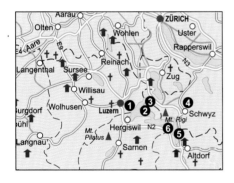

5 TELLSKAPPELLE

The church built in 1879 to commemorate Switzerland's legendary hero.

The road continues around the lake, but at Emmetten, turn towards Seelisberg and the:

6 RUTLI FIELD

It is also possible to visit here by boat. It is the most historic point in Swiss history.

Either go on to Lucerne by road or drop down into Beckenried, and use the ferry service back to the starting point.

Another way of using the Lucerne steamers is to travel:

Lucerne to Vitznau by boat;

Vitznau to the summit of Rigi by cable car;

Rigi to Weggis by railway;

Weggis to Lucerne by boat.

Houses of the Engadine

The Engadine house is unique and this route gives an opportunity to see the best villages.

Coming from Chur in south-east Switzerland, the first place with evidence of the *sgraffito* artwork is at:

1 TIEFENCASTEL

Many interesting buildings and church interiors of the Romansque style.

Both the rail and the road journey through to the Albulapass are enjoyable. Note the changes in the type of building, the nearer the Ober Engadine

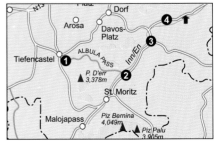

becomes. After the pass, the road and rail meet a T-junction: right for St Moritz and left for:

2 ZUOZ

A small historic village, once the home of the Planta family. The square is particularly good.

Next in this valley, is the town of:

3 ZERNEZ

Another village with fine examples of the Engadine culture.

4 GUARDA

This village is further on into the Engadine, and from here the route takes the traveller on into Austria, but it contains some of the best preserved houses in the area. Turn back along the same road and on to route 28 which goes back towards Teifencastel via Davos-Platz.

Three Lakes Tour

The three lakes in this trip are Biel, Neuchâtel and Morat. Starting at:

1 BIEL/BIENNE

Although not that interesting, there is a pleasant promenade and the novelty of a dual language. There are boats from here to St Peter's Island, but the road on the west shore goes alongside the lake past vineyards at:

2 TWANN

3 LIGERZ

(There are trips out to the island from both Twann and Ligerz.)

An alternative to the island visit is to spend some time walking in the vineyards, in the hills above Ligerz. Information for these walks is in the tourist office on the right of the road, just before the centre of the town.

From Biel, the main route travels straight on to Neuchâtel, but an interesting route would be to turn left across the Moos land, which is one of the flattest parts of Switzerland. From here it is a short distance to:

4 MORAT/MURTEN

A lovely lakeside town with old city ramparts and an air of a holiday resort. On the other side of the lake is another wine-growing town, Vully.

The minor roads meander south through the region, passing some superb castles and villages, before reaching:

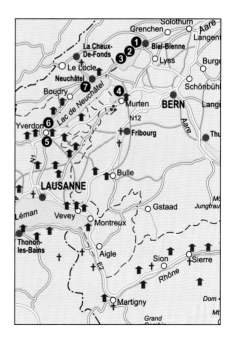

69

5 YVERDON-LES-BAINS

A larger town at the southern end of Lake Neuchâtel. It has good lakeside amenities and a health spa.

Leaving Yverdon, head up the western shore of Lake Neuchâtel to:

6 GRANDSON

A small romantic town with a fine schloss, it was here that the Duke of Burgundy fell to the first of his battles with the confederates.

Finally carry on into:

7 NEUCHATEL

A large town with some interesting buildings, a good marina and quay.

This tour can also be done using the services of the boat companies, as described in the section later in the book on Biel/Bienne.

Romantic Schloss' of Switzerland

This tour covers all the hill-top castles found in the Payerne area.

1 MORAT/MURTEN

Schloss and ramparts from the 15th century, and the scene of one of the Duke of Burgundy's disastrous battles.

2 LAUPEN

Hill-top schloss and scene of a battle in 1339.

3 FRIBOURG

Major town built by Zahringan, with a superb old town by the river.

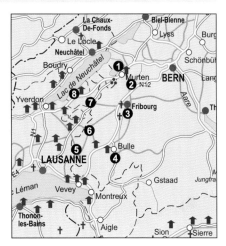

4 GRUYERES

Hill-top walled town, traffic free, and a very popular place for visitors. Cheese production demonstrations are at the bottom of the hill.

5 ORON LE CHATEL

A small town with a conspicuous castle alongside the railway station.

6 ROMONT

A small walled town dating back to the 10th century, with the schloss dating from the 14th century.

7 PAYERNE

A larger industrial town, this is the centre of the area. It does have some archaeological interest, and the town hall was a 14th-century château.

8 ESTAVAYER LE LAC

On the shores of Lake Neuchâtel, this walled town has a 13th-century castle, which is entered by a covered bridge.

The minor road route back to Morat takes in another two castles at Grandcour and St-Aubin.

Dams of Switzerland

There are four major dams in the Valais, all feeding off the waters from the high mountains behind:

1 ST BERNARD DAM

Use this trip to see the hospice and the kennels on the pass. The dam is to the right of the road, before the tunnels.

2 MAUVOISON DAM

The second biggest dam in the country. It is found by taking the right side of the valley out of Le Châble. It's a winding steep road, but the dramatic scene as the walls of the dam come into view are worth the effort.

3 GRAND DIXENCE DAM

This is Switzerland's finest engineering acheivement. It supplies four power stations and is reached by way of the Héremence valley, from the main road at Sion. Take the right fork at Vex.

4 MOIRY

A smaller dam in the beautiful Naviscence valley which runs south from Sierre. The small lane to reach the dam is to the right at Vissoie.

Glacier Passes of Switzerland

This is a longer route from Interlaken around and across some of the highest passes of Europe. It can only be done by road in the summer. Go from Interlaken and Spiez to Kandersteg and take the rail service through the Lötschenpass to Steg. Then take the road along the Rhône valley to:

1 GRIMSEL PASS

2,165 m (7,103 ft), the pass gives views of the Sidelhorn and the Oberaar glacier. Take route 19 on to:

2 FURKA PASS

2,431 m (7,976 ft). Views and excursions into the Rhône Glacier.

Follow the road down towards Andermatt, and then head north-west to Meiringen. This will go over the:

3 SUSTEN PASS

2,224 m (7,297 ft). This pass was created by Napolean to ensure the Bernese would carry their produce to Italy through Swiss territory.

The road continues into Meiringen, and then back to Interlaken.

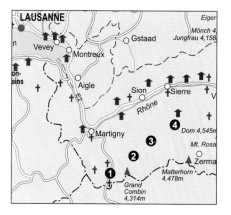

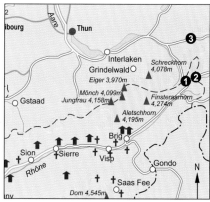

Roman Sites of Switzerland

Starting at Basel.

AUGST
A reconstructed Roman Villa; museum and display of silver treasure. The site of Augustus Raurica, founded in 44 BC, is to the north.

OLTEN
A number of small sites around the town, and at Winznau.

BERN
Capital of Switzerland, but retaining much of its old Roman history.

AVENCHES
Site of a Roman amphitheatre, and one of the finest sites in the country.

Towards Biel/Bienne, there are three sites just south of the city at Studen, Port and Moringen.

Museums

Some of the finest museums of Europe are in Switzerland. The best are:

ZURICH
The Landsmuseum. The greatest national collection.

GENEVA
The Red Cross Museum. History of this world-wide organization

BASEL
The Kuntsmuseum. One of the finest art collections in Europe.

LAUSANNE
The Cathedral Museum. The history of this famous cathedral.

World's Best Ski Centres

ST MORITZ
The highest and the sunniest resort in the Alps.

KLOSTERS
Famous resort with a high-quality background.

WENGEN
Skiing on one of the most difficult World Cup runs.

ZERMATT
Another historic resort with the Matterhorn as a backdrop.

CRANS MONTANA
Almost the perfect purpose-built ski resort.

VERBIER
The new town above the old village has every amenity, and a wealth of skiing in the four valleys.

Homes of Cheeses

APPENZELL
A soft dairy cheese.

GRUYERES
A particulary strong taste and smell.

EMMENTAL
Famous for its holes.

GLARUS
The cheese with the 500-year-old recipe.

Great Hotels of Europe

BASEL
Hotel Three Kings, with its historic visitors book, including Napoleon, and Queen Victoria.

LAUSANNE
The Palais de Lausanne. Scene of the signing of the Treaty of Lausanne.

ZURICH
Dolder Grand Hotel, just plain luxury.

MURTEN/MORAT
La Veiux de Manor. A superb setting, in a magnificent house.

Lausanne Wine Tour

There are 22 routes through the vineyards of Vaud, so any number of tours can be made up. The wine-growers are often pleased to offer samples of their wine.

East of Lausanne
Vevey–Corseaux–St Saphorin–Rivaz–Epesses–Cully.

Chardonne–Les Curnilles–Orgoz–Charmigney–Chardonne.

Chexbres–Le Signal–La Croix–Cheneaux–La Conversion.

Cully–Epesses–La Croix– Ligne–Riex–Cully.

Lutry–Savuit Ligne–Montagny–Lutry.

West of Lausanne
Marges–St Jean–Lonay–Echandens.

Morges–Monnaz–Vufflens–Denens–Lully–Tolochenaz–Morges.

Allaman–La Pecherire–Perroy–Rolle.

Allaman–Fechy–Bougy–Perroy.

Aubonne–Fechy–Bougy–Perroy.

Rolle–Bouge–Mont Dessus–Rolle.

Rolle–Bugnaux–Mont Dessus–Rolle.

Rolle–Begnins.

These are all walking tours, or possibly falling-down tours, depending on how many wines you sample!

Rack Railways

RIGI
One of the oldest in the world.

PILATUS
Recently celebrated its 150th birthday.

ZERMATT–GORNERGRAT
For views of Monte Rosa.

JUNGFRAU
Constructed in 1896, it cost £714,000.

The Basel Fasnacht will Surprise you, as Part of the City and the Country

The watchmakers of Switzerland have worked from this region for centuries, and their work can be seen at one of the finest museums in the country at La Chaux de Fonds. It is in part an industrial region, but it also offers one of the most peaceful parts of the country. Walking up on the plateau above St Croix, called the Siberia of Switzerland, proves just that, but to take in one of the most bizarre occasions of this normally sober country, try Basel in late February; it's not only the historical monuments that will appeal!

Basel

Whilst most holiday visitors to Switzerland come into Geneva or Zurich, heading for the mountains of the Valais and the Engadine, a number of people fly into Basel. For those travelling by road or rail this delightful town may well be the first port of call.

Basel was originally the Roman colony, Augusta Raurica, founded in

*T*he red stone spires of Basel Cathedral can be seen from most of the vantage points along the river banks. This is the oldest part of the town.

44 BC (the year Julius Caesar died), and it has always been an important site. Situated on the first navigable part of the Rhine (Rhein), its business and chemical industries have made good use of the river. Alongside the business wealth has grown a city of art and culture. Its **University**, founded in 1460, is the oldest and possibly the most prestigious in the country. Over 500 years ago the churchmen of Europe created the Ecumenical Council of Basel, and the recently restored 16th-century **Town Hall**, or **Rathaus**, must be one of the finest council offices in Europe.

Basel's modern reputation is probably for the pharmaceutical factories along the banks of the Rhine. Certainly, they cannot be ignored, giving the suburban landscape an industrial

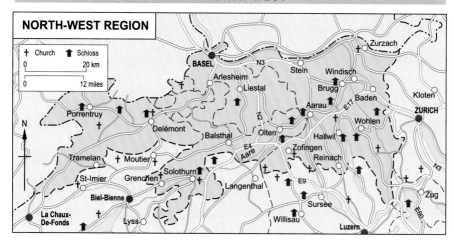

NORTH-WEST REGION

Church Schloss

0 20 km
0 12 miles

N

BASEL
Arlesheim
Liestal
Stein
Windisch
Brugg
Baden
Kloten
ZURICH
Zurzach
Porrentruy
Delémont
Aarau
Wohlen
Balsthal
Olten
Hallwil
Tramelan
Moutier
Zofingen
Reinach
St-Imier
Grenchen
Solothurn
Langenthal
Biel-Bienne
Sursee
Zug
La Chaux-De-Fonds
Lyss
Willisau
Luzern
N3
E4
Aare
N2
E17
N3
E9
E60

BASEL

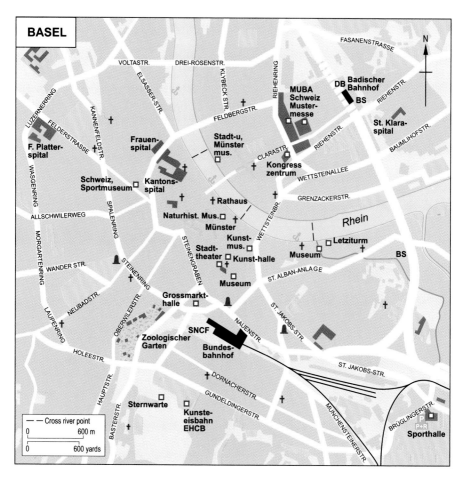

N

FASANENSTRASSE
VOLTASTR.
DREI-ROSENSTR.
KLYBECKSTR.
RIEHENRING
ELSASSER-STR.
FELDBERGSTR.
MUBA Schweiz Mustermesse
DB Badischer Bahnhof
BS
RIEHENSTR.
LUZERNERRING
FELDERSTRASSE
KANNENFELDSTR.
Frauen-spital
Stadt-u, Münster mus.
CLARASTR.
RIEHENSTR.
St. Klara-spital
BAUMLIHOFSTR.
F. Platter-spital
Schweiz, Sportmuseum
Kantons-spital
Kongress zentrum
WETTSTEINALLEE
WASGENRING
SPALENRING
Rathaus
GRENZACKERSTR.
ALLSCHWILERWEG
Naturhist. Mus.
Münster
WETTSTEINBR.
Rhein
MORGARTENRING
STEINENGRABEN
Kunst-mus.
Stadt-theater
Kunst-halle
Museum
Letziturm
BS
WANDER STR.
STEINENRING
Museum
ST. ALBAN-ANLAGE
NEUBADSTR.
Grossmarkt-halle
OBERWILERSTR.
LAUPENRING
Zoologischer Garten
SNCF
NAUENSTR.
ST. JAKOBS-STR.
HOLEESTR.
Bundes-bahnhof
ST. JAKOBS-STR.
HAUPTSTR.
DORNACHERSTR.
MÜNCHENSTEINERSTR.
BASTERSTR.
Sternwarte
Kunste-eisbahn EHCB
GUNDELDINGERSTR.
BRÜGLINGERSTR.
P P+R
Sporthalle

Cross river point
0 600 m
0 600 yards

outline. The city is used regularly for international trade fairs, which are held at the Swiss Industries Trade Halls.

Basel has also managed to combine three nationalities within its boundaries and the new international airport is being promoted as the *Europort*. On arrival you can choose which country you want to enter—Switzerland, Germany or France. International boundaries cut across the town, and on some local bus trips you can move between Germany and Switzerland quite regularly. This combination of three countries is not as much of a problem as you might think, and oddly, Basel does not have the bilingual signposting of Fribourg or Biel.

Basel/Mulhouse Europort

The airport has had a face-lift, to cater for what is an anticipated increase in traffic. Crossair (Switzerland's internal airline) use the airport as their base, and new routes may well be introduced into Basel. After choosing the Swiss passport control entry point, the best way into the city (if you are not hiring a car) is by the bus, which runs about every 15 minutes, and departs from the main entrance to the arrivals floor. The cost is low, and you have to buy your ticket from the machine at the bus stop. The driver does not have change or tickets, so it is as well to have some 2 SFr pieces handy. The bus takes you to the SBB railway

*M*ap of north-west Switzerland (opposite, above).

Town plan of Basel (opposite, below).

station (Swiss Railways), which is not quite in the centre of town, but is at a main tram terminal. If you are going to stay in the old town, you will need to use one of these trams to get there—it is a fairly long trek down to the river area.

Transport

The trams, whilst responsible for an unsightly array of aerial wires which ruin the aesthetics of your photographs, also provide an excellent, cheap service around the city and its outskirts. There is a mixture of tramways and tram buses, but both belong to the same system, and the routes are interlinked.

All the tram services operate on a prepaid fare system. The green or orange ticket machines are at every stop (the orange ones giving change) and are split into zones. You rarely need more than zone 1, which is a fare of around 80 centimes. (If you have a Swiss Card for the railways, you can use it for free travel throughout the city.) You can make two stops on the ticket, so if you want to spend a few hours going round the city, then the cost is fairly low. Alternatively, you can buy a day ticket, which will give you unlimited travel on the whole system. These are available from hotel receptions or from the BVB counter at **Barfusserplatz**.

Main Tram Routes

SBB Station (Bahnhof) and airport bus stop–Markplatz: Routes 1 and 8 (Messeplatz direction).
SBB Station–Kunstmuseum: Route 2
Markplatz–Zoo: Routes 6, 1 and 8.
Route number 3 will take you from

one side of the city to the other; from **St Albans Tor** to the **Spalentor**.

The main shopping centre is around the **Claraplatz** and the tram numbers 1 and 8 will take you there.

Ferries

It is not a long walk over one of the many bridges crossing the mighty River Rhine, but if you are between crossing points, or you fancy a short boat ride on one of the quaint ferries, there are four to choose from. They operate mainly in summer, travelling across the river by means of a tram-like overhead wire. The boats are small wooden gondola-like vessels, with a canopied area at the rear. Positioned between the bridges the three main ferries depart from a point about 100 m from the Hotel Drei Konige to **Klingental**, from the **cathedral** (Munster) area to Waisenhaus and from **St Albans Tor**, near the **Paper Museum,** to the **Kinderspital**.

At the eastern end of Basel is St Albans Tor, which was once one of the gateways to the city.

Driving

Basel is not a particularly good place to take your car, since most of the interesting areas of the city are traffic-free. If you are staying outside the city, then the public transport system should be straightforward enough to use. If you have to bring a vehicle into the town, then there are car parks on the City Umfahrung (the ring road). These are multi-storey car parks, and are probably the best places to leave your car.

Within the city, apart from the pedestrian precincts, there *are* non-prohibited times: Mondays to Fridays 1.00–6.30p.m. and Saturdays 11.00a.m. to 5.00p.m. The rest of the time the city centre is closed to traffic.

Tours

Basel is a fairly small town, so sight-seeing trips are quite short. The city coach tour takes one and three-quarter hours and leaves from outside the Hotel Victoria near the SBB Bahnhof.

The tourist office also operates trips out to the Black Forest, Alsace, and to the countryside surrounding Basel.

Walking

Undoubtedly the best way to see the sights of Basel is to take a tram to the **Markplatz**, and then walk. It is an easy city to walk around, through the small winding lanes of the old town, or as a summer stroll alongside the Rhine, from the **Mittiere Brucke** to the **Solitude Park**.

Throughout the city there are blue information boards with directions to the various sights and buildings. The tourist office runs city walking tours which ensure that you see all the historically and culturally important sites. For less able visitors the tourist offices provide a map and guide which will help to make a visit less difficult.

Banks

There are plenty of banks throughout the city, at main city areas such as Markplatz, Claraplatz, Spiegelgasse and Gerbergasse. For change, offices are open at:

Bahnhof SBB: 6.00a.m. to 11.15p.m. (closed Sundays);
Bad Bahnhof: 6.30a.m. to 8.30p.m. (closed Sundays);
Airport: Mondays to Fridays 6.00a.m. to 8.00p.m., Saturdays 6.00a.m. to 6.00p.m., Sundays 7.00a.m. to 8.00p.m.

Accommodation

Basel has a good range of hotels, although, as in most large towns or cities, the prices do tend to be slightly high. The symbols used relate to either the Swiss Hotel Association, or the Member of Basel Tourist Board (VVB). On average a room without shower will cost from 80 SFr, and with facilities from 150 SFr upwards. As with most Swiss hotels, the accommodation is clean, large, and generally good value for money. What part of the city you want to stay in largely depends on the purpose of your visit to Basel, but for the most pleasant, picturesque accommodation, the hotels at the side of the Rhine are the best. If you are looking for a quick getaway from the railway station, then there are seven hotels close by to choose from.

Basel is very full on the three days of the **Fasnacht**. This takes place on the first Monday after Ash Wednesday (late February/early March). Advance bookings for this period are definitely necessary as about 120,000 visitors flock to see the event.

The Old Town and River

There are three hotels recommended on the bank of the river opposite the cathedral:

Hotel Merian am Rhein: a beautiful building situated right next to the **Mittiere Brucke** (bridge) houses this four-star hotel. The restaurant and café are particularly pleasant, but beware of the rotating door and curtain combination, which confuses people coming during the winter when the curtain is pulled across. It can be defeated but needs some thought!

*T*he main bridge over
the Rhine at Basel connects
some of the newer amenities and
shops to the old Markplatz and
the cathedral, and is part of the
route of the Fasnacht.

Hotel Hecht am Rhein: since this one-star hotel is next door to the Meriam, the situation is similar. Facilities are fewer, but it is about half the cost.

Hotel Kraft am Rhein: this is a lively three-star hotel, with some lovely interior decor. Sweeping staircases, red carpet, and paintings on the wall contribute to a warm atmosphere. The rooms are somewhat small, and if you want to watch TV its position up on a shelf near the ceiling makes for awkward viewing. The restaurant is regarded as one of the best in Basel and certainly has plenty of atmosphere in the evenings.

On the opposite bank there is the five-star Hotel Drei Konige am Rhein. This is regarded as one of the finest hotels in Europe, if not the world. Its

The Terminus is fairly typical, offering comfortable rooms in the older part of the building or in a new extension providing higher quality accommodation.

Outskirts
On the outskirts of Basel there are a dozen hotels, which are cheaper than in the city, with prices at about 70–90 SFr for a double room.

Camping
There are no obvious camping areas around Basel—the nearest sites are at Rheinfelden to the east and at Vermes, on the way to Biel/Bienne.

Student Hostelries
There are a number of these in Basel:
Studentenheim Genossenschaft
Mensa Studentheim
Traugott Sandemeyer-Stiftung
Katholisches Studentneheim
Universitatsbibliothek Cafe
Alumneun
Boizentrum der universitat
Le Centre.

visitor's book makes fascinating reading with notables such as Queen Victoria, Dickens, Voltaire, and Napoleon among the guests, although it is doubtful that the latter paid his bills! The cost for staying in this hall of fame, which is said to have been an inn since 1026, is around 300–400 SFr per night for a double room.

Bahnhof and Area
Of the seven hotels around the Central Bahnhofplatz, the choice goes from the five-star Euler and Hilton to the three-star Bristol, Gothard and Terminus.

The Sights of Basel

The finest sights of Basel are probably to be found in the architecture of the **old town**. This architecture, along with a wealth of **museums** and a fine **zoo**, are its main attractions.

The Munster
The **cathedral**, founded in 1019, is largely 12th-century. Its imposing twin Gothic spires of red sandstone and its decorated roofs can be seen from most points of the city. To reach this major landmark, you will have to walk either

*T*he 12th-century cathedral at Basel remains one of the
outstanding sights of both the city and the country.

from the **Markplatz** or from the riverside. Both routes are well signposted, and each is a pleasant walk. Of the two routes, the small cobbled lane **Rheinsprung Augustinberg** has a number of old **calligraphy shops** on the right. The **Munsterplatz** is at the top of this lane, from where the full grandeur of the cathedral can be seen.

The main porches of the building are Romanesque, again from the 12th century. Like many of Europe's religious buildings, the upkeep and restoration work is a continuous programme, but generally the beauty of this fine cathedral is obvious even when there is work going on. Inside, the cathedral is divided into five aisles, with some 11th-century sandstone reliefs at the end of the south and north aisles. Adjoining the cathedral is the former **Bishop's palace**, and the Munsterplatz. This whole area is a very pleasant, quiet part of Basel.

The Town Hall (Rathaus)

This magnificent red stone building dominates the Markplatz, and has recently been restored to its former glories. The exterior walls are decorated with frescoes, as are the courtyard walls. The paintings originate from 1610, some 100 years after the ten-year construction of the building (1504–1514). Recent restoration has left the building, clocks and towers in superb condition, and one can only envy the council officers who work there.

On the Markplatz, the old town hums with activity in the shape of market stalls, musicians and the constant coming and going of the city trams.

From here, a short walk will take you to the **Peterskirchplatz**. All along

the old town lanes, there are small courtyards with fountains, medieval architecture and stately town houses. *En route* to the **Peterskirch**, you will see the **Fischmarkt fountain**, regarded as the most important Gothic fountain in Switzerland. On the edges of the old town are the **three gates**, of which the **Spalentor** is probably the most interesting. The overhead tramwires which encircle this fine piece of history do nothing to enhance its impact, but it remains an interesting sight.

On the other side of the city is the **St Albans Tor,** another of the city gates. In itself, this is relatively uninteresting, but just down the hill from here are the remains of the old wall and the **Paper Museum**.

The Museums

Basel boasts 27 museums. The major artistic and cultural displays in the city are held in the **Fine Arts Museum** and the **Kunsthalle**.

The Fine Arts Museum
St Alban Graben 16
Opening times: 10.00a.m. to 5.00p.m. The museum dates back to 1662, and has one of the finest collections of Swiss and German 15th- and 16th-century paintings. There are some 3,000 paintings covering the old masters, Holbein (Elder and Younger) and Witz, Impressionists and Post-impressionists. Works by Rodin, Renoir and Van Gogh are all on the first floor. But possibly one of the best collections is devoted to the 20th century. The people of Basel decided to buy two paintings by Picasso, which led to the artist donating another four pictures. Along with the Picasso (and baroque)

paintings, there are the works of the Cubists Juan Gris and Fernand Leger, as well as surrealists Dali, Miro, Ernst and Klee.

The museum has a fine collection of art dating from the 15th century right through to the 1990s. It is probably one of the most comprehensive collections anywhere in Europe, and well worth a visit.

The Kunsthalle
Steinenberg 7
Opening times: 10.00a.m. to 5.00p.m. The Kunstalle is almost next to the Fine Arts Museum, but is the venue for travelling and non-permanent art exhibitions. There are always plenty of posters and advertisements giving information on the current displays.

The Paper Museum (Papiermühle)
St Alban Tor
Opening times: Mondays to Saturdays, 2.00–5.00p.m.
This is a small museum, reached by taking tram number 3 to St Alban Tor and walking down a hill towards the river. On the way down towards the museum you can see one of the **old town walls**. The museum is at the far end of this wall, on either side of the **water-wheel**. The history of paper production and printing in the city goes back to the 1500s and this small working museum gives a good account of the industry.

As well as the exhibition area and the practical demonstrations on paper production in the past that take place in the museum, there is a café and shop.

Of the remaining museums, probably the most interesting are:

Paper Making

Basel preserves the great period of paper making at the small museum near St Alban Tor. The methods used are recreated, and visitors can see how rags were used as the raw material for the final product. Having been cut up, the rags were pulped into a coarse slurry by metal hammers in the stamping mill. The slurry was then reduced to a fine pulp, laid on felt and passed through a press. The resultant paper was finally hung out to dry before being sized (to stop the ink from running). Visitors to the museum can participate in the processes, as well as see exhibitions of typesetting and printing.

The Antique Art Museum (Antikenmuseum)
St Alban Graben 5
Opening times: Mondays to Saturdays, 10.00a.m. to 5.00p.m.
Take tram number 2. This museum displays Greek and Roman art.

Musical Instruments Museum (Musikinstrumente)
Leonhardsstrasse 8
Opening times: Mondays to Fridays, 2.00–5.00p.m., Sundays 10.00a.m. to 12.00p.m. and 2.00–5.00p.m.
Take tram number 3, Musik Akademie stop. This museum houses a good collection of early musical instruments, with a taped sound programme of the instruments being played.

Pharmacy Museum (Pharmazie-Historiches)
Totengasslein 3
Opening times: Mondays to Fridays, 9.00a.m. to 12.00p.m. and 2.00–5.00p.m.

Situated between the Markplatz and Peterskirch, about five minutes from the northern end of the Markplatz, this museum gives a history of the pharmaceutical industry, with a display of 18th-century medical equipment.

Historical Museum
(Historiches)
Barfusskirche
Opening times: 10.00a.m. to 5.00p.m.
This is near the Barfussplatz; tram number 3, trams 1 or 8 from SBB station or Markplatz will get you there. Various pieces of interest from Basel, including treasures from the cathedral, and fountain columns are on display.

The Natural History Museum
(Naturhistoriches)
Augustinerstrasse 2
Opening times: Tuesdays to Sundays, 10.00a.m. to 12.00p.m. and 2.00–5.00p.m.
This is on the right-hand side of Augustinerstrasse, walking up the lane which continues from the Rheinsprung, from the Markplatz to the Munsterplatz. Museum with minerals, dinosaur skeletons.

The Sports Museum
(Sportmuseum)
Missionstrasse 28
Opening times: Mondays to Saturdays, 2.00–5.00p.m.; Sundays, 10.00a.m. to 12.00p.m. and 2.00–5.00p.m.
Just beyond the Spalentor, on the way out of the city. Tram number 3 will get you there. An unusual collection of sport-associated items, including some racing cycles.

Caricature and Cartoon Museum
(Karikaturen Basel)
St Alban-Vorstadt 9
Opening times: Mondays and Saturdays, 4.00–6.30p.m.; Sundays, 2.00–5.00p.m.
Take tram number 2 to the Kunstmuseum stop, then take the right turn at the crossroads of Dufour Strasse and St Alban Vorstadt. The museum is on the left. Basel has a more than passing interest in this form of art, because of the number of cartoons and caricatures used in the Fasnacht. Displays vary throughout the year, highlighting cartoonists from different countries.

If this collection of museums is not sufficient, then there are also:

Architectural Museum
(Architekturmuseum)
Pfluggasslein 3
Opening times: Tuesdays to Fridays, 10.00a.m. to 12.00p.m. and 2.00–6.30p.m.; Saturdays, 10.00a.m. to 4.30p.m.; Sundays, 10.00a.m. to 1.00p.m.
Take trams 1 or 8, between Barfussplatz and Markplatz.

The Monteverdi Car Collection
Ober Wilerstrasse 20
Binningen
Opening times: Mondays to Fridays, 1.00–6.00p.m.; Saturdays and Sundays, 11.00a.m. to 6.00p.m.
This museum is on the outskirts of the city, past the zoo.

Basel Country Cantonal Museum
Altes Zeughaus, Zeugahusplatz 2, Leistal

Opening times: Tuesdays to Fridays, 10.00a.m. to 12.00p.m. and 2.00–5.00p.m.; Saturdays and Sundays, 10.00a.m. to 5.00p.m. On the outskirts of the city, past the zoo.

Most of the museums have special events lasting a month or more. For up-to-date information, the information office at the SBB or next to the Drei Konig Hotel (and the Mittlere bridge), has a leaflet giving details. It also lists *all* the museums. There is another leaflet available which gives details of all Basel's cultural activities.

If, after visiting this wealth of architectural and artistic splendour you are looking for a breath of fresh air, then **Basel Zoo**, or the **river port** are places of interest on the city boundaries.

The Zoological Gardens

Binningstrasse 40
Opening times: 8.00a.m. to 6.30p.m. (summer), 8.00a.m. to 5.30p.m (winter).

To get there, take tram number 2 from the SBB station, tram number 6 from the BD station and Markplatz or tram number 7 from Aeschenplatz.

There is a greater argument, these days, for not having zoos, and to a certain extent, I agree with that idea. However, if there are to be zoos, then Basel is as good as any. It has been in

The Basel Fasnacht

If the opportunity arises, one of the best times to see Basel in a different light is in February, on the first Monday after Ash Wednesday. The Basel Fasnacht will surprise you, not only as part of the city, but also as part of Switzerland.

It begins at 4.00a.m. on the Monday, and continues non-stop for 72 hours. The main theme is the parades of "cliques", groups of musicians. They stroll through the old town playing fifes and drums in a slightly military style. Their costumes vary from traditional chequered outfits to the most outlandish, bizarre attire. Grotesque masks, insect and animal heads complete this most un-Swiss scene. The parades start when the Markplatz clock strikes 4.00a.m., and wave after wave of these strange-looking people march through the city. Amongst the more traditional cliques are the *musicgrugge* bands. They are a more recent addition to the Fasnacht, and are based on a slightly off-key jazz and oompah band music. They inevitably have the most enormous sousaphones bringing up the rear, and one of the delights of the Fasnacht is to trot behind one of these bands each night. Encouraged by the rhythm of the band, supporters and general stragglers gather behind the musicians, who occasionally stop to give impromptu concerts, mostly in the middle of the street. At each stop, more people join the entourage, making for quite a crowd marching through the old streets of Basel.

During the day, parades of floats show off the banners and posters, many of which are send-ups of local and national dignitaries. There is a lot of political comment, with a fair amount of self-criticism. The whole event can become something of a trial, but the Fasnacht "players" carry on, day and night. It would be an unusual carnival (Fasnacht can be strictly translated to "carnival"), in any country. The fact that it is held in a city, and in a country, with a reputation for a stringent and rather staid attitude makes it an even more exciting sight.

existence since 1874, and its main claim to fame today is that it has successfully managed the reproduction of many rare and endangered species. Its success in this area has gained it an international reputation, with animals such as the Spectacled Bear and rhinoceros benefiting from its work.

For the children, there are elephant rides, a games area and a special "zoo" featuring smaller or domestic animals. In this area they can touch some of the animals. There is probably more freedom for the animals here, the zoo fitting in somewhere between the traditional zoo and the safari park.

There are feeding times for the animals, and to cater for the visitors there is a cafe and a restaurant. There is a good picnic area so, for a city zoo, a trip here can be a good day out for the family, especially on a warm summers' day when perhaps the many museums can prove too much.

At the colourful Basel Fasnacht the participants often parade as caricatures of themselves. This clique leader has opted for a military theme.

The Dreilandereck—Three Countries Corner

This is an interesting part of Basel, and indeed of Switzerland. From the vantage point where the three countries (Switzerland, Germany and France) meet, you can watch the huge commercial barges reaching their final destination. The point is marked by a futuristic pylon with the three national emblems on each of its three corners. There is, of course, a café, and if nothing else it is a pleasant place in which to take in the river scene.

Basel District

The countryside around Basel comes under a different jurisdiction from that of the city; it has its own cantonal centre and crest. To the north of Basel you are into Germany, at Lorrach and Weil am Rhein, and to the north-west

is France, at Mulhouse and Bourgfelden. Basel's outskirts from the *Swiss* sense are very much to the south and the east.

To the east of the city, on the route to Zurich, Bern and Lucerne, is the **St Jakob Sports Centre**. From this point you can either carry on east towards Zurich, or head south towards Delemont and the Jura. On this latter road you will see the turn-off for the **Augusta Raurica Amphitheatre**, at Augst. The site has been reproduced to give some idea of how the real thing looked, and features a **Roman house** and a **Roman hot bathroom** showing the system of underfloor heating. The site is still used for open-air events, and is one of the largest Roman amphitheatres in Switzerland, along with the amphitheatre at Avenches.

The way south will eventually take you into some of the most pleasant scenery of Switzerland. It has less

drama than the Alps, but also has less of the tourist "hype". It is quiet, the roads are virtually empty, and if your budget doesn't run to St Moritz prices, it is reasonably priced. You will get the impression that this could be the area where many Swiss take their holidays.

The route from Basel to Delemont is no more than averagely attractive. It probably was attractive earlier in the century, before man made his industrial mark on riversides. There are quite a few water-based industries along this road, which hugs the River Birse. There are a few highlights, such as the château at Zwinge, inconspicuously sitting next to a factory. It is not worth a special visit, but where else would it be allowed to remain standing? The road, railway and river all meander through to Delemont, the capital of the Jura Canton.

Delemont

Delemont is a fairly large town, and quite industrial. Its most famous industries are based on watch- and clockmaking. Typically, there is an old part of town which, despite the modern rôle of the city, gives some indication of its past. In the **old town** there are 16th-century fountains, the **Bishop's castle** and the **St Marcellus church**. Delemont could easily be passed by, although if the archaeology of the Jura region is of interest then you may well want to visit the **Museum of the Jura** here.

*E*ven on a river as busy as the Rhine it is still possible to do some fishing.

From Delemont the scenery improves and also the weight of the traffic lessens. This is the region known as the **Jura Bernois**, and its publicity boasts "a region free of mass tourism". This may seem an astonishing claim in a country which has prided itself on the development of mass tourism, but it is true, since from here to the rolling hills which drop down to Yverdon at the south end of Lac Neuchâtel, the atmosphere is less hectic, and you will not be forced off the road by pushy drivers on their way to the downhill ski runs every weekend.

You have two choices—the high road or the low road, although there is a small area of land which juts into France, where the city of **Porrentruy** is situated. Both routes, 18 and 6, lead to **La Chaux de Fonds**, and there is little to choose between them. You could also take the small roads between them to cut across country, either by car or by hiring a bike at any of the railway stations. The rail takes much the same course and you will find regional trains which will stop at the villages between Delemont and La Chaux de Fonds. The lower of the two routes will take you through some dramatic gorge scenery, while the higher road follows the ridge of the Franche Montagnes. Here you are skirting the French border, passing through some small towns at Montfavergier and Saignelegier.

Camping

There are a number of campsites along this route and around the region. All the campsites are non-classified, but they do take in caravans as well as tents. This is a good region for the more quiet campsites.

Montmelon-Dessous: between the main road (18) and St Ursanne. Open: 1 March–30 October.

There are two further sites to the west, nearer the French border at:

Tariche: open 1 March–30 November; Ocourt Moulin de Doubs: Open 1 March–31 October.

Continuing down route 18, either side of the road at Saignelegier there are campsites at:

Goumais: near Les Pommerats and the French border. Open: 15 April–1 October.

Saignelegier-Sous la Neuvevie: on the road to Tramelan. Open: 1 May–31 October.

The lower of the two roads, route 6, takes you through the **Gorges de Birse**, following the same river as previously on the road to Delemont. Again, the road, rail and river share the valley floor, and there is not a great deal of room for all three. The gorge cliffs are high and sheer, with wooded tops. If this route was not so busy with traffic, it would probably be more pleasant. However, it is a main road through to Delemont from the Biel and Neuchâtel industrial regions, so there are a good number of lorries on the road. A more leisurely route will take you through the more picturesque **Gorges de Pichoux**. This uses a minor road, but is well signposted (with the now European standard brown signposts), running from route 18 down to route 6. By taking this road you will avoid

the heavy traffic. Again, the gorges are deeply cut into the limestone, with fir trees clinging to the sides. This is one of those small areas not served by rail, but the PTT bus service runs from Tavannes, a small watchmaking town on the main road (30).

From here the road goes on through the **St Imier valley**, through the town of the same name and on to La Chaux de Fonds. St Imier is quite a large place and, if the town is approached from the the hills of Le Chasseral, its situation is something of a surprise. Unlike most towns involving a valley and a river, this town follows the length, rather than the width. Thus on the approach from the hills, the visitor is faced with an unusually long town.

St Imier

This town sits somewhere between an industrial watch- and chocolate-making centre and a tourist resort. It is already fairly high up, at about 800m (2,620 ft), but there is a funicular service to **Mount Soleil** at 1,290 m (4,232 ft). From here there is skiing, both downhill and cross country, and summer walking paths. There is a good view from Mount Soleil across to the **Chasseral**. In the town itself there is a skating rink, an outdoor swimming pool, a gliding school at Courtely and good fishing in the River Suze.

Accommodation
St Imier has three hotels, the Hotel de l'Ergual, the two-star Hotel de la Fontaine, and the Hotel Valaisan. The nearest campsite is La Cibourg, Clermont, which is about 15 km (9 miles) away towards La Chaux de Fonds. It is open all year round.

*T*here are just a few areas of Switzerland not dominated by mountains, such as this scene of fields north of Bern.

Sights

From St Imier there are some very good sights to be seen. The area is scattered with good walking paths, both short and long distance. If this is your first taste of the Jura, then you can begin to appreciate what an unspoilt part of Switzerland it is.

La Chasseral

This is the high point on the hills opposite St Imier, and is easily reached by car, bus, or on foot. The most direct footpath goes from Villeret, just outside St Imier, and goes through the **nature reserve** of Combe Grede. There are also paths from the town itself and a longer-distance path from Renan, about halfway between St Imier and La Chaux de Fonds. At the top of La Chasseral there are cross-country ski trails for winter, and more pathways which will take you over some quite high ground and down onto the vine-clad hills around Lake Biel. Another way of reaching the lakeside area from La Chasseral is to use the chairlift down to Nods.

Lake Biel (Bieler See)

Heading the lake, at the point where the River Aare flows in, is the city of Biel/Bienne. A double-barrelled name? Not really, since this city has the dubious honour of being the only city in Switzerland (or even the world) which cannot decide which language to use. So street names are marked "Rue de la Gare", and directly underneath "Bahnhofsträsse". This oddity apart, there is not a great deal to recommend about Biel/Bienne. It is a good starting point for a boat trip around the lake, it has

91

a nice promenade area, but essentially it is an industrial town, and quite a big one at that.

The town is well served with roads from Bern (about 30 minutes on the E27 motorway), from Delemont and Basel on route 6, or from the south and Neuchâtel on the N5. But the pleasures of this region are found outside the city walls of Biel/Bienne, along the lake-shore, and on the particularly unusual "island" of **St Peters**.

Biel/Bienne

The city's main claim to fame is its bilingual population, almost an equal split between French and German, with the latter having a small majority. Whichever way you come into Biel/ Bienne you will find industrial sites, not large ones, but enough to make you want to find the lake fairly quickly. There is an old centre of the town, with a **city hall** (Rathaus) which has the only **town gate** still in existence, dating back to 1530. The **church of St Benoit** (1451), the **"ring"**, the **Wauldleuten Guild House**, and a number of **fountains** make up the historic part of Biel/Bienne.

For a good view of the town and the lake there are two funicular and cable cars from Biel/Bienne to Macolin/Magglingden and Leubringen/-Evilard. The cable cars will not only give you a good panoramic view, but also provide good points from which to start walks through the **vineyards**, further down the lake.

Accommodation

Accommodation is plentiful in the city, since a fair proportion of its visitors are here on business. With 15 hotels to choose from, you can take your pick, but some will be of the sort where you may not be too sure which country you're in, never mind which city. Of this type there are:

Hotel Continental (four-star): Rue d'Aarberg;
Hotel Pullman Century Plaza (four-star): Neumarktsrasse 40–42.

On the older, more traditional side of the hotel lists, there are:

Hotel Schloss: at the junction of the Aarbergstrasse and the Route de Berne;
Hotel Weisses Rossli/Du Cheval Blanc: Madrentschstrasse/Route de Mache.

These hotels are in the higher price brackets. The best place to find the cheaper, but still good quality, accommodation is around the lake, in the wine villages.

All the villages on the western side of the lake, at Twann, Ligerz and La Neuville, have small picturesque hotels situated right on the lakeside. Some will be quite expensive, such as the Rousseay Hostellerie at La Neuville, but there are a number which offer reasonably priced rooms.

Camping

Camping is primarily on the western side of the lake, and situated on the hill above Lake Biel you will find some superb campsites:

Camping Preles: a four-star site on the road from Ligerz to Diesse, at Preles. Open: 1 May–30 August.

Fraso-Ranch Ligniers: a five-star site. This site is found by taking the road up into the vineyards from La Neuville to Ligniers. The site is on the road to La Praye.
Open: 20 December–31 October.

Down by the lake at La Neuville, there is a non-classified site:

Plage de Neuville: open 1 April–30 September.

Lake Biel

Whenever poets and lakes get together, a quotation always emerges. Lake Biel is no exception, since a poet has described Lake Biel as "the most beautiful thousandth of Switzerland". Only a country so keen on the precise could have worked out that Lake Biel is exactly one-thousandth of the land area of the country! The lake is indeed beautiful, and one its finest points is at St Petersinsel—**St Peter's Island**. Before reaching the island, by whatever form of transport you choose, there are some lovely villagesthat are worth visiting.

Twann is the first village of any note out of Biel, coming down route 5. There is also a regional train from Biel/Bienne, and the boat service runs from

*S*et amongst the vines in the hills above Lake Biel is Ligerz church. On a clear day you can see St Peter's Island.

May to October. The village has a number of good restaurants specializing in fish, and they also produce their own Twanner white wine. Further up through the vineyards the **Twannbach Falls**, at the **Gorges de Douanne**, are worth a visit.

Ligerz is the next village on the road, and the next stop on the boat or train route. This village is particularly picturesque, with an **old church** perched amongst the vineyards above the lake. The small lanes up to the church and beyond provide a whole network of paths through the vineyards, and give superb views of St Peter's Island and the lake. Also at Ligerz there is a **wine museum**, and a funicular which goes up to Preles.

La Neuville is the final stop before the island and Erlach, at the southern end of Lake Biel. La Neuville is more a small town than a village, having a variety of amenities, such as tennis courts, water sports, a marina and some good hotels. There is also a service directly to St Peter's Island from here which runs about every 30 minutes during the summer.

Erlach is the village from which you can either walk to the island or leave the boat. It is at the southern end of Lake Biel. The 11th-century **castle** (schloss) is above the village, and from here you can look down on the peninsula and St Peter's. It is one of the typical, beautifully kept castles of the region, vineyards surrounding its walls. In the town itself, which is a market town for the nearby prosperous market garden industry, there are shops, hotels and cafés. Down by the lake there are two car parks. One is the starting point for the walk to St Peter's, which takes about an hour. The other is near the **marina**, by the landing stage for the various boats. Just before the quay there is a **picnic area**, with a children's play park alongside. This is a good place for a summer's day out.

Although the boat service takes just one and a quarter hours to make the journey from Biel/Bienne to Erlach, you could spend up to a week exploring the surrounding area. The vineyards provide all the necessary footpaths around the region; in fact there are 250 km (155 miles) of signposted *wanderwegs*. Cyclists can make use of the flat ground to the south-east of the lake, where there are routes marked with red discs giving tours of 7–69 km (4.3–43 miles).

St Peter's Island (St Petersinsel)

This is the highlight of the boat trip for many visitors to the lake, although it is not exactly an island—you can walk along the peninsula from Erlach, but most visitors in summer would arrive by boat. Some famous people have stopped on the island, including Josephine Bonaparte and Goethe. However, the most famous figure to have used the island was **Jean Jacques Rousseau**, the Swiss philosopher. He was perhaps the sort of man who would seek refuge on an island such as this, since his theory that man is "born free, and is everywhere in chains" shows a certain dismay with the world. He actually only stayed there for two months in 1765, but this was sufficient to warrant his room being re-created for curious visitors. The island itself, when it was a real island, dates back to 1127, when the Cluniac monks built a **monastery** here. Now that very monastery is a restaurant and hotel, serving lake fish and local wine, so you can not only visit it, but can stay there as well.

Having savoured the natural delights of the lakeside at Biel, a major historical sight is nearby, and is well worth a visit. La Chaux de Fonds, reached from either St Imier or Neuchâtel, is the home of a fascinating museum— **La Muséé International d'Horologie**.

The International Museum of Horology
Rue de Musée 29
Opening times: winter 10.00a.m. to 12.00p.m. and 2.00–5.00p.m. (closed Mondays); summer 10.00a.m. to 12.00p.m. and 2.00–5.00p.m.
There are group reductions for 10 persons or more, and you can book a guided tour in advance, at a cost of about 50 SFr per group.

It seems only right that a country so dedicated to the subject of time—be it in the form of the science of horology, or simply a timetable—should devote a museum to clocks and watches. But this museum looks not only at clocks and watches, but also sundials and time-keeping instruments of every description. The museum houses the largest collection of time-pieces in the world, holds international conventions related to the industry and has an on-site restoration and repair workshop. The museum also provides training for future watch- and clockmakers.

The museum is situated towards the end of the Rue de Musée, about 10 minutes walk from the railway station (turn right outside the station). There is metered car parking outside.

Inside, there is every form of timepiece imaginable, from the early tower clocks that used fairly rudimentary weights to keep the clock ticking, through to modern electronic devices. There are also sundials, stop-watches, glorious regal French clocks, and marine chronometry. There is a recreation of an **astronomical clock**, made in 1985 by the Italian Luigi Pippa, who meticulously reproduced it from drawings made by Giovanni Dondi in the 14th century. The show cases are domes hanging from the ceiling or on pedestals. In the lowered lighting these globes give a space-like feel to the display. At the far end of the first level is the **workshop**, where you can look at the craftsmen carrying out repairs and restoration work. On the second level the floor is dedicated to the more common, recognizable watches, including some (to my mind) awful 1950s mantelpiece clocks. All the major manufacturers, such as Rolex, Logines, Omega and Swatch have donated a selection of their production for the display.

At the entrance there is a good museum shop where it is possible to buy replicas of some of the exhibits.

Outside is another Swiss oddity. A *carillon*, about 9 m (30 ft) high and made from 24 sound tubes. Apart from giving a very accurate time check in the form of a digital five-figure number, it produces sound—a modern variation on listening to the clock tick.

This museum won the European Museum of the Year award in 1978, and my only criticism is that although there is a section showing new acquisitions, some updating of the modern watch displays is necessary.

La Chaux de Fonds

The main reason for the Horological Museum being located in this town is that it was here that the industry grew up and is still centred. There are many small villages and towns in the Jura which have a watch industry but this is where Swiss clocks began. The history of the industry goes back to 1679, when Daniel Jean Richard repaired a watch from Neuchâtel. He moved on to manufacture watches, and so the area grew into the centre for this industry. The competition from the Far East has clearly had an effect on business, but there is still sufficient kudos to be gained from owning a genuine Swiss watch, especially a hand-crafted one, to keep the industry moving.

In the same road as the horological museum, there is the **Museum of Fine Art,** which has just been restored to its

A foretaste of the elegant architecture to be found in Neuchâtel can be seen here at the quayside. There are also castles and mansions further inland.

former glory. The sight of the building from the street off Robert Leopold Avenue (the main road) is very impressive. Also, at Rue Chevrolet, there is a **peasant museum**, where arts and crafts of the Jura region are on display. Rue Chevrolet is named after the man whose name appears on so many American cars. He was born in La Chaux de Fonds in 1878. One other industry for which the city is famous is the production of postage stamps. All the confederation's various stamps are made here.

Apart from the museums, the town is not very interesting. Its main avenue is a wide thoroughfare, with average department stores.

The other major town of the Jura is **Neuchâtel**, and in fact the road between them effectively creates a line separating the Jura Bernois and the Jura Vaudois. This heads into schloss country, where the romantic castle architecture appears at every opportunity. Between here and Morat/-Morten in the Fribourg region, there is a wealth of castles, vineyards, and châteaux.

Valangin

For starters, you could make a visit to the château in this small village, with its typically styled town clock. Standing proudly, tall and elegant at the beginning of the main street is the château. It is now a **wine museum**.

Opening times: 10.00a.m. to 12.00p.m. and 2.00–5.00p.m.

This is a convenient place to visit, since the village is just off the road between La Chaux de Fonds and Neuchâtel. It is also a good place to visit if you are using the splendid minor road which cuts across from St Imier. If you are travelling directly from St Imier to Neuchâtel, this is the road to take: there are hardly any vehicles on it, and you see some beautiful scenery and small farming villages *en route*.

One way or another, Neuchâtel will crop up in your itinerary, whether as a point from which to explore the lake, or on your way to the Jura. Whatever the reason, Neuchâtel makes an interesting town to visit.

Neuchâtel

From my very first visit to Neuchâtel, there has always seemed to be road works or some improvement scheme in operation. There is certainly a lot of effort going into making the town as popular as the lively resorts of Lac Léman and Geneva, for these would seem to be its competition. The lake is as big, its south-western side has as many attractive castles and places as Geneva or Lucerne, yet it does not attract the same numbers of tourists. The council is obviously keen to put this right, thus the new **marina**, the **Papiliorama** (butterfly) tropical garden, and the emphasis on providing many new facilities.

Notwithstanding all this new development, Neuchâtel is a charming French town. It is relatively quiet, but with a large student population it has a good atmosphere. In the area around the **Arts Museum** (it, too, is having a face-lift), the tall mansions remind you of Paris and all that is French.

Along with the relaxing and quiet **promenade** area, Neuchâtel's most attractive feature is its **architecture**. In the centre of the town and around Beaux Arts there are the mansions and town houses of the 17th and 18th centuries. Dating further back are the **Collegiate Church** (La Collegiale) and **castle**. The two, although built over different periods, are on one site.

Open: 1 April–30 September.
Weekdays: 10.00a.m. to 4.00p.m.
Sundays: 2.00–4.00p.m.
Guided tours are available.

The Collegiate Church is the older of the two buildings, having been started at the end of the 12th century. It was consecrated in 1276. One of its finest features is the **cenotaph** of the Counts of Neuchâtel from the 14th and 15th centuries. The **castle** part of the complex was not finished until the 16th century, when the various wings were added. The **prison tower** and the walk along the walls give good views over the town and the lake. The prison tower is on the opposite side of the road to the castle.

In the centre of town there is a superb building, the **Maison des Halles**, featuring a wonderful **oriel window**. Looking into the square from the promenade side this Renaissance building really looks the part, since this was the old market square and halls. The ground floor is now a restaurant, which naturally gets very busy, especially at weekends.

To see the best of the **old town**, which has quite a number of interesting sights, a walking tour is arranged by the local tourist office. The tours run in the summer and last for about two hours.

The **Papiliorama** tropical garden is a fairly new attraction, situated at the Marin centre, about 6 km (3.7 miles) from Neuchâtel.

Open: summer 9.00a.m. to 6.30p.m; winter 10.00a.m. to 5.00p.m.

There are more than 1,000 types of butterfly flying about in these gardens. Added attractions to this new venture are exotic birds and fish, dwarf alligators, turtles and an exhibition of giant insects and spiders. There are regional trains to Marin, apart from the boat service and PTT buses.

Museums

Neuchâtel has four main museums:

Museum of the History of Art
Quay Leopold Robert, near the port.
Opening times: 10.00a.m. to 12.00p.m. and 2.00–5.00p.m.; Thursdays 10.00a.m. to 12.00p.m. and 2.00–9.00p.m.

Museum of Ethnography
4 Rue St Nicholas
Trolleybus numbers 1 or 3. A ten-minute walk from the centre, it is situated near the Collegiate and castle.
Opening times: 10.00a.m. to 12.00p.m. and 2.00–5.00p.m.

Museum of Archaeology
7 Avenue DuPeyrue
Near the Palais Dupeyrue, and five minutes' walk from the main railway station.
Opening times: Wednesdays to Sundays 2.00–5.00p.m.

Museum of Natural History
14 Rue des Terreaux
Trolleybus number 6 from the railway station, in the direction of the town centre, or about five minutes' walk.
Opening times: Wednesdays to Sundays 2.00–5.00p.m.

Accommodation

Two of the more expensive places in the town are:

Hotel Beaulac, a four-star hotel on the Quay Leopold Robert.
Hotel City, another four-star establishment in an equally central position at Place Piaget.

The brand new Eurohotel is at the Avenue de Gare.

For atmosphere, right in the thick of things, the hotel to be at is the Hotel Marche in the Place des Halles.

There are some hotels outside the city, such as the Chaumant and Golf Hotel, but they are expensive. At **Theille** there is a Novotel, which does good deals for families in particular, but this is fairly close to the industrial side of the area.

Like Biel/Bienne, some of the nicest hotels (and restaurants) are to be found on the shores of the lake and around the vineyards. Most of them are non-starred, or are one- or two-star, but this should not put you off. In Switzerland the minimum standards are excellent, and ratings are usually given for amenities like televisions and mini-bars. The rating has nothing to do with the cleanliness or size of the rooms. At **Colombier**, for instance, a village with a nice château, only 7 km (4.3 miles) from Neuchâtel, there are four hotels, all of them quite small, but offering good accommodation at reasonable prices of 35 SFr upwards. In the smaller hotels you often find the breakfast is the simple one of rolls, jam and coffee, rather than the buffet breakfast served in the larger hotels.

Camping

For campers, there are the sites at Preles and Lignières previously mentioned. There are also sites nearer the town at:

Colombier Paradis Plage: a four-star site, right on the lake.
Open: 1 March–31 October.

Cortaillod Petit-Cortaillod: another site on the lake, with fewer facilities. A two-star site.
Open: 1 April–30 September.

Marin La Tene: this three-star site is to the north of the city near St Blaise and Marin. It has excellent sporting facilities, including five indoor tennis courts, squash and mini-golf.
Open: 1 April–30 September.

Le Landeron: there are two sites here, Camp le Peches and Bellerive. They are both four-star sites, and are situated in the area between the lakes of Biel and Neuchâtel.
Camp le Peches opens 15 March–16 October.
Bellerive is open 1 March–31 October.

On the promenade area Neuchâtel has been expanding, and the lakeside will be better equipped for visitors in years to come. It stretches from Monruz at the northern end, down Serrieres. The **port** is near the centre of the town, and from here you can make day trips out on the lake or, if you wanted to go further afield, you could go by **canal** from Lake Neuchâtel to Lake Bien, or from Lake Neuchâtel to Lake Morat in the Fribourg region. The summer services run from 2 June to 28 September, with four departures in the morning and four return trips in the afternoon. The boats initially go south, calling in at the western shore towns of Cortaillod, Bevaix, Gorgier Chez le Bart and St Aubin, before crossing the width of this huge lake to reach Estavayer du Lac. From here there is another vessel which travels to Yverdon-les-Bains at the most south-westerly end of the lake. The two departures at 11.30a.m. and 4.45p.m. are more direct, and do call in at the small villages.

Three Lakes Tours

Neuchâtel ia a good place to begin one of these tours, but you could start at either Biel/Bienne or Morat. A more detailed description of **Morat** is given in the Fribourg section, but it is included here to give some idea of the boat services available.

The three lakes of Neuchâtel, Bieler See and Morat are interconnected by canals, making it possible to travel

quite a way by boat, if not in the Jura, then certainly alongside it. This is a relaxing way of moving through the country, and also gives the opportunity to see the small wine-producing villages at **Twann**, **Erlach**, **Vully** and **Vaumarcus**. To add to this, you have the pleasure of seeing the châteaux from the best viewpoint.

The vessels of the Societé de Navigation sur les Lacs Neuchâtel et Morat run throughout the year. The winter timetable is not as extensive as the summer, but the fact that it runs at all points to there being a local need for these connections. You are not on a special tourist boat, but a regular local service. Bear in mind also that your Swiss Pass rail card is good for these journeys. The services available are:

Neuchâtel–St Peter's Island–Biel
A journey time of nearly two hours, making two stops before going into the canal for Lake Biel. The boat then makes the same stops as the normal Biel services. From Biel there is another service through a further canal to Solothurn, which takes another one and a half hours. There are three departures from Neuchâtel and two from Biel throughout the year.

Neuchâtel–Morat
This trip takes around one and a half hours and, although the canal between the lakes runs through flat countryside,

*A*lthough as large as many other lakes in the country Neuchâtel remains a backwater compared with Geneva or Lucerne.

it is an excellent way of going from the Jura to Fribourg in a leisurely fashion. The stop at **Motier** is the one from which to see the **vineyards** at Vully, and is on the opposite bank to Morat. In the summer there are five departures from Neuchâtel, the first being at 9.45a.m. There are six back from Morat, but the 2.45p.m. departure goes directly to Neuchâtel, non-stop. In the winter the reduced service means just two departures from Neuchâtel and three from Morat. Again the 2.45p.m. is non-stop.

Linking the Lakes

Linking all three lakes—Crosière sur les trois Lacs—takes a whole day. For instance you can leave Morat at 11.30a.m., stop at Neuchâtel for one and a quarter hours and arrive at Biel/Bienne at 4.35 p.m. The winter timetable runs from 30 September to 1 June, although this is variable (within a couple of days) from year to year.

Although most of the tourist offices have details and timetables, in the event of there not being any information the company is based at:

Société de Navigation sur la Lac
    Neuchâtel et Morat S.A.
Case Postal 1460
2001 Neuchâtel
Tel: 038 254012; Fax: 038 247961.

Special Trips

There are any number of special trips on the lake, such as musical trips, barbecue sailings, and all manner of serenaded boat journeys. The prices vary but typically a musical evening from Estavayer du Lac costs around 16 SFr, and will have a restaurant on board.

Walking

As with the Jura Bernois, the countryside around Neuchâtel offers the very best in walking. The tourist office issue a footpath guide *Itineraires Pedestres*, which gives rough outlines of walks around Neuchâtel, Biel and Morat lakes. The Morat walks are in the Fribourg section, but to give some idea of the sort of leisurely walking to be done around Neuchâtel, here are a few examples:

Neuchâtel–Sernieres, 40 minutes;
Sernieres–Auvernier, 35 minutes;
Auvernier–Cortaillod, 1 hour 20
    minutes;
Cortaillod–Port de Bevaix, 50
    minutes;
Port de Bevaix–Chez le Bart, 1 hour
    45 minutes;
Chez le Bart–St Aubin, 30 minutes.

The full walk will take you down the western shores of the lake towards Yverdon, past the **châteaux** at Cormondeche, Boudry and Bevaix. In total, according to Swiss walking times, it would take about five and a half hours, not including stops for refreshment. So it would make a good day's walk, with the opportunity of going back on the boat or over to Estavayer, on the opposite shore. The permutations for walking/boat/bus travel in the region are endless, given the range of transport and pathways available.

The lakeside of Neuchâtel is picturesque, but the hills behind, from the vineyards of Boudry, Bevaix and Valingan to the forested countryside of the Val de Travers and the gorges of the Doubs, are ideal for exploration. This is a great expanse of quiet, unspoilt landscape, which I hope will remain so. There are small intrusions, in the shape of ski-lifts around St Croix, but generally, from La Chaux de Fonds southwards, the area has been left without too much development.

One of the most popular places to visit from Neuchâtel is the **Vue-des-Alps**. At an altitude of about 1,288 m (4,226 ft), with little between it and the alpine peaks, the view from this point is impressive—on a good day. I've driven across Vue-des-Alps when you could barely see the trees, never mind the Alps. However, choose a good clear day and you will not be disappointed. At the summit there is a restaurant and picnic area. It is a good place for a picnic, since it is roughly midway between the lowlands and the higher regions of the Jura.

Les Doubs and Les Brenets

This is the very edge of western Switzerland, where the River Doubs forms the frontier with France—in fact if you take a wrong turn along one of the roads around here you are likely to end up in French territory.

Dubius

This was the name given to the River Doubs by the Romans, clearly because, as rivers go, it is a "doubter". Without the benefit of high-level satellite photography, the Romans were somewhat confused by this river which changes direction four times. From its source at La Mouthe to the point where it enters the Saone is about 86 km (53 miles). But the actual length of the river is slightly longer at 430 km (267 miles), and when viewed from above it forms the shape of a letter M.

The main point of interest in this area is the **Saut du Doubs**, the deep ravine and gorge which runs from the area around the Swiss town of **Les Brenets** to a point where it returns to being a narrow river. The journey to Les Brenets is quite spectacular as you go between deep cuttings in the rock. Most visitors come from **Le Locle**, a small town just 8 km (5 miles) from the Doubs. Le Locle has a **horological museum**, which is internationally known, but is nothing like the size of the one at La Chaux de Fonds. Coming from Le Locle there are plenty of signs to Les Doubs, the most important turn being the one on to a minor road at **Col des Roches**. If you carry straight on you are into France. Coming back into Switzerland so soon after having left it can prove slightly awkward and too interesting for the ever-curious Swiss border guards.

The road down from Col des Roches eventually opens up to give a wide panorama of the valley, the lake, and the town of **Les Brenets**, which sits in a huddle on the hillside. At the **quay**, there are boats making the return trip through the meandering steep gorges to La Saut du Doubs. The boats are operated by Jean-Claud Durig, 2416 Les Brenets, tel: (039) 321414; he has the information on schedules.

Alternatively, there is a forest walk of about an hour each way. The **waterfall** of the Doubs is along a forest path, a short way from the point of the boat landing stage.

The best views of the Doubs are said to be on the French side, so it may be worth going over there to see the waterfalls. Certainly on the Swiss

side many of the views of the gorges are blocked by trees, and it is only at the restaurant at Les Roches de Mauron that a good view of the river appears.

The region from the Doubs down to Yverdon—La Brevine—at the southern end of the Jura, is one of the nicest areas of countryside in Switzerland. Apparently it is also the coldest in winter, registering the lowest temperatures in the country. It has no dramatic hill climbs, not too many multiple hairpin bends to negotiate in a car, just rolling, forested, wide-open country with the odd village here and there. It's a pleasure to drive around, and cyclists and

*F*orming the north-western border between France and Switzerland, the River Doubs meanders through the forest-clad gorge.

walkers will find the region ideal. The **plateau of Brevine** is a short distance from the turn-off for Le Locle, following the signs for **Fleurier**. If approached from the lake or eastern side, you will be in doubt as to the height of this plateau, having climbed quite rapidly from the lowlands around Yverdon.

As for sights and points of interest, there is only the landscape. The plateau is what it is, pasture land for the high grazing of horses and cattle. There is the odd hostelry, and at the highest point of just over 1,000 m (3,280 ft) there is the town of **La Brevine**. There is a small **lake** at Lac de Tailleres, and further down, in the Val de Travers, there is a **nature reserve** near **Noiraigue**. But there are no chairlifts here to get you to the top at Le Soleil; the path is the only way and will take you about one and a half hours to walk.

The main town in the area is **St Croix**, which is at a halfway stage between the heights of the Brevine and the lake area of Yverdon.

St Croix/Les Rasses

The town of St Croix lies in a valley at about 1,066 m (3,497 ft), so it could be regarded as a winter resort for those looking for a less hectic skiing holiday,

with shorter queues. It has a lift system which will take you up to **Le Cochet** at 1,483 m (4,865 ft) and **Les Petit Roches** at 1,583 m (5,194 ft). As well as the downhill, for which there are ten ski-lifts, there are 80 km (50 miles) of cross-country tracks, so although it's nowhere near the size of the average Alpine resort, it does offer an quieter alternative.

Come the summer, the area offers superb walking through forested hills. The town is more or less surrounded by undulating hills. For the long-distance walkers, Le Croix is on the **Jura Summits path**. Among these forests and small peaks there is an unusually large number of hostelries: 15 mountain and country restaurants cover this small area, so it is unlikely that you will go hungry.

As a town, St Croix has a few historical attractions, based largely on its history of precision engineering, and in particular its work with musical boxes. There is a **museum** devoted to the area, showing local crafts, geological specimens and a good collection of musical instruments, but perhaps a more interesting visit is one to the International Centre of Mechanical Art

International Centre of Mechanical Art
Rue de l'Industrie 2
Opening times: Tuesdays–Sundays
1.30–6.00p.m.
The centre looks not only at the local history of **musical boxes**, which gave St Croix the name "The Village of Sound", but all manner of the world of music with movement. Many of the ingenious models, figures and oddities which stand up, turn on and switch off were generally made for no other

*I*n the far distance is the town of Les Brenets, and the starting point for the river trips down the Doubs.

Health and Spa Towns

Switzerland is world famous for its health properties, guaranteed to make you feel 100 per cent better, until you get the bill! The basis for this reputation as a healthy place is genuine, and anyone who suffers from chest complaints or breathing problems such as asthma will know that a spell amongst the mountains of Switzerland will make them feel considerably better—and that's free. But, as only Switzerland can, this reputation has been commercialized to produce any number of health spas, hospitals and treatment centres.

Leukerbad has natural sulphurous springs, as does the lake-side town of Yverdon. Each of the resorts boasting a health spa or treatment centre will not be hiding any lights behind bushels, but if you are looking for more private treatment, there are adverts in the Swissair Gazette. As an example a hotel in the Bernese Oberland, the Schwefelbergbad, offers acupuncture, ozone therapy and a few others which I know little about!

purpose than to satisfy the inventive mind of a Jurese craftsman. It makes a fascinating visit.

The region from St Croix to Lake Neuchâtel is largely forested, hilly countryside which eventually opens out onto the lowland area, and **Yverdon**.

Yverdon-les-Bains

This is the most westerly part of Lake Neuchâtel and is actually in the canton of Vaud. It is something of a crossroad in travels around the Jura, Fribourg and Vaud cantons. It is also a well-known spa town, and still offers thermal health treatment in the form of baths and treatment centres. At the

Centre Thermal the water comes from a depth of 500 m (1,640 ft), through a variety of geological formations, to emerge at a pleasing 29°C (84°F). The baths date back to Roman times, although the building has been slightly updated. It now features an array of high-tech therapeutic equipment to relieve respiratory and rheumatic ailments. Even if you are not a sufferer, the chances are that you would come out of here feeling a lot better.

Apart from its **beach** (yes its beach!), which in summer attracts sunbathers who can imagine that the waters lapping the shore are those of the Mediterranean, there is also the **old town**. The **main square** and the **castle** are the most interesting parts to visit.

In the square is the main tourist office, offering plenty of information on the town and attractions of the area. One such place, still on the western side of Lake Neuchâtel, is **Grandson**.

This is a fairly typical town of the region. It boasts a good, well-kept **castle**, **vineyards**, two **museums** and a lakeside situation. It is remarkable how many of these Swiss towns each keep up such a high standard; you could pick any one from a dozen such towns and not be disappointed.

Château du Grandson

Opening times: summer 9.00a.m. to 6.00p.m., winter 10.00a.m. to 5.00p.m. (Sundays only.)

The castle at Grandson is a grand affair, and was the site for one of Switzerland's major battles. The Duke of Burgundy and his defeated armies left in something of a hurry, persuaded to some degree by confederate soldiers, but without most of their armoury.

Thus the castle has an excellent collection of **artillery** and **treasure**. The battle was, however, in 1476, so some credit must go to someone for hanging on to the treasure for so long. Also in the château there is a **motor museum,** which has some splendid vintage cars. The star attraction is the white Rolls Royce belonging to Greta Garbo.

Camping
This region is another good area for camping, and there are sites by the lake or further up in the hills near St Croix. When identifying the region look for **Nord Vaudois.**

Bullet Les Cluds: this is one of the sites in the mountains, and is in the hills below Le Chasseron. It is a four-star site. Open throughout the year.

Yverdon les Bains Iris: a three-star site situated at the marina for Yverdon, very convenient for the town.
Open: 1 April–30 September.

Grandson Pecos Grandson: another top quality five-star site, right on the lakeside.
Open throughout the year.

Corcelettes Belle-Rive: about 1 km ? miles) off the main N1 road from Lausanne to Neuchâtel, east of Grandson. The turn is to the right towards the lake. The site is actually at the lakeside, and is a three-star site. Open: 1 April–30 September.

For information on the eastern side of Lake Neuchâtel, and the area towards Lausanne and Geneva, refer to the sections on Central and South-West Switzerland, and the cantons of Vaud and Fribourg.

For the Best Views of the Alps, Jura, and the "Cradle of Switzerland"

Central Switzerland includes almost everything about the country in a neat compact area. It has enough water to run several ferry services, as many castles as you can take, and a small collection of mountains. It features the oldest rack railway, the birth of the confederation, and in Lucerne, Interlaken and Bern, enough sights to fill several trips. The Transport Museum, Mt Pilatus and the city named a world cultural landmark, are within hours of each other; no wonder it's the most popular destination in Switzerland.

Bern

This, the political centre of Switzerland, is less like a capital than that of many other countries. In fact many people are not too sure as to which is the capital of Switzerland—the commercial city of Zurich or Bern. To confirm that this is the administrative centre of the country, the **Federal Palace** is here, although this is the only indication of its role in Swiss politics.

*T*he parliament building at Bern is impressive, with the cantonal shields running along the front.

Bern is one of the most beautiful cities in Europe, if not in the world. It has a unique distinction in that its **old town** is entirely protected under a UNESCO conservation order—it has been listed as "A World Cultural Landmark".

The old town, which sits in the bow of a sharp U-turn in the River Aare, is a museum of 14th–16th-century architecture. The old arcades, housing modern designer interiors, are the oldest and the largest covered shopping areas in Europe. Amongst the fine old town houses and shops are colourful street fountains, towers and churches. All credit must go to the authorities who have kept Bern in such superb condition, and well-deserving if its unique status in Europe.

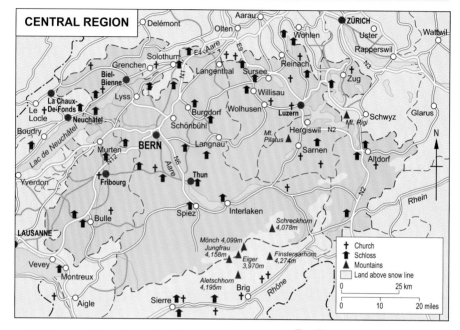

Map of Central Switzerland.

With a position almost in the centre of the country, Bern has developed as a crossroads for the rail and road system. Journeys from Geneva to Zurich and from the Jura to the Engadine use Bern as a change-over point. This means that if you are travelling around Switzerland on a rail pass you can see an awful lot of Bern railway station. Not that it isn't a pleasant place; simply that it appears to be involved in most cross-country trips. As an air destination, Bern has not developed as rapidly as Zurich or Geneva. There are direct flights here, by Dan Air, who also offer onward coach transport to Thun, Interlaken and Speiz.

Bern was created in 1191 by Duke Berchold the fifth of Zahringen, who chose the strategic site "to create a city". It was named after the first animal to be captured in a hunt—a bear, which also gave rise to the city's crest of a bear. It also seems to justify

keeping two bears in a pit near the river, who by the looks of them sincerely wish the Duke had captured a goat or a deer back in the 12th century. Bern joined the confederation in 1353 and expanded through the 14th and 15th centuries at a rate which would hold it in good stead at a later date. Its major setback was in 1405, when a fire destroyed most of the original city. The rebuilt town was made largely of sandstone, and the old section of today's Bern has remained virtually unchanged since that date. The expansion programme, and its role in the politics of the country, were rewarded in 1848 when the city was declared by popular vote to be the Federal Capital.

Transport

Like Basel, and so many of Switzerland's cities and towns, the last thing you need in Bern is a car. The public transport system is excellent, and in such a small city, where nearly all the interesting sights are in the centre, the motor vehicle really has no place. Inevitably the most popular form of transport is the tram, with the railway station at the centre of things. Much of Bern's old town is pedestrianized, so the chances are that if you are not on a tram then you are on foot.

By Rail

If you arrive by rail, the main exit of the station will take you out to the **Bahnhof Platz**. This is the main point of departure for the tram system, and across the platz, at the **Bubenbergplatz**, are the en route trams.

Einstein

Although not of Swiss nationality, Albert Einstein lived for many years in Bern. His house can still be seen at 49 Kramgasse, and information on this area is found in the Bern walking tour. His fame is for the theory of relativity, but perhaps his most useful contribution was in America, having been forced to live there by the activities of Germany and the Nazis. When in America he was persuaded by a group of scientists to write to President Roosevelt to warn of the dangers of uranium research being carried out in Germany, and stressing the urgency of investigating the use of atomic energy in bombs. Albert Einstein lived from 1879 to 1955.

T own plan of Bern.

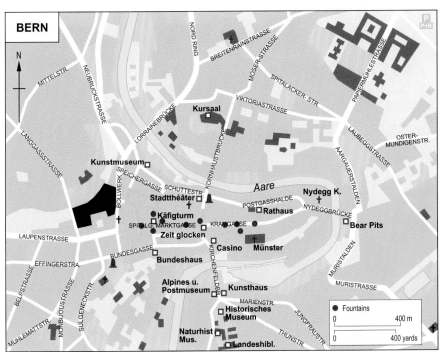

The Unterbrücke in Bern is one of many bridges crossing the river into the old town.

By Road

Travelling to Bern by road is very simple, since the city is surrounded by motorways. Travelling from Thun and Interlaken on the N6, come off at Bern–Ostring; from Basel, Zurich and Lucerne on the N1 leave at Bern–Neufeld; if travelling north from Geneva and Lausanne on the N12, then the best junction to use for Bern is the one at Bern–Bumpliz or Weyermannshaus. At Bumpliz and Neufeld junctions and on the Papiermuhlestrasse, near the Wankdorf junction of the N6, there are park and ride services which I would recommend.

If you have to bring your car further into the city there are a number of covered and open car parks at Laupenstrasse on the south-west side, at Lorrainbrucke to the north, at Laubergerstrasse in the east and Monbijoubrucke to the south. In order to keep Bern as it is, motor transport must be kept to a minimum, so you should use the perimeter car parks if you possibly can.

Since the main points of interest are all within walking distance, the tram and bus routes are only useful if you are going from one end of the city to the other. To go from the **Bahnhofplatz** to the **Bear Pits** (west to east) then take bus number 12 or tram number 3. Going across the city in the other direction, say from **Thunplatz** to the **Viktoriaplatz** (south to north) then use tram number 11.

Walking

Undoubtedly the best way to see Bern is to wander the streets on foot. The information office gives out a city map, which includes a walking tour with a suggested route. The sights are marked, with an easy to follow key in six languages. It gives an excellent guide to the layout of the city, as well as information on the outskirts. If the idea of following a carefully prepared route doesn't appeal, then Bern is easy (and small) enough to discover your own way around. Dark, old alleys with well-worn steps lurk between the main streets, giving the visitor a feel for the age of this antique city. To go from the river area to the cathedral and the old town does involve a lot of steps; disabled visitors can only move easily

112

when on the main streets. Unfortunately, there are also steps involved around the arcades, but there is a lift from **Aarstrasse**, at the riverside, up to the gardens adjacent to the cathedral.

Banks
The main banking area is around the **Bundesplatz** and the **Barenplatz**. Opening times:

Mondays–Wednesdays, 8.00a.m. to 4.30p.m.
Thursdays, 8.00a.m. to 6.00p.m.
Fridays, 8.00a.m. to 4.30p.m.

You can also change currency at the railway station (Bahnhof).
Opening times: 6.00a.m. to 9.00p.m. (January–March).

6.00 a.m. to 10.00p.m. (April–December).

Post Office
The main post office is at **Schanzenstrasse**, near the Bahnhof and the Bubenbergplatz.
Opening times: Mondays–Fridays, 7.30a.m. to 6.30p.m.
Saturdays, 7.30–11.00a.m.

Accommodation
Bern's accommodation is surprisingly central, so you can stay in the old part of the town without any difficulty. There are a number of hotels on the perimeter of the city, but most of them are right in the middle of the old quarter. Being a political and business centre, the city caters for all manner of

From Ancient to Modern— Switzerland's Architecture

As with its food, language and history, Switzerland draws from its neighbours when it comes to architectural styles. The links with the cultures of Italy, Germany and France have left their mark in nearly every aspect of Swiss life, and none more so than the architecture of the country. However, while there would seem to be little that is strictly Swiss in the more historical buildings, there is a distinct style of Europeanism in the design of the newer, more modern architecture.

There are few countries where such an easy comparison of architecture across the ages can be made. Unlike many of its counterparts, it has neither been assaulted by bombardment nor ruthless property developers. Switzerland's historic buildings are there for all to see, and in many cases, the modern trend of conservation and "listed buildings" has been the norm in Switzerland for centuries. Why knock down a perfectly good building to replace it with something not as good, would seem to be the motto. One of the great things about looking into the architecture of this country is the vast range of levels at which the visitor can explore. On the domestic scene, the differences in the style of house is fascinating. From the grand, big houses of the rich Engadine farmers to the stone-built cottages of the Ticino.

The Engadine house is something quite unique, not only in its decoration of sgraffito, which is very different from frescoes, but also in the way in which the house was used. More than one family would occupy the house, and areas were set aside for animals, stacking of hay and the like. But the most obvious feature of the Engadine building is the colourful pictures on the walls. The actual colour is put in later, because the technique of producing the picture is carried out by the stone mason. The rough grey plasterwork is coated with a limewash, after the plaster has dried out. He then scrapes away the lime to highlight the grey plaster underneath. The scraping produces a relief, which is then painted. Usually the pictures take the form of floral or heraldic designs. This type of decoration is the most elaborate of the Swiss domestic building, but there is a wealth of skillful wood carving on the Bernese Oberland farmhouse. These huge structures can be seen at their best in the farmlands between Bern and Lucerne, and one of the first things to notice is the way in which the housing part of the building appears almost as an addition. At one side there will also be a steep ramp, for the tractor to drive into the barn area. The roof and front of the building owe something to the Tyrolean design, with long low eaves, under which the winter wood will be stored. Across the front of the building is the elaborate woodwork, which, depending on the wealth of the owners, is either an arched affair or a simple boarded front. These structures, along with the other big farmhouses of Lucerne and the Valais, contrast completely with the simple stone houses in the Italian regions.

The Ticino farmhouse is built with 1 m (3 ft) thick walls, and is made of rough stone. Today, there are plenty of examples of the older stone farmhouse, in areas where the owners have left to live in the more prosperous areas of the region. The result is that amongst the rich church architecture, which draws all its influence from the Italian Catholic Church, there are groups of dilapidated stone houses. Gradually, many of these

*On the way up to the top of the cathedral there are a number
of views over the city of Lausanne.*

Stein am Rhein features the unusual sight of an open-air art gallery. Most of the inns have a story to tell on the façade of the building.

dwellings are being converted to holiday homes, so popular are these centuries-old cottages.

What would Switzerland be without its schlosses? These castles, some almost too perfect to be true, attract visitors to Switzerland continually. The settings are invariably picturesque, and unlike many countries the majority of these castles have been well maintained. Some, like some of those on the shores of Lake Morat, are private homes, but most of the larger ones are open at some time to the public. In the region around the Payerne, between Oron le Chatel through to Morat, you can visit and enjoy up to a dozen of these romantic castles. Gruyères is a famous schloss, and here you will find a good museum which traces the history of the various occupants of the castle. The schlosses to be recommended are: Chillon, Coppet, Gruyères, Hallwil, Morat, Oron, Sion, Speiz, Tarasp, Vufflens and Vaduz. They all have a story to tell, be it a historic battle, or famous dungeons. There can be no better country to tour than Switzerland if there is an interest in real history.

This history is all too obvious in most of the major cities of Switzerland. With the exception of Geneva, and maybe Zurich, there are some wonderful examples of early townships, and how they have developed can easily be seen. Bern, Basel, Lausanne, and Lucerne have all conserved their architectural heritage to an almost uncanny degree. Bern has been given a listing as world cultural landmark and Basel kept the maze of historical buildings at its heart for centuries. Basel also has a marvellous collection of architecture in its 12th-century Gothic cathedral and the later 15th-century Rathaus. Lausanne teems with history around its cathedral area and, in more recent times, down by the lake at Ouchy. In this city there is such a variety of architecture that a visitor could almost choose a period and find it in Lausanne. The obvious influence here is French, with rows of shuttered villas typical of any French city.

In the northern cities of Schaffhausen, Stein am Rhein and St Gallen, the emphasis is on the ornate frescoes, which date back centuries. The most striking are in Stein where, in an arena of art, there are a dozen or more high terraced houses and inns covered in fine artwork. In this region probably the finest Rococo cathedral is found at St Gallen. This magnificent building dates back to 1755, although it is built on a site founded by an Irish monk in AD 720. The cathedral is at the centre of an otherwise ordinary industrial town, but because of that appears so much grander. The Abbey, alongside the cathedral, also has an impressive Rococo interior, so for those interested in this period of architectural decoration, St Gallen is a must.

While most visitors to a country such as Switzerland are normally in search of historical features, this country has also come to display an imaginative side to its architecture. The Red Cross Museum in Geneva has managed to create an atmosphere consistent with its theme, even to the extent of it being slightly underground. The restaurant and terraces at the top of the Jungfrau are as good an attempt as any to make a building blend in with its surroundings. No country is perfect, and where Switzerland has let itself down is in its previous mountain-top buildings. The likes of the Pilatus and the Schillhorn restaurants and hotels do nothing to enhance the views, but some credit has to given for building anything in these places.

In all, Switzerland offers far too much in terms of architectural interest. Castles, churches, cathedrals, houses and museums are all there to be discovered.

visitors, from diplomats to campers, so the choice of hostelry is wide.

There are two five-star establishments, one of which, the Bellevue Palace, is next door to the Federal Palace—make sure you go in the right palace! To benefit from the really old section of the city, the four most convenient hotels are situated on the **Gerechtigkeitsgasse**. They are not only very close to the best shops, but they are also near the cathedral and the river. The four hotels are:

Hospiz zur Heimat (two-star)
Belle Epoque-Garni (four-star)
Goldener Adler (three-star)
Nydeck (two-star).

Other hotels worth considering are the Goldener Schlussel (two-star) on the Rathausgasse, and the Kruez (three-star) at Zeughausgasse.

Student Accommodation
This can be found at:

Studentheim Concordia, Postgasse 47
Studentenlogierhaus "Fellergut",
  Muhledorferstrasse 15
Studentenlogierhaus "Tscharnergut",
  Walmannstrasse 15
Mensa des Studentheims der
  Universitat, Gesellschaftsstrasse 2
Logierhaus des Bernischen, Langgas-
  strasse 75.

There is also a youth hostel at Weihergasse 4, open all year:
7.00–10.00a.m. and 5.00–11.00p.m.
Mondays to Saturdays;
7.00–9.00a.m. and 5.30p.m. to midnight on Sundays. The telephone number is 226316 (area code 031).

Camping
For campers there are two sites:
Eichholz Campsite, Wabern: this is 3.5 km (2 miles) south-east of the city, on the road to Belp.
Open April–October.

Eymatt Campsite, Hinterkappelen: situated 5 km (3 miles) north-west of the city on the road to Wohlen.
Open throughout the year.

Both sites are non-classified, but are available for tents and caravans and have facilities for the disabled.

The Sights of Bern

Bern has the distinction of being a world cultural landmark. On a stroll through the **shopping arcades**, past the **prison tower** and the **clock tower**, it is easy to see why that award was made. There are obvious symbols of the medieval architecture, but there also nooks and crannies, off the main streets, small details on buildings kept but not forgotten. All this adds up to a unique city, where even the underground concourse of the railway station has a monument to the past—some of the **foundations of the Christoffel Tower**, which was the western gate of the city, built in 1344. The remains were discovered when the foundations for the new railway station were being prepared, and rather than cover them with fresh concrete, it was decided to keep them and build around them. This is a good reminder to other city councils that simply because such remains lie in the path of a building programme, the answer is not always

*A*t the head of the Kramgasse, the clock tower
is one of the most famous clocks in Switzerland.

found with the demolition expert or the concrete supplier. To see the walls, come down the escalator from the Burgenplatz. You will find drawings and a potted history of the development of the town—not bad for a station.

Most of Bern's famous (and not so famous) sights reel off before you, as you walk through the town. The most obvious place to start your walk is from the **Bahnhofplatz**, down the **Spitalgasse**, under the **prison tower**, into the **Marktgasse**, and then on by way of the **clock tower** and the **Kramgasse**. From the end of the street, by the **Nydeggbrücke** (bridge), you can decide to go over the bridge to give some encouraging words to the bears, or to turn back up through the **Junkerngasse**, to the **cathedral** and the **Munsterplatz**, or turn left and come back via the **Rathausgasse**. Either way will give you a good view of this medieval town, and on both the routes you can take in the **arcades** and the **fountains**.

The Fountains

Whilst wandering through the **old town** you will see, at fairly evenly spaced intervals, **street fountains**. Each of these fountains is named, and they were added to the city in 1545. In the summer, the flowers and the fountains give Bern an almost village atmosphere. Among the fountains there are some odd ones, like the **ogre fountain**, which depicts rather a nasty looking man devouring a small boy. However, to give some balance to this, there is a fountain devoted to **Anna Seiler**, who provided the city's first hospital. I am including the fountains in the order you would see them when walking from the Bahnhofplatz:

*T*he fountains of Bern appear throughout the old town but this is probably the most famous—the Ogre Fountain.

Spitalgasse to Barenplatz
Piper Fountain.

The Prison Tower, Barenplatz
This is the first **tower** you come to after walking down the **Spitalgasse**. Built in 1256, it was the second extension to the city but was given its role as a prison in 1641.
Opening times: Tuesdays–Sundays, 10.00a.m. to 1.00p.m. and 2.00–6.00p.m.
Thursdays until 9.00p.m.

Barenplatz to Marktgasse
Anna Seiler Fountain and Musketeer Fountain.

The Clock Tower, Kramgasse
The first extension to the old town was the western gate, built in 1218, which is one of the city's best-known features. Posted in the form of cards to all corners of the globe, the clock tower of Bern always looks attractive. Whether it was always as picturesque as this is doubtful, since the timepieces were added in 1530. Below the main clock face is the **astronomical clock** and alongside this is the **figure play**. From May until October you can take a guided tour into the tower, but the real beauty of the whole building can be best seen from the **Kramgasse**, especially in the morning when the sun (should it happen to be shining) lights up the figures and the gold work of the clock. The chimes start at four minutes to the hour, and you can guarantee that a small crowd will be gathering, each and every hour to watch the bear cub figures filing past to the sound of the Fool's bells. Only the Swiss can come up with such delights as this, although on close inspection the figure play and the astronomical clock are beginning to look a little faded.

Kornhausplatz
Ogre Fountain.

Kramgasse
Zahringen, Einstein and Samson Fountains.

*T*he Clock Tower can be seen from the inside as well as the outside. This is a detail of the figures on the clock tower.

Gerechtikeitsgasse
Justice fountain.

The Arcades

From the Kramgasse and the clock tower it is as easy as not to take a stroll through the streets around the centre, and take in the shops in the arcades. In total there are 6 km (3½ miles) of undercover shopping, the largest in Europe. The fact that this modern convenience was built in the 14th century makes it even more remarkable. The arcades go from the Bubenbergplatz, down the Spitalgasse, the Marktgasse, the Kramgasse and on to the Gerechtikeitsgasse. This is the main street, but parallel streets and areas around the Rathausgasse are also arcaded. At number **49 Kramgasse** you will find the house in which Einstein wrote his theory of relativity, although the only mathematical exercise you are likely to get nowadays is in counting how many litres of beer you have drunk in the bar now residing here.

Munsterplatz
Moses Fountain.

The Cathedral

This is one of those cathedrals which began life in one century but took several more to finish. The official beginnings were in 1421 but building was still going on in 1573 and it took until 1893 for the tower to be completed. Despite this drawn-out programme, it is an excellent example of Gothic architecture. On the drum of the main entrance is a scene of the **Last Judgement**, by Erhard Kung, with 234 figures. There is a staircase to the tower from where there are good views.

Summer opening times: Mondays–Saturdays, 10.00a.m. to 12.00p.m. and 2.00–5.00p.m.
Sundays, 11.00a.m. to 12.00p.m. and 2.00–5.00p.m.
Tower: Mondays–Saturdays, 10.00–11.30a.m. and 2.00–4.30p.m.
Sundays, 11.00–11.30a.m. and 2.00–4.30p.m.

Winter opening times (November–Easter Saturday): Tuesdays–Fridays, 10.00a.m. to 12.00p.m. and 2.00–3.00p.m.
Saturdays, 10.00a.m. to 12.00p.m. and 1.00–5.00p.m.
Sundays, 11.00a.m. to 12.00p.m.
The tower closes 30 minutes before the cathedral, as with the summer times.

The Bear Pits

Over the **Nydeggbrücke**, on the right-hand side, you will see the bear pits. It is traditional to keep bears in a pit, since it is the heraldic animal of the city. Personally, I cannot see why this tradition has to be upheld. The bears are obviously unhappy, kept down in a deep, walled pit, mainly for the pleasure of visitors. The sight is not one which needs to go on much longer.

Viewpoints

There are a number of viewpoints outside the old town which give lovely views of the houses and cathedral. Turn left or right at the bear pits, and walk up the hill to **Aargaurstalden** or towards the **Englische Anlagen** alongside the river. Both are good vantage points, just off the town. Bern is also a city of bridges, and in the turn of the river there are eight of them (if you include the railway bridge). The old

ones, like the Nydeggbrücke, give a really good view down on to the roofs of the old town. There are plenty of refreshingly green areas of the city, a tribute to the way in which Bern has developed. In fact, greenery extends all the way round the old town. A good viewpoint from which to see the **Federal Palace** is from down by the **Dalmazibrücke**, a small bridge to the south of the city. In the afternoon the sun shines directly onto the façade of this imposing building.

The Federal Palace

All the crests of the federation line the dome of the federal palace, which is in the style of Florentine renaissance. On a guided tour of the building the workings of Swiss democracy are explained, but these are curtailed when the parliament is in session (four sessions per year). The guided tours are also suspended on official holidays and special

The cantonal shields displayed on the front of the Bundeshaus in Bern.

occasions. You can, however, go into the public gallery during sessions. Tours of the federal building last 45 minutes.

Weekdays, 9.00a.m., 10.00a.m., 11.00a.m., 2.00p.m., 3.00p.m. and 4.00p.m.
Sundays, 9.00a.m., 10.00a.m., 11.00a.m., 2.00p.m. and 3.00p.m.

Just outside the front (river side) of the palace there is a terrace with benches, offering—on a good day—a good view of the Alps.

Museums

There are four museums of particular note in Bern:

Museum of Fine Art

Hodlerstrasse 12. This museum has the largest Paul Klee collection as well as 14th–16th century Italian work. The Swiss art dates from the 15th century through to the present day, and the French artists are represented by some famous names including Cézanne, Matisse, Braque and Picasso.

Bernese Historical Museum

Helvetiaplatz 5. The second largest historical museum in Switzerland. It has one of the country's most important ethnographic collections. There are also religious treasures from Konigsfelden Abbey, and the original sculptures from Bern Cathedral.

Museum of Natural History

Bernastrasse 15. Three claims to fame for this museum: the largest diorama of mammals and birds in their natural habitat, a very good mineral collection, and the original lovable St Bernard dog—Barry.

Swiss Alpine Museum

Helvetiaplatz 4. Anyone interested in the history of Alpine mountaineering would enjoy a visit to the museum. It has the largest collection of topographical models, as well as equipment and information on the scientific exploration of the Alps. The Swiss Postal museum is housed in the same building, displaying one of the world's largest collections of postage stamps.

The Outskirts

Around the outskirts of the city there are a number of pleasant sights: castles, villages and even a minor (by Swiss standards) mountain. At 858 m (2,815 ft) **Gurten** is not going to compete with its neighbours across the Mittelland, but there is a terrific view from the top. To go to the mountain take the number 9 tram from the Bubenbergplatz in the direction of Waben. From here there is a rack railway. The views extend across the city and to the Bernese Oberland. There are ramblers' paths and a children's area at the summit.

This part of the country has a castle or the remains of one around every corner. The nearest ones to Bern are at Allmenginden, Gumlingen, Rubigen, Worb, Koniz, Munchenbuchse, Muri and Zollikofen.

There are also some archaeological ruins at the **Enge Peninsula** which are under excavation. The site has revealed part of a Helvetian town and a Roman amphitheatre and baths. To get to the ruins head out towards Biel—the ruins can be found by following the signs at the Mathauskirche.

From Bern, there are a number of lovely sights in the form of towns, lakes and countryside. The area is good cycling country, has well-marked routes for walking, and offers cruising as part of the **Three Lake Cruises** (Neuchâtel, Biel and Morat). For motorists there are good motorways from Bern to Morat, Lausanne and Fribourg. As with many of the towns around Neuchâtel there has been a lot of conservation and restoration work on ramparts, châteaux and churches.

In this area you will see the unique Bernese Oberland **farmhouses**. Look out for them around the small villages of **Kerzers** and **Walperswill**. They are not so much houses as huge barns with a building attached.

One of the favourite spots for many Bernese is **Morat**, only 30 minutes' drive from the centre of Bern, and undoubtedly one of Switzerland's best-kept secrets. I suspect that this is where many of the townspeople of Bern come for weekends and their holidays.

Morat/Murten

As in a number of towns and cities of this area, Morat suffers from the bilingual nature of its population, thus the need for the two names. Generally it is more commonly known as Morat.

The town's layout has remained intact since the 12th century, when it was founded by the Dukes of Zahringhan. As part of their trilogy of strategic sites, Morat joined with Bern and Fribourg.

Morat's other historical fame comes in the form of a rather bloody battle which took place some 200 years after the town was created. After a devastating defeat at the hands of confederate soldiers at **Grandson**, on the western shores of Lake Neuchâtel, the Duke of Burgundy decided to lay siege to Morat, until the confederate soldiers arrived to see him off again. The Duke fled, leaving a massive toll of dead—some 8,000 soldiers. He apparently did not have the strategic mind of the Dukes of Zahringhan since most of his men drowned in the lake after being hemmed in by the advancing armies.

Today, Morat is a peaceful town, and within the town walls there are arcaded shops, hotels, and restaurants. There is a slight leaning towards the holiday resort type of shop here and there, but most are high-quality confectioners, tea shops and goldsmiths. Outside the walls are all the amenities of the lake, which is not too big: swimming pools, indoor and outdoor, campsites and, over on the other side of the lake, the vineyards of the Vully wine.

The Ramparts

The walls, or ramparts, of the old town run from the **Deutsche Kirche** (German church) along the length of the town almost to the castle. At points along the ramparts there are the old look-out towers, some of which you can go up. Beware of the low beams, and the old steps—there has been little added (or taken away) since they were put up 800 years ago. From the last tower, at the western end, there is a good view out across the castle to Murtensee—Lac de Morat. The castle itself is only open in part to the public, but the ramparts are there to enjoy at any time. There is no charge or restriction on walking along them.

The Historical Museum

The museum is situated next to the castle, at the site of the old **water mill**.

Opening times: May–September, 10.00a.m. to 12.00p.m. and 2.00–6.00p.m.
October–April: Tuesdays–Sundays, 2.00–5.00p.m.
January and February: Saturdays and Sundays only, 2.00–5.00p.m.

The museum has been developed to recreate the way it looked in the 18th century. It has some temporary exhibitions, but in its permanent collection it has Roman relics and much of the Burgundian treasure left by the fleeing Duke of Burgundy.

On the ramparts around the city of Morat/Murten, the old keyhole look-outs can still be seen. This is where the Duke of Burgundy came to grief for the second time.

Accommodation

Normally a town of this size would have a good hotel and few average ones, but here you can find superb hotels in the old town, and a hotel which I would rate as one of the nicest in Switzerland. In the old town there are:

Hotel Murtenhof, next door to the castle. They also have apartments.
Hotel Krone, right in the middle of one of the main streets.
Hotel Schiff, just outside the town walls, near the marina.

These three hotels are all in the three-star range, places where you can enjoy the atmosphere of the old town without forsaking any comforts. One particular hotel stands out among the ten hotels in the area, and that is **Le Vieux Manoir**. Its situation on the shores of the lake is superb, and it is a large manor house, beautifully decorated throughout, with huge rooms and furniture to match. Although a four-star hotel the prices are no more than you often pay for a lesser hotel in a city.

Camping

Morat/Murten Camp, Lowenberg: situated on the lakeside, just outside the town. A three-star site.
Open: 1 April–31 October.

The Lake

Lac de Morat—or Murtensee—is ideal for a good family holiday. Not being a large expanse of water like the lakes at Geneva or Neuchâtel, it is good for windsurfing, yachting and all manner of water sports. Morat has a small marina, a promenade with mini-golf, and grassy areas by the lake for picnics.

Over the other side of the lake is the small village of **Vully** and the high vantage point at **Mount Vully**. From here there are views across the lake and to the Alps. The boat service runs all year from **Motier** (Vully) to Morat and vice versa, about once an hour. The journey time is 15 minutes. The hillsides of Mount Vully are covered in vineyards, from which one of the more famous Swiss wines is made.

Excursions from Morat

From Morat there are some good excursions, some of which would interest cyclists, others historians.

In the region between the three lakes the land is probably the flattest in Switzerland. There is the odd bump here and there to make the journey more interesting, but in the main it is market garden country and it is known as Grossmoos.

A good starting point for a cycling trip around this area is **Kerzers**, and on all the lanes in the area cycling routes are marked with a dark red disc, and a cycle logo. The routes vary from fairly short trips around the local villages to journeys of some distance between the towns. Kerzers itself is central to many of the lanes, but there are plenty of small lanes connecting farmhouses which can also be used. Travelling across from Kerzers to the **Bieler See** and **Erlach** takes you over canals and through farm land where the only evidence that you are in Switzerland is the huge Bernese farmhouses. A typical route is from **Kerzers** to **Munschemeir** (via the **Agrisroilmoos**) to **Treitch**, **Bruttelen**, **Vinelz** and **Erlach**, a trip of about 20 km (12.5 miles, with a gentle climb between Bruttelen and Vinelz. If cycling is something you would like to do just for the day, then bikes can be hired from the railway station. This is true of all stations, not just the ones in this area.

For those interested in history, this part of the country has some of the oldest sites. **Fribourg** is one of the most historic cities of the region, and a couple of kilometres down the road from Morat there is the town of **Avenches**. Here there is an excellent Roman amphitheatre which, unusually, is not in the middle of a field miles from anywhere but at the end of the main street in the town.

Avenches

Oddly, this town is in a small part of the canton of Vaud, although it is quite distinctively in the Fribourg region. Its main street is typical of the market towns which are dotted all over the region: a pleasant main street around which are fountains and a château. The main feature of this town, at the end of the rue Centrale, is the **Roman amphitheatre**, which has been partly and tastefully restored. Work continues at the site, but it is good enough to give a really good idea of this landmark. The original seating of the theatre has been extended using modern materials to give the impression of how the site looked, while all the buttresses which were added in the 3rd century have been kept clean and in good order.The amphitheatre was probably constructed in the 2nd century to seat around 8,000 spectators. The arena was used for the usual Roman sports: gladiator versus bear, lynx or lion. The whole structure covers 115 m x 87 m (380 x 285 ft)

and was carved out of the hillside. The site is open for any visitor to wander around at will, and there is a museum nearby.

The museum is open from 9.00a.m. to 12.00p.m. and 1.00–5.00p.m. It is closed on Wednesdays in winter.

Aarberg

Aarberg is another place worth visiting in this area. Its bridge is centuries old, as is the old medieval town. Once across the bridge you enter the town's main street, which is almost like a huge courtyard. All the buildings in this town centre are well-preserved.

Further to the south-west of Morat the region is commonly known as the valley of **la Broye**, and is covered in detail in the section on Vaud and South-West Switzerland. For most visitors to the Morat/Neuchâtel and Bern area the medieval city of Fribourg is an essential part of their tour.

Fribourg

The Dukes of Zahringhan could certainly pick a site. Here, as in Bern, the defences are almost totally natural: a deep gorge, the town enclosed by the bend of the river and look-out towers dotted around the perimeter. Fribourg was the handiwork of the fourth duke; the fifth duke created Bern some 40 years later.

Unfortunately, the delights of the historic part of Fribourg are not entirely obvious as you arrive in the city. There is a fair amount of urban sprawl to negotiate before arriving in the centre of the city, and it's not until you

*F*resh fruit is often brought into the villages and towns directly by the farmers. This is in the village of Aarberg.

nice patisseries). You will then come into a large square where the tourist information office is situated—turn immediately right into the square, and it is on the right-hand side by two bus stops. This is a **place Georges Python**, and it is from here down to the river that Fribourg becomes interesting.

The **rue de Lausanne** is quite an attractive shopping street and leads on to the **Grenette**, an area which abounds in beautiful Gothic architecture. Walking into the square from the rue de Lausanne there is the cathedral, Hotel de Ville, and les Cordeliers, the Franciscan monastery. Carrying on past the cathedral there is a steep cobbled street down to the river, and the oldest and possibly the most interesting part of Fribourg, with old squares, leaning houses and the old covered wooden bridge. Not far from the bridge to the right are the towers, so you can go back up to the main road and the new bridge via the old tower steps. An alternative route back takes you around the bend of the river to further lookout towers and the church of **Lorrette**.

venture from the main square down the **rue de Lausanne** that the real Fribourg reveals itself. The closer to the river and the further down you walk the older the buildings are, and it is in this area that French turns to German. Fribourg is another of these bilingual towns—here the river has created the language barrier.

Although it is quite a hilly walk basically down and then back up the hill, it is well worth the effort. If arriving by rail, cross over the **place de la Gare**, and walk down the **rue de Romont**. This is a main shopping street, with department stores and the usual array of fast food outlets (as well as some

---

Jean Tinguely

As a complete contrast to the supposed national trait of staid conservatism, Jean Tinguely is one of the most creative sculptors of this century. At 65 he is still raising eyebrows with his exploding ironmongery, and has exhibited in New York's Museum of Modern Art and Moscow's House of Artists. His "Homage to New York" caused the biggest stir when shown in 1960, when the self-destructing machine disintegrated with much smoke and fire. He was born in Fribourg, and still lives near his native city.

There are a number of vantage points from which to see the extraordinary layout of Fribourg, the best being from the **Zahringhan bridge** which gives a good view down on to the old town, and down by the **River Saarne**. The latter really shows the high rocks—almost cliffs—upon which the city was built. The walk around Fribourg is quite short, but it can be strenuous for the less fit, so there is a funicular from Neuville back up to the rue des Alpes, which is fairly close to the place Georges Python. There are also a good bus and tram services, which will have you back up the hill in no time., and with a lot less effort.

Of the main buildings in Fribourg the most interesting are:

The Cathedral of St Nicholas

This magnificent 13th-century Gothic church dominates the lower part of the city. As with many of these structures, it was several centuries in the building and in fact, from the original stones

*T*he best of Fribourg's architecture is down the hill towards the river, but the place de Ville is almost at the heart of the old town, near the cathedral.

being laid in 1283, 200 years went by before the 75 m (250 ft) high tower was complete.

Hotel de Ville

The town hall, the cobbled square and the gleaming gold clock make for a very complete scene. The building itself is 16th century, and there are few intrusions of the modern world here. Without any cars present, you can imagine the scene has changed little down the centuries.

L'Eglise des Cordeliers

This building housed the Franciscan monks and dates back to the 13th century. The **chancel** is particularly good, with oak stalls dating from 1280.

Museums

There are four museums in Fribourg, two of which are fairly specialized:

The Museum of Art and History
Rue de Morat 12.
Opening times: Tuesdays–Sundays, 10.00a.m. to 5.00p.m.
This museum contains some of the finest religious and medieval sculptures in Switzerland.

The Museum of Natural History
Chemin du Musée, Boulevard de Perolles.
The boulevard runs from the station towards the Perolles district. Tram number 1 goes in this direction.
Opening times: 12.00–6.00p.m.

There are two other museums: the **Sewing Machine Museum** and the **Puppet Museum**. Both are quite specialized and the opening times vary, so it would be best to check at the tourist office. (Tel: (037) 813175.)

Accommodation
Of the best hotels, there is only one where you could say you have the atmosphere of Fribourg. This is **Hotel Duc Bertold**, a four-star hotel next to the main bridge across the River Saarne. A delightful position, right in the heart of old Fribourg.

Most of the other hotels of any interest are scattered around the higher part of the city. The Faucan, which has no star rating but is cheap, and La Rose, a three-star hotel, are in the older part near Les Cordeliers.

The old covered bridge at Fribourg leads to the city walls, and the "German" side of the language barrier.

Camping

The two nearest campsites to Fribourg are:

Dudingen Schiffenensee, just to the north of the city, and not far off the main N12 to Bern. This is a three-star site. Open all year.

Marly la Foliaz, a non-classified site, on a minor road. After crossing the main bridge over the River Saarne at Fribourg, follow the signs to Marly. Take a right turn after Marly, on the road to Le Mouret.

Another site in this area is Montecu le Mont, a non-classified site on the road between le Mouret and Giffers. There is a bus service which takes this route on its way to la Roche and Bulle. It leaves Fribourg about every 40 minutes, and the first bus is at 6.34a.m., the last at 9.14p.m.

Excursions

From Fribourg there are some good places to visit, and given the choice between battling down the motorway to Gruyères or using the back road via la Roche, I would choose the latter.

If you need an overnight stop on this road, there is a hotel at **la Roche** which may not be entirely obvious. It is called La Belvedere and its situation gives a superb view from any one of the rooms, which are quite cheap at around 35 SFr for a single room, 70 SFr for a double. It has a good restaurant, but the owner speaks no English. To get there look out for the sign on the left as you travel from Fribourg to **Bulle**. The hotel is at the top of a fairly windy single-track lane.

Another favourite spot for a day's visit is **Schwarzsee—Lac Noir—** although some people also come here during the winter for a holiday. It has a fairly extensive system of nine lifts, taking you up to the **Kaiseregg** at 2,185 m (7,169 ft), **Les Reardets** at 1,922 m (6,306 ft) and the **Schwyzberg** at 1,628 m (5,341 ft). It is only when it has been a good year for snow that Schwarzsee attracts tourists wishing to ski, so the more likely visitors here are those who come from Fribourg in the summer on a day trip.

V̦iew down to Old Fribourg Town.

From the lake, which is very picturesque and is surrounded by the mountains mentioned, there are plenty of walking paths, and the lake can be used for boating, swimming (although it is possibly a little cold!) and generally enjoying clean country air. There are some terrific walks here, most of which skirt the lake either along the shore or up in the hills. They cater for both the casual stroller and the more serious hiker, and the local tourist office can arrange a six-day walk which takes in the Schwarzsee.

The Six-Day Walk—Itinerary

Take the bus to **Planfayon**, a town which heads the valley leading to Schwarzsee. From here the hike—known as the Itineraries des Prealpes Fribourgeoises, and symbolized by a grouse strutting, wings astride, through the mountains—takes you over the hills rather than through the valley.

The walls of Gruyères are just off the main street, and the view looks down on the surrounding countryside to Bulle.

by accident that the climax of the trip is in the Gruyères, Chatel St Denis region. Of all the superbly conserved towns in this canton, probably the most famous and the most dramatic is the hilltop town of Gruyères.

The second and subsequent days take the walkers through **Singine** country, southern **Veveyse** and the beautiful **Gruyères**. In total it is about a 100-km (62-mile) hike, marked out by the symbol of the grouse. There are some climbs on the route but nothing too strenuous, and your main luggage is sent on to **Charney** where there is a full day for relaxation. Needless to say it is a well-organized affair, and there are three categories of accommodation to choose from. Up-to-date information on dates and prices is available from the Fribourg tourist office.

This walk probably takes in some of the best of Fribourgland, and it is not

Gruyères

The first good point about Gruyères is that it is traffic free, even if you are staying in a hotel within the town walls. There are three car parks on the main road up to Gruyères but in summer and on holidays the top ones will be full. Gruyères is as popular with the Swiss as it is with foreign tourists, so it can get quite busy.

The town is reached from the road between Bulle and the towns of the Moleson and Granvillard. Drivers will have no difficulty in finding the town, since it sits on a hilltop which, unless the weather is particularly bad, can be seen some distance away. There is also a bus service from Bulle or Fribourg.

In the true spirit of the best of Switzerland's romantic architecture, the **castle** at Gruyères has pointed towers at every corner and dominates the entire valley. Once inside the town's fortifications the whole appearance is like a theatrical set—possibly *too* perfect. If it were not for the throngs of visitors, and the Gruyères cream tea shops, you could believe you were in another time. The town was constructed between the 12th and the 16th centuries. After walking through the town's main, and only, street, there is the castle.

Gruyères Castle

In all, 19 counts reigned in Gruyères castle between the 11th and the 16th centuries, but only the **dungeons** remain as part of the original building. This does not detract from the fact that it is a well worth a visit, with re-creations of a feudal kitchen, guardrooms and a superb collection of 18th-century furniture.

Opening times: summer, 9.00a.m. to 6.00p.m.
Winter, 9.00a.m. to 12.00p.m. and 2.00–6.00p.m.

Cheese Dairy

Whilst Gruyères as a town is undoubtedly attractive, most people think of its cheese rather than its castle. Famed the world over, it is one of only two very well-known Swiss cheeses—the other one being Emmental. Gruyères is the one without so many holes in it. You can see the whole process of cheese production at

T he main street at Gruyères is (almost!) traffic free, and leads up to the castle and museum.

the bottom of the hill. When you reach the junction with the main road, turn left toward Moleson and the cheese factory is just on the right, after the railway lines.

This is not an old-fashioned cheese dairy where you might expect to see men carrying cheeses around on their heads. It is a modern production house, but it does give an interesting insight into the whole industry in Switzerland. As an example of good public relations and multi-lingual presentation it is excellent. There are stairs to the **gallery** which overlooks a production floor and has three sides, the fourth being used for the visual display. Each side offers commentary in a different language: German, French, and English. The presentation lasts about 20 minutes, and from the gallery you can also see the cheeses on their racks. Visitors who have difficulty with stairs will be pleased to know that the staircase has a chair-lift alongside it. Entrance is free.

Swiss Cheese

To the surprise of many there are more than two cheeses in Switzerland. Gruyère and Emmental are the most famous, but there are plenty of other types in fact, from all over the country. The oldest cheese of Switzerland is Sbrinz, and is one of the hardest around, whilst over in Glarus there is a soft green cheese called Schazeiger. The recipe for this one is over 500 years old. Appenzell has two types, and the Jura has the Tête de Moine, eaten scraped. Mountain cheeses come from the Valais with a variety named after the valley Bagnes, while down in the Italian regions of the Ticino there are three types called Piora.

Around Gruyères

Around Gruyères there are quite a few resorts for both summer and winter vacations. At the head of the valley is the town of **Moleson**, which is the base for lifts to the mountains of **le Moleson** (2,002 m; 6,568 ft) and **la Vaudula** (1,668 m; 5,472 ft). There is only a limited number of runs, which for the enthusiastic skier may be less than satisfactory. However, there is a good cross-country course which takes the skier up to 1,520 m (4,987 ft) at **Plan Francey**. The balance with a lot of these lower altitude resorts of Switzerland is that they do not attract the mass market so, in theory, the area is less crowded and lifts easier to use.

This area is probably more suited to the summer visitor and to accommodate them Moleson has tennis courts, mini-golf, horse trekking, walking and archery. There is a number of small towns around Moleson, such as **Pringy**, **le Paouler**, **les Rybes**, and **Epagny**. None has the spectacular setting of Gruyères, but add up to an interesting, less-crowded area of the country. The main town of the region is **Bulle**, which has a very impressive **château**. Just when you thought Bulle had nothing to offer, this delightful building appears on the road out of town on the way to the N12. If you intend to stay in the Gruyères region this would make a good excursion.

The Gruyèrian Museum (Musee Gruerien), Bulle

The museum is housed in a low, modern building just to the side of the castle. Its collection is very much based around the culture and history of the Gruyères, and to that end it is a very

The old chapel at Juan could be one of the smallest around—it has enough room for about 12 people.

agricultural museum. Cowbell collars, cream spoons and butter moulds make up the display, along with a small collection of paintings and regional furniture.

Opening times: Tuesdays–Saturdays, 10.00a.m. to 12.00pm. and 2.00–5.00p.m.
Sundays and Public Holidays, 2.00–5.00p.m.

Charney en Gruyères

To the east of Gruyères is another valley area, which has a number of pleasant towns for winter or summer holidays. This is Charney en Gruyères, and it encompasses two valleys and a good-sized mountain which is well served with lifts and ski runs.

The town of Charney itself is quite small, situated on an artificial lake. The lifts go to **Mount Voutnetz**, at a height of 1,626 m (5,335 ft). There are several smaller lifts from here, giving access to the northern side of the mountain. Its capacity is slightly larger than the system at Moleson but is mainly downhill skiing, with only a small cross-country trail. From Charney the valley to the east goes to the **Juan Pass** and the small town of **Juan**. This little town is really hemmed in and gives the impression of being one of the more forgotten places in Switzerland. It is on the way to the more famous region around **Zweissimmen** and the **Simmental valley**, but is not a bad place to stop before heading on to the Juan Pass, since there is a good **waterfall** here and one of the smallest **chapels** you are likely to find. The waterfall is to the right as you head towards the Juan Pass. Further along the road, the older part of the town appears, and just on the left is a small chapel, built around the turn of the century, almost next to a working **water wheel**. The chapel has four pews, and seems capable of seating only about 12 people.

Accommodation

There are some excellent hotels in the Gruyères, the most expensive of which are in Gruyères itself. The novelty of staying in a hotel in the main street of Gruyères is attractive, and to meet this need there are two hostelries, Hotel de Ville and Hotel Fleur de Lys.

These are both two-star establishments, one on each side of the main street. There is nothing to choose between them in terms of facilities, although the Fleur de Lys claims to have a parking area. To be strictly accurate this is outside the walls of the city, but it *is* reserved for patrons.

All the hotels in Gruyères will cost you at least 100 SFr per night, but even more expensive is the three-star Des Chevaliers. There is no doubting the quality of this hotel, situated just outside the city walls, but it will cost 150–210 SFr per night, which I feel is rather overpriced.

Out of Gruyères, prices drop to more reasonable rates, although you do not have the same setting as the hilltop town. The largest towns of Bulle and Broc have a number of good hotels, such as the Alpes, Rallye and Tonnelier in Bulle, which all offer accommodation at about the 90 SFr mark.

Moleson has surprisingly few hotels, but **Charmey** has a four-star hotel by the name of Hotel Cailler. **Juan**, too, has only one hotel registered, aptly named the Wasserfall, where rates are a reasonable 50–70 SFr.

Camping
For campers there are two good sites, one of which is on Lac Gruyères:

Gumefens Camping du Lac: this three-star site is not far off the old main road between Bulle and Fribourg—do not take the motorway. The site is easily seen from the road and is on the lakeside.
Open: 15 May–15 September.

Epagny-Gruyères les Sapins: one of those special four-star sites in a remarkable location, within a stone's throw of Gruyères.
Open: 1 May–30 September.

The Juan Pass
To move between the Fribourg canton east to the lakes of Interlaken and the rest of central Switzerland, there is a convenient, but little-used pass—the **Juan Pass**.

For those travelling by public transport, do not despair at the realization that there is no railway: the local regional bus services operate between Bulle and towns on the other side of the pass. Once over the pass, the whole of Central Switzerland opens up and you can travel on to the Brunig Pass and Lucerne.

*T*he Juan Pass is one *of the quieter passes in the country, yet has some fine features like this waterwheel at Juan.*

The Juan Pass is not very high—a mere 1,509 m (4,951 ft)—so it is rarely closed in winter. At the highest point there is a rest area and quite an active ski centre and camping and caravan park. This small ski area is used well into March, and the caravan park is open throughout the year. Although it does not give the impression of being a high-quality site, it is rated with five stars.

The run up to the top of the Juan Pass is gentle, through forests and the previously mentioned town of **Juan**. It is not a helter-skelter, 20-hairpin road, so you can enjoy the scenery at your

leisure, whichever direction you are travelling in. Going from Fribourg across to Simmental takes you from a very definitely French region to one where German is the native tongue. Signposts will reveal the differences, but try asking for something in French on the other side of the pass!

The road down to the valley of the River Simme offers beautiful views of the small towns of Reidenbach, Boltingen and Pfaffenned, amongst the green fields and red roofs of this sharp vale. To the right and south are the resorts of Zweissimmen, Gstaad and Château d'Oex, which are covered in detail in the section on South-West Switzerland. A left turn will take the traveller northeast towards **Interlaken**, via the Simmental valley.

The road from the Juan Pass through the Simmental valley is delightfully easy, and there is a good alternative for cyclists. The main road runs on a higher plain on the northern side of the river, but to the south of the valley there are numerous lanes running between the small villages. Along the main road there are, periodically, covered wooden bridges leading to these hamlets, and both the road and the lanes are relatively flat for easy cycling. On each side of the valley the mountains reach over 2,000 m (6,560 ft), but only one is accessible by funicular railway—the **Stockhorn**.

This area is the real heart of Switzerland, and nowhere could typify the concept of Swiss tourism better than **Interlaken** and **Lucerne**. Of the two, Interlaken is slightly less commercial, and you can find some small, quiet villages along the banks of the Thuner See and the Brienzer See.

Interlaken

The town of Interlaken sits, not surprisingly as its name suggests, between the two picturesque lakes Thuner See and Brienzer See. At the extreme end of the lakes are the towns of Thun and Brienz, but the attractions lie in the valleys around the lakes and on their shores. Interlaken itself can be considered an ideal place to be based for trips out into the surrounding mountains, boating on the lake, and any number of spectacular day excursions. The organization here is geared to provide information and arrange visits within the region, rather than in the town itself.

However, the town is pleasant enough, with promenade walks, a small central square and events in the evenings such as the "William Tell" play and cultural performances at the **casino**. The choice of things to do in Interlaken is great, but the area really scores highly in the opportunities outside the town.

Out of Interlaken: Winter

The tourist office have recently put together a programme of sporting possibilities designed especially for skiers and other winter-sports people. Having decided that they cannot compete with the major winter resorts they have organized excursions to places away from Interlaken.

Apart from the trips to the mountain tops of the **Jungfrau** and the **Schilthorn**, which winter sports enthusiasts would take anyway, there is a whole range of activities including snowboarding, Telemark skiing, monoskiing, glacier skiing, off-piste skiing,

and possibly the most bizarre activity invented for some time—bridge jumping. This apparently involves hurling yourself from one of the many high bridges, while attached to a nylon cord. There is also "Crazy Week" organized by the Swiss ski school at **Wilderswil** (tel: 223019), where they promise that everything that *can* be done on snow, *is* done—which is enough to make the mind boggle!

Out of Interlaken: Summer

Interlaken has traditionally been more of a summer resort (hence the winter activity programme), so it is not surprising that there is a whole host of excursions and activities aimed at the summer visitor. There may have been a tendency in the past for Interlaken to

From the hill near the railway station, Spiez Castle stands out against the Thuner See.

be associated with the middle-aged coach tripper, but there have been serious attempts to attract the younger tourist: among the horse-carriage rides and the trip to the model cheese dairy, arrangements can be made for hang gliding, paragliding, accompanied mountain treks and climbing, a new tennis centre, open-air fitness course and horse riding.

For the evenings, there are cultural shows in the grounds of the **Kunstall** (casino), and there is also the "William Tell" play, which attracts great numbers every year.

Information about these winter and summer activities can be found, along with the relevant phone numbers, in a brochure called *Interlaken Activ* available from the Interlaken tourist office.

The Jungfrau

The most obvious trip, in any season, is to the top of the **Jungfrau.** This is one of the highest points in Europe, has the highest rack railway in the world, and provides spectacular views of the **Eiger**, the **Monch** and the Jungfrau from a panoramic restaurant. It can hardly be ignored. The height of the station is 3,454 m (11,333 ft), so it is quite a feat of engineering to have provided a mountain railway to this peak.

Your Swiss Pass is not valid for the whole of the journey up the Jungfrau: it will take you as far as **Lauterbrunnen** or **Grindelwald**, but after that you have to pay. Look around for package trips, taking in a number of places, since the basic rail fare up the Jungfrau is expensive.

The rail journey starts from Interlaken Ost (east), but it can also be reached from the station at Interlaken West. The trip takes in some of the finest scenery in the country, going through the villages of Wengen, Lauterbrunnen and Murren. In fact, you can go by one of two routes: one through the Lauterbrunnen Valley, which will take you via Wengen and on up to Kleine Scheidegg; the other is to take the Grindelwald train and go via Grund to the same station. Whichever way you go, you can choose to return via the other route. The changeover point for the last leg of the journey is at Kleine Scheidegg, where the train will pull you from 2,300 m (7,612 ft) up to the **Jungfraujoch** at 3,454 m (11,333 ft). Although it would be a most spectacular journey to travel across the glaciers of the Eiger, unfortunately even Swiss ingenuity has only been able to provide a route by burrowing through the mountain. There are, however, stopping points along the way where windows have been put in at underground stations. You can leave the carriage and look over the mighty glacial deposits on the face of the Eiger. Despite having a thick window between yourself and these great balls of ice, the scene is inspiring. There are two such stops, one at **Eigerwand** and the other at **Eismeer**. The train creeps up to its destination at Jungfrau and it is not surprising that many visitors wonder at the reason for building such a railway—surely not as a mere tourist attraction? The railway was in fact made to service the research work being carried out on the Jungfrau glacier, and although the first impressions are of a new, bright restaurant and visitors' centre, not too far away is the older **Sphinx building**.

In the true tradition of Swiss determination to cover its peaks with restaurants, the Jungfrau rates as one of their finest achievements. Here you can sip coffee while gazing out over one of the largest glaciers in Europe. To your right the winds will create flurries of powder snow on the tips of the Monch and the Eiger, and should you wish to sample the air there are terraces where it can be very warm or very dangerous. The danger comes from icicles that can hang directly over the terrace viewing area. In these cases the terrace will be closed. There is an

*T*he last leg of the train journey to the summit of
the Jungfrau, shortly before the train vanishes into the tunnels
in the Eiger.

*T*he new "Top of Europe" restaurant at the top of the Eiger is ideally designed to give the best views—without getting cold!

area where you can go no matter what the weather, and to some extent this is where you can appreciate the height, the cold and the solitary nature of a high peak. Do not go out on this "plateau" if you are not well wrapped up in warm clothes, or suffer from vertigo, heart problems and suchlike.

A corridor runs from the second floor of the restaurant towards the **ice palace**. Just before the ice palace a door leads out onto the mountain itself. For many this will be the only time they will be able to stand actually on a mountain of this height, rather than on a concrete platform, and it is exhilarating. On a blustery day, the temperature can be around –9°C, with winds upwards of 65 kph (40 mph), so

you must take some care. Remember also that at this height it makes little difference whether it is summer or winter, it can still be bitterly cold in August. There is a path up to a viewing point where you can look down on the glacier and the restaurant, and up at the now very close mountain tops.

Significantly, there is a visitor's book in the corridor near this opening point out onto the mountain, and it is quite interesting to read some of the comments. "We have survived the Jungfrau" said one group from Australia.

Without detracting from those who have scaled these peaks, this excursion from the warmth of the restaurant can leave the visitor feeling as though they have been close to the real thing. It is worth the effort.

On the other side of the wonderfully designed restaurant is the old Sphinx building, which can be reached by a series of underground passages. On the way to the Sphinx is the small exhibition area showing the work of the glacial researchers, who have worked on this mountain for many years. To reach the top of the Sphinx there is a manned lift and at the top another terraced area that looks directly down on the glacier. At the back is the wide range of the Alps stretching away for miles. Dominating the building is the **Monch**, only slightly shorter that the Jungfrau at 4,099 m (13,449 ft).

Other attractions at the top of the mountain are the polar dogs and a cross-country ski school. These are mainly summer attractions, so that despite a temperature in the 80s down in the valleys, you can ski or go dog sledding on the glacier. There is also the opportunity to climb the final 100 m (328 ft) to the actual top of the Jungfrau. Led by an experienced mountain guide, the trek takes about four hours. Information is available from the tourist office or the Alpine Centre in Interlaken.

In the summer you can spend a whole day on the Jungfrau trip. Using the variety of rail services to see the villages along the route, coupled with the amenities on the mountain itself, you can easily enjoy a day which will give you a taste of the world at nearly 3,700 m (12,000 ft).

The Schilthorn

Although a good 1,200 m (4,000 ft) lower than the Jungfrau, the Schilthorn is another good excursion for those who yearn for the "high life". I doubt whether you would want to do both mountain tops, but it has been said that the panoramic view from the Schilthorn is a greater attraction than the pure height of the Jungfrau. It also has the (slightly overworked) fame of

having been used for one of the "James Bond" films. Why this has any bearing on the attraction of a place baffles me, but you cannot read much about the mountain without being reminded of this.

The route from Interlaken to Schilthorn is very similar to that to Jungfrau, but you stay in the Lauterbrunnen valley and go on to **Murren**. From here there is a spectacular cable car system which will take you to the summit, with a change at the mountain restaurant at **Birg**. The views from the top of the mountain are stunning, helped by the fact that you can still see the valley floor far below. Added to this is the revolving restaurant which has recently been enlarged and refurbished to accommodate more people and provide a secondary revolving surface. If the improvements carry on in this vein there is a good chance that the Schilthorn restaurant will also feature as a fairground attraction!

In visiting the mountain tops, you will also have seen some of the finest scenery in Switzerland. It is pure Alpine country with deep narrow valleys, searing snow-clad mountains, cow bells, Edelweiss, and pretty shuttered chalets. This scene appeals to many thousands of visitors to the Interlaken region every year, and you cannot ignore the fact that it is indeed beautiful. The tourist trappings which can sometimes go with it may not appeal,

One of the finest views of the Alps is from the terrace of the Sphinx building on the Jungfrau (overleaf).

and if this is the case then the un-limited walking paths between the mountain cafés soon take you away from such things.

Walking

The two valleys are the **Lauterbrunnen**, which comes complete with a raging **waterfall**, and the **Grindelwald** valley. Both villages are relatively large, cater-ing for winter and summer visitors, and one of the real joys of this region is being able to get into the mountains very quickly. At Grindelwald it is no more than a ten-minute walk from the railway station before all the village chalets are left behind and you are out in the hills.

Grindelwald particularly has some superb walks, and the hikes can be fairly short, from the village to Ober-haus, or more ambitious six-hour af-fairs which will take you up on to the high ridges of the Faulhorn. These walks take you to some of the most picturesque parts of the country, and it would be hard to surpass the scenic beauty of the Bachalpsee, with the Schreckhorn and the Finsteraahorn as a backdrop.

In the event of not wanting to, or not having sufficient time to, walk back to your starting point, there are the chair-lifts at First, Egg and Bort, and there are bus services to Bussalp and Grosse Scheidegg.

Switzerland is an agricultural land, even though it has crowded many of its mountains with lifts. Fortunately, some areas remain as they are, in the hands of the farmers.

High Flying in the Alps

For those in a hurry there are a number of good helicopter services in Switzerland. The helicopter was once regarded as one of those "beyond reach" forms of transport for the rich and famous, and although it is a spot of self indulgence to use them to fly into Zermatt they can be of great help by simply taking you to an otherwise difficult area. Particularly in the winter, some of the helicopter companies will fly groups to the mountain slopes at very reasonable rates, since their main occupation of carrying large loads into the mountains is summer based.

Bohag Helicopters at Zweisimmen are typical in that throughout the summer their Lynx choppers carry timber, cement, and steelwork up to new developments on the high slopes, but have little to do in winter. Operating from a small landing site at Wilderswil, on the road between Interlaken and Grindelwald, they offer flights up to the high slopes of the Jungfrau, with some spectacular views of the Eiger. The cost is probably less than you would think, at around 75SFr. These machines are also the ones which operate for the mountain rescue service, which is not a recommended way of trying a flight in a helicopter, especially with the costs for the rescue being fairly and squarely lodged with the unfortunate victim!

The other way of using the unique abilities of the helicopter is in the skiing area. An increasing number of skiers are taking up heliskiing, whereby the aircraft will take the skier up to untouched snow fields, way above the normal pistes. Clearly, your skiing ability has to better than average since you will be skiing on virgin snow. This is for the more adventurous sports person who is looking for the extra excitement offered by non-piste skiing. There are heliskiing facilities at most of the big resorts like Verbier, Crans Montana, Interlaken (Grindelwald) and Saas Fee.

The local tourist office has recently introduced a walking passport (*wanderpass*) for summer visitors. Walking is free, and the passport is also free, so why have one? The idea is that following a series of suggested routes or itineraries, you can, after completing the walks, be awarded small momentos of your efforts. The passport is stamped at places such as boat landing stages, railway stations or by the local bus driver. Upon completing a total of five walks the proud passport holder is entitled to a Golden Boot, and so on until you graduate, with the presentation of a gold-plated boot emblem and a certificate for walking all ten itineraries. This is as close as you can get to organized walking, but for younger visitors it adds some flavour to the trips. For less experienced walkers, or casual strollers who cannot resist a challenge, it may just be the thing to remind you of how you ended up with such sore feet. The wanderpass is available from railway stations.

If walking on the mountains does not appeal, then there is a choice of forest walks alongside the Brienzer See or the Thuner See. A particularly good walk is on the northern shore of the Brienzer See, where you can go from Bonigen to Iseltwald, and then on to Geissbach. This side of the lake is well wooded and Iseltwald is a quiet, beautifully positioned resort. If your journey proves too arduous, then the lake steamers call in at all the towns on the lakes. Whilst Brienz is largely affected by its timber-felling trade, making it a

*F*rom the small village of Oberried it is possible to make excursions on the Brienzer See lake.

slightly less-likely resort, just along the road from here is the small village of **Oberried** (one of quite a few in the Bernese Oberland). The main road from Brienz to Interlaken runs across the higher part of the village, but down from here, by way of the narrowest lanes imaginable, is a small promenade. At one end there is the landing stage, and the point from where the local fishermen push out into the lake. It's a peaceful little backwater, away from the more touristy Interlaken. A pleasant day out would be to go by lake steamer from Oberried across to Geissbach. Here there is a hotel, and a series of **waterfalls** which you can walk under. From this point the paths are clearly marked for the route to Iseltwald through the forests. After

refreshments in the village, you can take the ferry back to Oberried, should you need to collect your car, or travel on by bus to Interlaken.

For those on longer walking tours, the mountain restaurants and hotels at Faulhorn, Waldspitz, Bort and Grosse Scheidegg have simple accommodation available.

Grindelwald, too, has a good range of hotels and guesthouses, from the five-star Grand Regina to the one-star Blumlisalp.

Camping

The campsites in the Grindelwald and Lauterbrunnen valleys are down in the warmer, flatter part of the countryside,

*S*ome of the walking paths alongside the Brienzer See go under waterfalls, such as this one at Geisbacht.

Spiez Castle, on the Thuner See, dates back to the 10th century.

so for hikers travelling in the mountains these may not be the sort of places to stay. However, for the more leisurely walker who is likely to return each night, there are some perfect sites.

Grindelwald Eigernordwand: a four-star site with plenty of amenities and close to the town.
Open throughout the year.

Grindelwald Aspen: a slightly higher site at 1,111 m (3,645 ft), with simple amenities—a two-star site.
Open throughout the year.

Grindelwald Gletscherdorf: a four-star site about ten-minutes walk from the centre.
Open throughout the year.

Grindelwald Weisse Spinne: a non-classified site in the valley.
Open: May–September.

Grindelwald Sand: the second non-classified site in the area, with simple facilities.
Open throughout the year.

In the Lauterbrunnen valley there are sites at:

Stechelberg Breithorn: this three-star site is at the far end of the valley.
Open: 1 May–30 September.
Closed in winter.

Stechelberg Rutti: another three-star site at the end of the valley.
Open: 1 May–30 September.

Lauterbrunnen Jungfrau: situated in a beautiful position in the heart of the valley, this is one of the five-star sites with all facilities.
Open throughout the year.

The Lakes

For many visitors to this region, the point of coming here is to enjoy two beautiful lakes, either as something to look at or to use in the many forms of water sport. Of the two, probably the **Thuner See** is the more scenic, and there are more possibilities for travel between villages on this lake. The **Brienzer See** is certainly dramatic, but only one shore, the side which runs from Brienz via Oberried and Ringgenberg to Interlaken, can be fully utilized. On Thuner See you can boat across from one side to the other and there are plenty of small villages as well as delightful places such as **Speiz**.

For the water-sports enthusiast just about every type of sailing, boating, sailboarding and windsurfing is possible on these picturesque waters. Again, there have been considerable efforts to attract the younger visitor, since until recently not many people got wet.

Of the villages on the lakes Iseltwald and Oberried are interesting, if a little quiet, and Thuner See is more lively, with Speiz as one of its best shoreline towns.

Speiz is built on a very steep hill, and if you arrive on the train there is a fairly long trek down to the harbour area. In summer the best way to arrive would be by ferry from Interlaken or Thun. The quay area is also the hub of the village, which is largely centred around the medieval **castle**. From the castle gardens there are good views down to the lake and the harbour. The castle is open:

May–October 10.00a.m. to 12.00p.m. and 2.00–5.00p.m.
Closed Monday mornings.

Accommodation in the Interlaken Region

The variety of accommodation in this well-established resort is wide ranging. It is one of the few Swiss towns that has catered for the cheaper, mass-tourist market, so there are some fairly ordinary places here—that is, by Swiss standards. There is also one of the few examples of hotel follies, in the shape of the Hotel Metropole. Disregarding the fact that it is, apparently, a good hotel, it is a tall monotonous building, sticking out like the proverbial sore thumb. At some stage in Interlaken's town-planning history, the builders were not told that you simply do not build hotels like that in the Swiss Alps. But there it is, and it does give you an easily identifiable landmark if you are unsure of your whereabouts. The **tourist office** is located under the Hotel Metropole, so it is easy to find.

The Metropole is a four-star hotel, but if you are looking for a more traditional Swiss hostelry, then there is a good choice in the luxury category. At the very top of the range there are two fine old hotels—the Grand Victoria-Jungfrau and the Grand Beau Rivage. Both are imposing hotels in Swiss Victorian style, and you will be paying in the region of 400 SFr for a double room at either. In the more realistic market the choice is endless, with 15 three-star hotels to choose from, all around the 100 SFr per room mark.

Throughout the region, and in Interlaken itself, there are chalets and apartments to let, and for those travelling on a tight budget who are not camping there is the Balmers Herberge. This is situated about 15-minutes walk out of the town, and is tucked away behind some small shops. The bus to Bonigen from Interlaken west will take you there, and you should leave the bus at Matten by the ice rink. The Balmers Herberge is a traditional Swiss chalet building, and provides dormitory accommodation for around 26 SFr per person.

Camping

Campsites abound in the whole of the Interlaken region, some of which are well out from the lakes in mountain resorts such as Grindelwald.

Interlaken Thuner See: this is Manor Farm site, situated on the lakeshore and is a top of the range, five-star site. Open throughout the year.

Interlaken Alpenblick: a three-star site on the Lombach River, about 2 km (just over a mile) along the road from Interlaken to Thun. Open throughout the year.

Interlaken Hobby: another site situated on the strip of land between the two lakes. A four-star site. Open 1 April–31 October. Closed in winter.

Interlaken Lazy Rancho: a four-star site, again on the River Lombach between the lakes.
Open 1 April–31 October.

Interlaken Jungfrau: one of the all-facility sites in the five-star category in the same area on the River Lombach.
Open 1 March–31 October.

Interlaken Sackgut: a simpler two-star site for tents and caravans between the lakes.
Open 1 April–30 September.

Interlaken Jungfraublick: this site is a little further out than the rest, near the district of Matten. A four-star site.
Open 1 March–30 September.

Slightly further out from the main town there are two sites at:

Wilderswil Oberoi: situated at the head of the valleys to Grindelwald and Lauterbrunnen, the site is four-star.
Open 15 March–15 October.

Lütschental Danys Camp: between Zweilütschinen and Lütschental, on the way to Grindelwald, this a beautifully situated four-star site.
Open 1 May–31 October.

For those who want to take advantage of the lakeland, then there sites around both Thuner See and Brienzer See:

Bonigen Seeblick: a four-star site set in extensive woodland.
Open 1 May–30 September.

Bonigen Terrasse: a three-star site with limited facilities.
Open throughout the year.

*E*ven in the depths of winter the cattle market at Interlaken is a regular event.

155

Bonigen Seeruhe: a non-classified site for camping only.
Open 1 May–30 September.

Iseltwald du Lac: in one of the most picturesque positions on Brienzer See, a four-star site.
Open throughout the year.

Ringgenberg au Lac: not too far out of Interlaken, a four-star lakeside site.
Open throughout the year.

Ringgenberg Talacker: a four-star site at the Interlaken end of Brienzer See.

Brienz Aaregg: at the lakeside, the town of Brienz is fairly large. The campsite is a good one with a five-star rating.
Open 1 April–1 November.

Brienz Seegarti: an inexpensive, non-classified site on the lakeshore.
Open 1 May–30 September.

Out from Interlaken

Interlaken is a centre for the Bernese Oberland, but spreading out from here, towards Bern or to the Brunig Pass, there are points of interest. Thuner See has a number of **castles**, three of which are near the town of Thun. The one at **Oberhofen** offers all the characteristics of the romantic Swiss castle, sitting right on the water's edge. Oberhofen dates back to the 12th century although it was restored and improved between the 17th and 19th centuries. Inside there is a collection of period furniture, and art from the Bernese Oberland.

Going in the opposite direction provides you with an altogether different interest—the **Brunig Pass**, over to Lucerne. The journey takes you along the shores of the Brienzer See and then up and over the Brunig Pass at a height of over 1,000 m (3,280 ft) and past two very scenic lakes at Lungern-see and Sarnersee, before dropping down into the Lucerne area. There is a choice of travelling by road, bus or car, or by the Brunig railway which recently celebrated its 100th birthday. The train is one of those delightfully slow affairs, and gives you a much greater impression of the height of the pass than the road can. It also runs throughout the year, whereas the road

is occasionally closed in winter. The train service runs from the Interlaken east station and takes just under two hours. You can also travel by rail to Lucerne by going to Bern and changing there, but it is a far less interesting trip, and certainly not nearly as scenic.

Before reaching the flat lands running towards Lucerne there are several small villages along the road and the railway line. Since the two run almost next to each other, there are no disadvantages to either form of transport. The Lungernsee is a beautiful lake, which has the **Wilerhorn** as a backdrop. Further along the small villages

The Brunig Pass between Interlaken and Lucerne is a superb route, by rail or road.

of Giswil and Sachsein are good stopping-off places on a tour. Accommodation costs in these smaller villages are considerably lower than in the main towns of Lucerne and Interlaken. A good example is the Bahnhof Hotel (nearly every Swiss town or village has one!), where a single room is in the region of 45 SFr and a double about 60 SFr. In this particular hotel the rooms are enormous and include such delightful touches as a *chaise longue* in each room.

Coming into Lucerne from this direction is not too interesting; flat farmland in a wide open valley. There are more picturesque routes into the town from the north, but probably the finest way to see Lucerne is from one of its many lake steamers.

Lucerne

Like Interlaken, this is one of the most famous tourist cities of Switzerland. For years it has been the destination for the packaged Swiss holiday, and to some extent this still shows. Rather unpleasant commercial treats such as a yodelling accordion player dressed in leather trousers at Alpnachstad do nothing to dispel this atmosphere.

Most western travellers have gone through that period. However, Lucerne is trying to change its image slightly and some of its long-established attractions are still worth looking at, particularly the **Transport Museum**, **Mount Pilatus** and the innumerable variations on the lake steamer trips.

The **old town** also boasts some of Switzerland's most historic constructions, notably the **Kapellbrücke**, which provides a walkway across the river entering the **Vierwaldstattersee** (Lake Lucerne).

The Kapellbrücke in Lucerne is not only an historical feature, but also a useful short cut over the river.

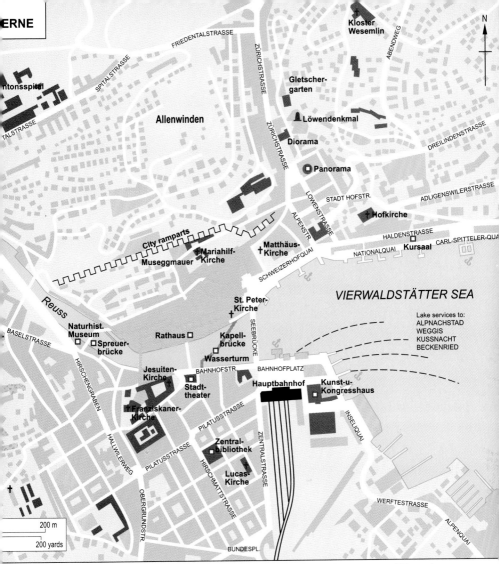

Town plan of Lucerne.

The Kapellbrücke

This was built in the early part of the 14th century and, although it is an interesting feature to look at from outside, the paintings on the inside portraying Swiss and local history are the real feature. There are 112 pictures in the apex of the roof, which were put in during the 17th century. They have been carefully restored so they can be easily seen, and once again it is good to be able to view historic places in the a normal working environment, not in a specially preserved, museum-like way. The bridge is used constantly and the only people stopping to admire the pictures are the visitors—for the locals it is just a part of their city life.

Further up from the lake are the old city walls—the **Musegg Ramparts**—which have the same towers as the

The city walls of Lucerne are among the most interesting sights in the city, with footpaths alongside. It is also possible to walk along the walls.

bridge below. There are restricted times for walking the walls which stretch from the River Reuss almost to the **Alpenstrasse** in the centre of the city. The walls are open during the summer from 8.00a.m. to about 7.00p.m.

Lucerne does have some less-famous sights, such as the **Jesuits' church** near the railway station and the **St Leger Cathedral** behind the quays and the casino, but the real history of this region lies in the Kapellbrücke, the city walls and its being at the very beginnings of the Swiss confederation, for

this region is known as the Cradle of Switzerland. It was on the other side of the lake from Lucerne, in the cantons of Uri, Schwyz, and Unterwalden, that the first pact was made to form the confederation. Surprisingly, there is no reference to these events in the city itself, although it does have a large number of museums devoted to all sorts of other things.

Museums

The best and by far the largest museum in Lucerne is the excellent **Transport Museum**. Switzerland has devoted much of its resources and time to perfecting the art of travel in most of its varying forms. If any country deserves to have a museum dedicated to moving people from one point to another by land, water or air, then it ought to be Switzerland.

Transport Museum (Verkehrshaus)
Lidostrasse 5.
Open all year (except Christmas day) 9.00a.m. to 6.00p.m.
This is approximately a 20-minute walk from the centre of town, along the **Nationalquai**, past the casino, to the Lidostrasse. The museum is on the left-hand side of the minor road but cannot be missed due to the huge picture of a smiling SBB conductor gracing one of the walls. Alternatively, tram number 2 or bus 24 (Hermitage) will take you to the front entrance.

Inside the museum there is every form of transport imaginable, from penny-farthing bicycles to space capsules. Although this covers all the types of transport, interest must be centred on the development of Switzerland's rail, road and air systems. Some of the early Swissair aircraft are displayed in a courtyard, with steam trains and cars. A visit is a really good day out, and a great opportunity for the grown-ups to play trains again under the pretence of educating their children.

Historical Museum
Pfstergasse 24.
Featuring local and national history.

Museum of Fine Art
Robert Zund Strasse 1.
Paintings from the 16th century to the present.

The Picasso Collection
Am Rhyn Haus, Eingang Furrengasse.
A collection donated to the city in 1978.

Richard Wagner Museum
Richard Wagner Weg 27.
A museum devoted to the composer who scored *Siegfried Idylle* here between 1866 and 1872. Also a collection of musical instruments.

Bourbaki Panorama
Lowenstrasse 18.
A panoramic display of a battle in the Franco–German War of 1870 which was fought in Switzerland.

Glacier Garden
Beim Lowendenkmal.
A sort of geological and natural history display featuring the oldest relief map in Switzerland and a historical model of Lucerne.

Other Attractions in the Area
Unlike Interlaken most of the attractions of the region lie either in the city, or within the area encompassed by the scenic lake. **Vierwaldstattersee** is a lake of real interest and character, mainly because it has headlands and bays jutting in and out of its waters. In travelling on the lake you are actually going through passages and round bends to get to the destinations. The trip to Alpnachstad is one full of interest and only a short trip from Lucerne. The lake is a hubbub of ferry boats, pleasure cruisers, yachts and fishing boats without being overcrowded. The local people use these services regularly to travel from Weggis, Vitznau and Brunnen to Lucerne.

All the lake steamers and ferry services operate from the quay outside the railway station, as do most of the bus and tram services. Lucerne railway station has just been revamped and now the whole public transport system operates from this central area. The Swiss Pass can be used on the lake steamer services and on the Lucerne urban transport system.

One of the best ways to use Lucerne and its lake is to make round trips using the boats, trams and trains. You can easily spend a day going over the lake by boat and returning by bus or train, and one of the most popular round trips is to the summit of **Mount Pilatus**. But the real "round trip" can only be made in summer, when the old rack railway is operating. In winter this is closed so you have to journey to the top of the mountain by the cable car from **Kriens.**

Round Trip Itinerary
The itinerary for a good summer's day out between May and November is: Lucerne–Alpnachstad by lake steamer, Alpnachstad–Mount Pilatus Summit

*P*ilatus Hotel and restaurant commands an outstanding view of the Alps to the south and the Jura to the west.

by rack railway (the steepest cog railway in the world), Mount Pilatus–Kriens by cable car, Kriens–Lucerne by tram number 1.

You can make the trip in the opposite direction, and an alternative to the boat is to use the railway to Lucerne. This is a very popular excursion

from Lucerne and you will have to watch out for the yodelling troubadour at Alpnachstad, but given a good clear and quiet day it is a memorable trip.

Mount Pilatus

Mount Pilatus is a mere 2,132 m (7,000 ft) high, but because it is very much on its own the views from the summit are outstanding. It goes without saying that there is a restaurant at the top, and you can also stay the night here in what must be one of the more unusual hotels of the world. There are two paths with fairly steep steps up to the weather stations. From here you get magnificent views of the Alps, the Jura and particularly the Cradle of Switzerland, looking north-east towards **Weggis**. This is the region which heralded the beginnings of the country in 1291. The journey on the cable car is as exciting as the railway since it really hangs out in the middle of nowhere on the upper stages. Look out for the remote **church** on the right as you go up.

Mount Rigi

A similar trip can be made to the mountain on the other side of the lake at **Mount Rigi** (Rigi Kulm). This is one of the most spectacularly shaped mountains of the country, with heavily wooded sides. There are several ways of reaching the mountain, by way of Weggis, Vitznau or Arth Goldau. The **rack railway** from Vitznau was the first to be built in Europe, in 1871, so here is a chance to sample some of the original Swiss engineering genius. Probably the easiest way to go up the Rigi from Lucerne is to take the train to Arth Goldau, where you can connect directly with another rack railway to take you to the summit. Another alternative is to go from Lucerne to Weggis by lake steamer, and then on to the cable car which goes to the station at Rigi Kaltbad whence you can join the railway. Around the Rigi area there are 14 hotels. As with the Pilatus trip, you can make a day of it by going:

Lucerne—Weggis—Rigi Kaltbad—
Rigi Kulm—Vitznau—Lucerne.

This trip must offer the greatest variety of modes of transport available of any excursion.

Historical Sites

While Lucerne and its waters are some of the most picturesque in Switzerland, the whole area is one of great historical importance to the Swiss and its confederation beginnings. The northern shores are where the cantons of Uri, Schwyz and Unterwalden made their pact to create the confederation. There are, as you can imagine, a lot of **William Tell**-based sights in this area, with the **Tellskapelle**, between Brunnen and Altdorf being the most popular. There has been some development work and improvement taking place here, so a new centre will soon be open. In the more prosaic history of Switzerland one of the most revered sites is the **Field of Ruttli**, which is simply a small field in a very remote spot on the shores of Lake Lucerne. Accessible by boat, it is the field on which a more finite independence was gained for the three forest cantons in 1315.

All along the shores of the lake there are small villages, each with its own tremendous view, each with its own collection of facilities and hotels. One of the most interesting aspects of lake Lucerne is its shape. Unlike any other lake, it has headlands and deep coves which create a scene of outstanding beauty. The scenes can vary from a misty flat water , with ghostly mountains rising from the shore, to an almost Mediterranean blue, the mountains stark against the skies. For boating and yachting enthusiasts, it is a challenging water to sail, and it can become quite rough on a windy day. The lake is one of Switzerland's most popular holiday destinations, so it can become somewhat busy, since the attractions are all on someone's itinerary

*T*he museum in Schwyz houses the most historical document in Switzerland—the confederate charter.

each and every day. It is difficult to travel around Lucerne without meeting coach parties doing the rounds. This popularity is reflected in the cost of hotel accommodation, but there are some splendid places to stay in the area if you wish to stop.

Accommodation

In Lucerne
Many of the hotels are geared up for the group travel market, so rooms can be difficult to find at the height of the season. The railway station has a hotel reservation system, situated on the lower level of the station, and you can at least find out how much the various places cost. There is a telephone by the

The Most Famous Apple since the Garden of Eden
The legendary figure of William Tell is the main character in a play by Schiller, and is probably the most famous of all Swiss, even as a fictional person. The story of how William Tell was recruited by the Austrian governor to shoot the apple from his son's head is world known, and has if nothing else given Switzerland a source of income from Tell theme products. Lucerne is the place to be beseiged with Tell-like artifacts, but if you would like to see an enactment of the play then Interlaken is the place. Every summer, the full version of Freidrich Schiller's play is performed in the Rugen woods. There is a covered seating area in the arena, and room for some 2,300 people. The play is performed at the Tell Open Air Theatre from the end of June to the beginning of September, prices from 12 SFr to 26 SFr. The tickets are on sale from the Tell office, Bahnhofstrasse 5, Interlaken CH-3800.

list, which gives you a location reference, the cost of the type of room and the phone number (as well as a picture) for each hotel. From here you can call the hotel and reserve a room, should there be one available. If the hotel is full, the information panel will have the room rates shown in red. For available accommodation the panel is green. The **tourist information office** is close to the station, so if you want more detailed information on hotels or any other information it is close at hand. Leave the station on the left side, as you face the front of the building, and turn into **Zentralstrasse**. The information office is on the right, about 20 m (20 yds) down the road.

The hotel list for Lucerne is extensive and covers the top-grade luxury establishments through to the simplest one-star place. Top of the list comes one of those delightful Victorian residences which also occupies one of the best positions in the town. The **Hotel Schweizerhof** on the **Schweizerhofquai**

looks right out over the bay in which Lucerne sits. It is near the casino and the promenade and, should the need arise, there is a Rolls Royce for guest use (at a price, I'm sure). It is not as expensive as a similar hotel in Zurich, even though it is graded as five-star, but it will still cost you about 380 SFr for a double room, per night. Further along the Schweizerhofqui is another five-star hotel, the **Grand Hotel National**, and while the position is not as good, it does have its own indoor pool.

So much for the luxury. The majority of the hotels in Lucerne are in the four- and three-star category, mainly to cater for the tourists. It's very difficult to say which hotels are better than others in Lucerne, partly

*L*ake Lucerne can change character with its deep bays and headlands.

because they can differ from year to year. Most of the hotels are gathered in groups on the cathedral side of the town, or on the other side of the bridge around the **Pilatus Strasse**. None of them, however, has the position of the bigger, more expensive hotels by the promenade.

A typical four-star hotel is the **Metropole**, which has a good central position at the junction of Pilatus Strasse and Zentralstrasse. This is in the 250 SFr per night range, so it is still expensive.

Of the three-star places the **Zum Weiessen Kreuz** on the Furrengasse comes in at a very reasonable 120 SFr per night—reasonable by Lucerne standards, that is.

Around Lucerne

The towns and villages around the lake are also quite costly and at a place such as Beckengried, which is about a 20-minute drive from the centre of the city, most of the hotels charge between 90 and 150 SFr per night. At Buoches, a slightly less touristy town, there are three hotels, one of which is reasonably priced. This is the Hotel Sterner, which charges about 50 SFr for a single room and 85 SFr for a double. It has no view and is on one of the streets off the main road; it is, however, clean and comfortable, and has a good restaurant to recommend it.

Camping

The region abounds with campsites, most of which are situated near the lake. As with hotels (and all forms of accommodation), there is a great influx of visitors in the summer so advance booking is advisable.

Most of the sites are of the multi-facility, four- and five-star type, although the nearest to Lucerne is the only non-classified site.

Lucerne Lido: very close to the city and the transport museum. This is a non-classified site.
Open throughout the year.

Merlischachen Rebmatt: to the north of Lucerne, near Meggan. A four-star site.
Open 1 April–31 October.

Merlischachen Unterbergiswil: almost next to the previous site. This one is three-star.
Open 1 April–30 September.

Vitznau, Vitznau: on the opposite shore line to Lucerne between Weggis and Gersau. A five-star site with every facility.
Open 1 April–15 October.

Brunnen Hopfreben: a two-star site in a very convenient spot for connections to Lucerne.
Open 30 April–25 September.

Brunnen Urmiberg: another two-star site next door to the previous one in Brunnen.
Open 1 April–31 October.

Sisikon Ruoss: Sisikon is a small village on the road down to Altdorf. The site is on the lakeshore and is a four-star site.
Open 1 May–31 October.

Fluelen Camping Urnsee and Surf-centre: this village is only a short

distance further on than Sisikon. A four-star site.
Open 1 January–31 October.

Altdorf Remo Camp: a four-star site at the head of the lake and another convenient place for travel around the region.
Open throughout the year.

Alpnachstad Erholungszentr: Alpnachstad has very good connections for Lucerne and is also the base for the mountain rack railway. Good steamer service here as well. A four-star site.
Open 1 April–30 September.

Hallwilersee

Central Switzerland is a difficult area to define, and you could easily include regions of the eastern side and the more southerly places towards the Gothard Pass. These will be detailed in

One of the many romantic Schlosses around Lucerne. This one is on the route down from Mt Pilatus to Kriens.

the appropriate north-east and south-east sections of this book, but one area which is most definitely central, and slightly off the beaten track, is around another lake—Lake Hallwiler (*Hallwilersee*). It is not that far from Lucerne and it could be a good excursion from the city. It is headed at the northern end of the lake by the **Château Hallwil**, another of those romantically designed Swiss castles. The castle is situated on the river from the lake and is reached by turning off the main route 26 from Lenzburg to Lucerne. The castle is on the right-hand side, and there is a car parking area and a bus stop on the left of the road.

Opening times: April–November
9.30–11.30a.m. and 1.30–5.30p.m.

This castle has an interesting feature in that there are two buildings, each on a small island, or with a moat around each. After crossing into the courtyard of the first building, you can then go over another drawbridge to the next building. Around the whole castle is a wide moat, with ducks and swans. Inside the building there are displays of furniture from the 17th and 19th centuries.

If it were not for a visit to Hallwil, the chances are that the eastern side of this lake would be missed, which would be a pity because it's another of those small, rarely visited areas which walkers and cyclists find ideal. From the castle there are walks through the trees, along the side of the river, and along the shores of the lake. For wind-surfers and water-sport enthusiasts, these smaller lakes are sometimes better for their sports than the large ones.

At about the halfway mark of the lake there is the Hotel Seerose from which a ferry operates to Hallwil and to other villages. This is all there is at this part of the lake, but as a centre for travel around the north part of central Switzerland it is ideal. You not only have a lake for whatever you like to do on the water, but there are walking paths to Hallwil and south to **Mosen**. It is close enough to Lucerne for a livelier day or night, and is well off the normal routes. The Hotel Seerose looks to be a good-quality hotel, with rooms at around the 120 SFr mark, and there is a **campsite** at Mosen: Mosen Seeblick, at the southerly end of the lake. This is a five-star site,

which will benefit from all the points just mentioned. It is open 1 May–31 October.

If you are touring the area around Lucerne and staying within the central regions, then lakes will be very much on your itinerary. It may be at this point that you will realize that Switzerland has as much water as most countries, and a lot more than others. As any Swiss will be quick to tell you, the jokes about the Swiss Navy are not justified, since all of these lakes have ferry services operating on a year-round basis. It may not be sea water, but one still needs a boat to get across.

Other Lakes in the Area

To the south-west of the Hallwilersee there is a smaller lake, the **Sempachersee**, with the small town of **Sursee** at its head. Its has an interesting town hall (Rathaus) which goes back to the 16th century.

Travelling east will take you onto the **Zugsee**, which almost connects with the Vierwaldstattersee and Lucerne. There is a causeway on which the N4 runs down to **Schwyz**. The main town on the Zugsee is, not surprisingly, **Zug**. It is a small town, with some interesting features, particularly the gardens along the shoreline quays. On a clear day from here you can see across to Rigi, Pilatus, Burgenstock and Stanserhorn. Zug has developed from a small trading town to one of the more important industrial towns of the country. Meanwhile, it has managed to retain its older section and one of the most pleasant sights, apart from the lake and gardens, is the **central square**—Kolin—and the blue-striped roof to the **Zytturm Tower**.

Some Will Come to Ski Down Them, Some to Climb Them, While the Rest Will Simply Admire Them

"Head for the mountains" is the motto for the south-west, but there is more, a lot more, including Lausanne with its magnificent cathedral, Château Chillon, and the beauty of Lac Léman. The international city of Geneva has more than it appears, with the Red Cross Museum being outstanding. However, the south-west also has the Valais, the highest mountains of the Alps, and come what may the world will be skiing here as it has done for a century.

The most popular area of Switzerland for over a century has been the Alpine region around Lake Geneva (**Lac Léman**). The **Valais**, the **Diablerets**, **Montreux**, **Lausanne** and **Geneva** have been firm favourites of all Europeans, and especially the British, for many years. This popularity has helped in some ways, but has also detracted from the natural beauty in other ways. The skiing industry has left an indelible mark on the countryside. In the effort to attract more and more visitors hardly a mountain has been left without a lift system of some kind on its slopes. Villages such as **Verbier**, **Crans Montana**, **Saas Fe** and **Zermatt** have been transformed to accommodate the thousands of snow-hungry downhill skiers, whose main concern is how deep the snow is and if the pistes are well prepared. On the positive side, this has brought a prosperity to the villages which could never have been imagined, and in some cases has lifted a village to international status.

Many Swiss have undergone a change of heart regarding downhill skiing, and these people are now returning to the traditional use of skis as a

Log storage is important to the Swiss mountain villagers, and all the chalets have a good winter stockpile.

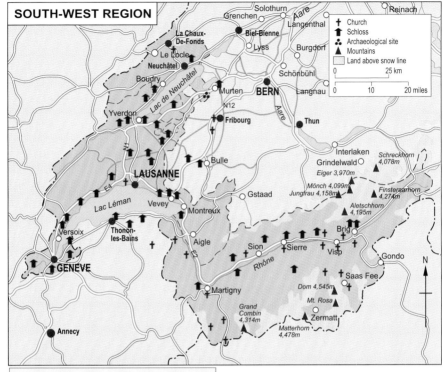

SOUTH-WEST REGION

Legend:
- † Church
- ⬆ Schloss
- ⚒ Archaeological site
- ▲ Mountains
- ▢ Land above snow line

0   25 km
0   10   20 miles

*M*ap of south-west Switzerland.

When Did Skiing Start?

Although winter sports, that is tobogganing, had been taking place in the Alps for some time, skis were only introduced to Switzerland in 1859. Some years later in 1884, the Brangger brothers travelled from Davos to Arosa on skis, and to give the trip some international publicity repeated the journey in 1885 with Sir Arthur Conan Doyle. He wrote of the experience in *Strand* magazine, so by the turn of the century British downhill skiing was on its way. The race element was introduced later, due partly to the fact that it took so long to climb back up to the top of the slopes. In 1934 Erich Konstam introduced the first ski lift, which was the T-bar design. Switzerland's mountains have not looked the same since, to the extent that there are now 210 ski resorts in the country.

way of touring the countryside. This is not *langlauf* (cross-country skiing), but touring using the type of ski seen on the mountains 150 years ago. It may be too late to save some of the mountainsides from permanent damage, but is a definite change of emphasis for the country which brought skiing within the reach of millions.

The vast majority of visitors to the area arrive in Switzerland at Geneva Airport. The details of this excellent airport have been covered in an earlier section, but to reiterate the facts, you can travel on to any of the resorts of the Alps from Geneva, by rail, or by road. The airport is about 20 minutes

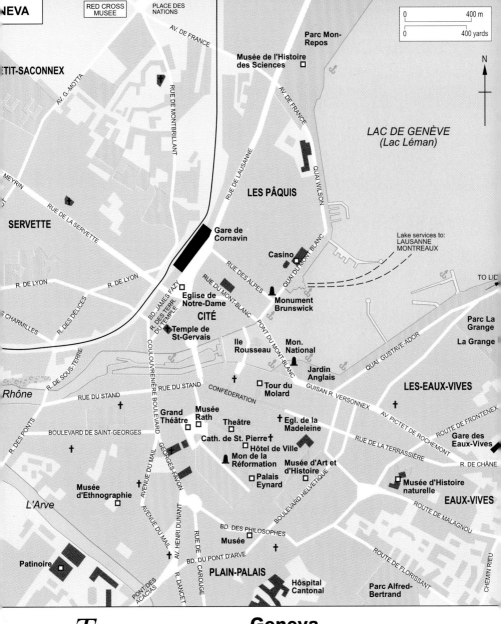

RED CROSS
MUSÉE

PLACE DES
NATIONS

AV. DE FRANCE

TIT-SACONNEX

AV. G. MOTTA

RUE DE MONTBRILLANT

Parc Mon-
Repos

Musée de l'Histoire
des Sciences

AV. DE FRANCE

LAC DE GENÈVE
(Lac Léman)

MEYRIN

RUE DE LAUSANNE

LES PÂQUIS

QUAI WILSON

RUE DE LA SERVETTE

SERVETTE

Gare de
Cornavin

Casino

Lake services to:
LAUSANNE
MONTREAUX

QUAI DU MONT-BLANC

TO LI

R. DE LYON

R. DE LYON

RUE DES ALPES

Monument
Brunswick

Parc La
Grange

CHARMILLES

R. DES DÉLICES

RUE DU MONT-BLANC

Eglise de
Notre-Dame

La Grange

BD. JAMES FAZY

RUE DES TERR.

CITÉ

R. DE SOUS-TERRE

Temple de
St-Gervais

Ile
Rousseau

PONT DU MONT-BLANC

Mon.
National

QUAI GUSTAVE-ADOR

Rhône

COULOUVRENIÈRE BOULEVARD

RUE DU STAND

CONFÉDÉRATION

Jardin
Anglais

GUISAN R. VERSONNEX

LES-EAUX-VIVES

RUE DU STAND

Tour du
Molard

R. DES PONTS

Grand
Théâtre

Musée
Rath

Théâtre

Egl. de la
Madeleine

AV. PICTET DE ROCHEMONT

ROUTE DE FRONTENEX

BOULEVARD DE SAINT-GEORGES

AVENUE DU MAIL

GEORGES-FAVON

Cath. de St. Pierre

Hôtel de Ville

RUE DE LA TERRASSIÈRE

Gare des
Eaux-Vives

Mon de la
Réformation

Musée d'Art et
d'Histoire

R. DE CHÂNE

Musée
d'Ethnographie

AV. HENRI DUNANT

Palais
Eynard

BOULEVARD HELVÉTIQUE

Musée d'Histoire
naturelle

L'Arve

RUE DU PONT D'ARVE

BD. DES PHILOSOPHES

EAUX-VIVES

ROUTE DE MALAGNOU

Patinoire

AVENUE DU MAIL

Musée

R. DE CAROUGE

PLAIN-PALAIS

ROUTE DE FLORISSANT

CHEMIN RIEU

PONT DES
ACACIAS

R. DANCET

BD. DU PONT D'ARVE

Hôspital
Cantonal

Parc Alfred-
Bertrand

0   400 m
0   400 yards

N

*T*own plan of Geneva.

Geneva

Geneva is probably the least Swiss of
all the large centres of the country. It
has a very cosmopolitan population,
helped by its association to the international bodies which have made their
headquarters here. This aspect of Geneva is one its more interesting features.

away from the city, but with the rail
and road system being as they are,
there is no need to go into the city centre to continue your journey.

*T*he flags of France and Switzerland cross regularly on the waters of Lac Léman.

That, along with its position on the shores of Lac Léman, have made it a busy place, although I would doubt if many people would make it a centre for their holiday. Its centre has little of the historical parts found in most Swiss large towns, although there is a very small area off one of the main streets which does have some interesting historical buildings.

The main attractions of Geneva would seem to be its shops, the promenade, with the superb swimming-pool complex at the eastern end, and its international status. The **international buildings** are interesting, and with the European Headquarters of the United Nations (UN) here, there is good reason to make your way up the hill to the area allocated for these centres of diplomacy. All the headquarters are gathered in a small section of the city, mainly in large old buildings, but some in glass and concrete skyscrapers, undoubtedly intending to impress.

Amongst the world of political comings and goings, just around the corner from the UN building is one of the most effective and moving showcases of humanity I have ever witnessed anywhere. Anyone visiting Geneva should go there.

174

La Musée de la Croix Rouge (The Red Cross Museum)

Open: 10.00a.m. to 5.00p.m.

The entrance fee may seem expensive, but you must appreciate that this goes into assisting in the organization's expenses as well as the cost of running the museum. The museum is situated, symbolically, in a sort of underground bunker, next to the original **Red Cross Hospital**. The first striking impression is given by the statues in the courtyard at the entrance to the building. A huddled group of stone figures are reflected in the glass panels around the courtyard. Also reflected in the glass are the two flags of the organization, the Red Cross and the Red Crescent.

The museum is informative, it gives an interesting account of how, and more importantly why, the Red Cross began. The effect of thousands of dead and dying soldiers on the battlegrounds of Europe led to its formation. The audio-visual programme which gives the historical story is one of the best I have ever seen, and it is important that you see it through to the very end. It's quite a surprise! The museum is slightly confusingly laid out, and you have to follow the course through the museum carefully. Emotions vary, as you pass through the chronological layout of the displays, and one can only wonder at man's inhumanity to man on occasions. It should not be an upsetting or depressing experience, because this museum shows the positive side of war and suffering: it is about what is being done, and to emphasize this fact there is a global panel from which you can select any country in the world to find out how the Red Cross is involved.

*T*he flags of the Red Cross and the Red Crescent are always reflected in the mirror glass of Geneva's Musée de la Croix Rouge.

Although it may not be your idea of a good start to a holiday, or even a way of spending your spare time on a business trip, I cannot recommend a visit to this museum highly enough. It is an experience to be remembered.

Other Museums

There are a number of the more conventional museums in Geneva.

175

Museum of Art and History
Boulevard de Helvetique.
Open: 10.00a.m. to 5.00p.m., closed Mondays.
This is one of the better museums following the history of civilization from prehistory to the modern world. It covers archaeology, art from the 15th century and local period furniture.

Ariana Museum
Place des Nations.
Currently undergoing refurbishment but is likely to be open from 10.00a.m. to 5.00p.m. daily.
The collections are of ceramics and pottery, showing Delftware, as well as more modern artifacts.

Museum of Modern Art
Boulevard de Helvetique.
Open: 10.00a.m. to 12.00p.m. and 2–5.00p.m., closed Mondays.
Housed in a 19th-century mansion, the museum has one of the best collections of French and European paintings from 1880 through to 1930.

Museum of Musical Instruments
Boulevard de Trenchées.

Watch and Clock Museum
Rue St Laurent.
Open: 10.00a.m. to 12.00p.m. and 2–5.00p.m., closed Mondays.

Most of the historical museums are in the area called **Les Trenchées**, and on the **Boulevard Helvetique**. There are regular tram services there from the town centre and railway station. The trams from the station go from islands in the middle of a very busy road, so it is advisable to use the subway.

Sights in Geneva
The previously mentioned **international headquarters** are another point of interest in Geneva. It is doubtful if you would be particularly taken with the **Centre for Nuclear Research**, but many visitors are keen to see the **United Nations Building**. It is situated at the **place des Nations**, and is easy to find. There are armed guards at the gate; very friendly ones, but none the less, if you are not on a guided tour but simply want to have a stroll around the lawns, look at the building and see the symbolic **globe**, then you will have to leave your passport with them. You can collect it on leaving. It is a very pleasant walk around the gardens, and if you take the right-hand road as you face the main entrance you will come to the globe, symbolizing the unity of the nations under the wing of the UN. From here there are also good views across the city.

You can go into the building on a tour. The building was originally used by the ill-fated League of Nations, and was built between 1929 and 1936. The guided tour will take you into the **assembly rooms**, the **council chambers** and various **galleries**.

It can be a pleasant walk back into the town by way of the **Avenue de la Paix** and the **Rue de Lausanne**. This wooded area skirts the lake, and there are some good views from the parks named Villa Barton, La Perle du Lac and Parc Mon Repos. Once through these parks, you will come onto the **Quai Wilson** and the **Quai du Mont Blanc**.

The latter quay is one of the nicest parts of the city for a stroll, with light breezes coming from the lake. It also

*O*ne of Geneva's attractions is the fine French architecture.

gives a good view of the spectacular **fountain** of Geneva (*Jet d'Eau*). It rises to 145 m (475 ft), and is one of the most famous fountains in the world. It only sends its plume of water skywards during the summer, so if you are here in winter you will miss it.

To reach the fountain take the **Pont du Mont Blanc** over to the **Promenade du Lac**. On the city side of this promenade, or the inland part, is the only really historical section of the city. Gathered around the Rue de Fountain and **St Peter's Cathedral** (*Cathédrale St Pierre*) are a few of the older buildings of Geneva.

St Peter's Cathedral

Built originally over the 12th and 13th centuries, it was rebuilt in the 15th, and the reformist Calvin has the honour of having a named seat here. Calvin made Geneva his home, and dictated his ways and theologies from here. There is a good view of the city from the top of the tower.

Also in this area are the **Reformation Monument**, as a remembrance of the Reform Church, the **Town Hall**, built in the 16th century, and **St Germanus' Church**, some parts of which date back to the 4th century. This part of the city is more or less pedestrianized so it can be a pleasant walk around. Further down towards the lake there is the **Rue de Marché**, which is the busy main shopping street of Geneva. It is not too far to walk from here to the gardens near the fountain, and I think this aspect of Geneva is one of the best. It has some good open areas for simply sitting around and watching the day go by. There is always plenty of activity on the lake to gaze at.

The Lake Area

There are not many cities which have the likes of **La Parc de Grange** within their perimeters. It has three outdoor swimming pools for all ages, including infants. The bigger pools have diving boards and within the park there are cafés, wooded areas for picnics and odd games facilities like table tennis tables. There is a tram directly to the park, or you can reach it by a small boat which leaves from the Quai du Mont Blanc. The entrance fee is included in the cost of the ticket on this service, and it is a really good way to arrive at a leisure park: no standing on

*T*he highlight of a summer trip to Geneva is seeing
the world's highest fountain.

a crowded tram, simply board the small ferry boat (which makes other stops in the "bay" area around Geneva), and step off into the park.

The bigger lake steamers, are of the old paddle steamer type seen on the lakes of Europe in yesteryear. Some newer craft do operate, but for most visitors it's the old-timers which appeal. They do a round trip of the lake, starting in Geneva, calling in at **Montreux**, **Morges**, **Lausanne**, **Evian les Bains** and **Thonan**. The last two stopping points are in France, so if you intend leaving the boat at either of these, don't forget your passport. There are also plenty of cross-lake services to choose from, especially further down at Lausanne and Montreux. The company which operates the steamers is:

Compagnie Générale de Navigation sur le Lac Léman
17 avenue de Rhodenie
CH-1000 Lausanne 6
Tel: (021) 6170666.

They will have up-to-date sailing times, and prices for excursions and standard tickets. Remember though, your Swiss Pass is valid for travel on the steamers, as it is for the Geneva urban transport system.

Accommodation

Hotels

Geneva has plenty of hotels, as you might expect. What it lacks is the less expensive pensions and low-star quality places. A good majority of its visitors are diplomatic, industrial and conference guests, who are not too bothered about the cost of anything.

Their needs are catered for in the big hotels along the quays, and around the park areas of suburban Geneva. The average tourist or traveller is at a slight disadvantage here, although there are plenty of places for students. Of the cheaper hotels there is the **Hôtel Mon Repos** (two-star), which is near the UN building. The more expensive, but central, **Hôtel Les Armures** is down near the cathedral, although it claims to be in a very quiet part of the city.

If you are young enough to qualify, some of the three-star hotels do a special package for travellers between 18 and 26, the price of which is dependant on your age. If you are 19, then a share of a double room will cost you about 36 SFr each, with a single supplement of about 15 SFr. The 25-year-olds pay about 52 SFr, so the younger you are, the cheaper it is. This package is detailed in a leaflet supplied by the Geneva tourist office at the railway station, and the current participants of the scheme are the Hotels **Drake**, **International Terminus**, **Le Grenil**, **Mon Repos**, **Plan les Oautes** and the **Tor**. All are three-star hotels and, although they probably will not offer you the best room in the house, at least you should get a comfortable night's sleep. For the older guests, these hotels will cost in the region of 100 SFr.

Camping

There are some campsites quite close at hand in the Geneva area, and one which is very close to the city. The nearest site is:

Geneva Conches Sylvabelle: only 3 km (1.8 miles) from the city centre, this is a non-classified site. Buses will take you there; for drivers it is on the route de Florrisont out of Geneva on the way towards Conches.

Open throughout the year (April–October for tents).

Also in the area there is:

Camp Geneva-Vesenaz Pt à la Bise: this site is about 7 km (4 miles) from the city on bus route E, and is another non-classified site.
Open: 1 April–30 September.

Camping de l'Abarc: on the route de Vernier, and only 4 km (2.5 miles) from the city. Bus 6 will take you there.
Open: July–September.

The largest site in the area is at **Mies**.

Mies La Buna: coming off autoroute N1 at Chavannes de Bogis, the site is past Mies, and on towards Versoix. It is a three-star site.
Open throughout the year.

Cycling

The flat lanes and roads around Geneva provide quite good cycling possibilities, although I would not recommend biking it too much in the city. Geneva is one of those through-traffic cities, and most of its drivers seem to be in a hurry. You can hire a bicycle from the railway station or from:

Procycle SA
17 place Montbrillant
Tel: (022) 7342622.

These cycles are available from April to October only, although you would be able to hire one at any time from the main station (*Hauptbahnhof*), tel: (021) 7326100.

Out from Geneva

From Geneva Airport, it is as easy to travel north as it is to the city. If you are on the train, you will go to the city whichever way you are travelling, but don't let this confuse you; the train *does* go in the right direction eventually. The nearest city to Geneva is **Lausanne**. The route up to Lausanne is marvellous, and here you are into some of the most intensive wine-growing regions of the country. All along the shore of the lake terraced vineyards stretch up into the hills. **Châteaux** sit among the greenery, with all the charm of the best romantic pictures. From Geneva to **Montreux** there are villages reputed throughout Switzerland for their wine, and a trip along this stretch of Lac Léman is well worth it.

Swiss Wine

It can hardly be described as a major contributor to the national economy, but Swiss wine makes up about 36 per cent of that drunk in the country. When travelling through Switzerland, it is very noticeable how many hillsides are used for the cultivation of the grape, although it only amounts to between 5,665 ha and 14,570 ha (14,000–36,000 acres) of land in total.

The most popular are the white wines which have less of the acidity of their German counterparts. Of these the favourite is probably the slightly sparkling variety from the shores of Lake Neuchâtel. When poured from a height, the foam of the wine forms a star, a trick at which some waiters are particularly adept.

Coppet and the Romantics of Europe

Situated on the road between Geneva and Nyon, is the small village of Coppet. Its main attraction is the château, which became a court to the intellectuals of Europe. Madam de Stael spent years in exile there during the French revolution. Amongst the many visitors to the château were Byron, the French painter Constant and the historian, Edward Gibbon. The château is much as Madame de Stael left it, and is open daily, except Monday. A feature of the museum is the half piano, half violin in the music room.

Most of the villages on the way between the two cities have a quay or port as well as the landside vineyards. This adds to the delight of the places, and typical of such towns are **Nyon**, **Rolle** and **Morges**. At Nyon you can see the small port, whilst at Rolle there is a 13th-century castle, built by the Prince of Savoy. This whole area is very French, and no towns are more so than **Morges** and **Vufflens le Château**. These two towns are back some way from the lake, being greatly associated to the wine industry. Unfortunately, the grand château at Vufflens is not open to the public.

From Vufflens the road or railway will take you down to **St Sulpice** and its Romanesque 11th-century **church**. This is open to the public.
Opening times: 9.00 a.m. to 6.00 p.m.

*T*he magnificent Lausanne Cathedral is one of many fine buildings in the city. The tower can be climbed by spiral staircases for a small fee.

St Sulpice is on the very edge of Lausanne, which sits at the very heart of French Switzerland.

Lausanne

This is my favourite Swiss city. It has style, character and charm. The lakeside promenade, the steep streets up the hill to the town centre and the richly decorated cathedral all make Lausanne a special city. It attracts art, it has an active nightlife, and in summer it is delightful to sit in the gardens at the **Ouchy quayside**. Ouchy is the port area of the city, where all the lake steamers come in, *en route* to Geneva and Montreux. It is also from here that you would take a ferry over to France, at **Evian les Bains**. Having said all this, your first sight of Lausanne may not be that impressive. If you arrive by rail, then there is little sight of either the cathedral or the promenade since Lausanne is built on a terraced hillside which is quite steep. The

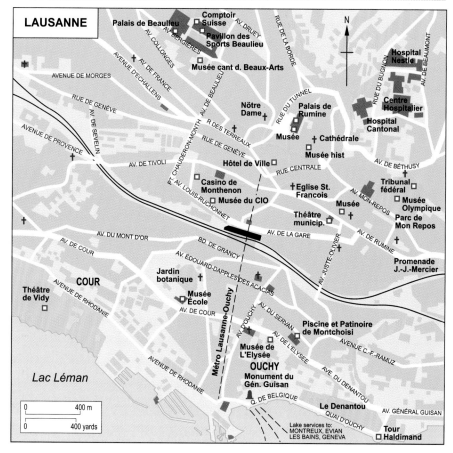

T own plan of Lausanne.

railway station is about midway between the top of the city and the lakeside. If arriving by road, the chances
are that you will enter the mid-area.

Thankfully, there is a simple solu-
tion to the problems of being on such
a steep hillside, and Lausanne has its
own **funicular railway (metro)** which
runs from **Ouchy,** via the **place de Gare**
(railway station), through to the main
shopping area in the centre. It is quite
cheap, and it saves a lot of climbing.
There is an efficient tram system as
well, and if you want to go right up to
the cathedral and the château, then
you will need to use one of these.

*T his modern work of
art is easily seen from Ouchy
promenade and the lake.*

182

The site on which Lausanne stands was originally used by the Romans, as a crossing point and staging post for traffic from Italy to Gaul, and from the Mediterranean to the Rhine. Invasions by the barbarians led to the population moving up to the hills, and so the city grew on the terraces above the lake. The cathedral dates back over 700 years, and is the oldest remnant of the city. There are 14 museums, seven art galleries and 14 theatres—quite a cultural city. There is also a **botanical garden**, a **zoo** and a **vivarium**. There is enough interest about Lausanne to fill a number of trips, and if you want to spend a night or two in total luxury one of the top hotels in Europe is here.

Museums

Cantonal Museum of Archaeology and History
Palais de Rumine.
Open: 10.00a.m. to 12.00p.m. and 2–5.00p.m. The latest discoveries of the Vaudois district.

Decorative Arts Museum of the Town of Lausanne
4 avenue Villamont.
Open: Mondays, 1–6.00p.m., Tuesdays, 11.00a.m. to 6.00p.m. and 8–10.00p.m., and Wednesdays–Sundays 11.00a.m. to 6.00pm.
Temporary exhibitions of graphic art, glass ceramics and folk art.

Cantonal Museum of Fine Arts
6 Palais de Rumine.
Open: Tuesdays, Wednesdays, 11.00a.m. to 6.00p.m., Thursdays 11.00a.m. to 8.00p.m., Friday–Sundays 11.00a.m. to 5.00p.m.

The collection consists of 18th-, 19th- and 20th-century artists from the French-speaking areas of Switzerland. Represented are Ducros, Gleyre, Bocian, Bieler, Vallotton and Soutter.

Lausanne Historical Museum
Ancien Eveche, 4 place de la Cathédrale.
Open: 11.00a.m. to 6.00p.m.; Thursdays, 11.00a.m. 8.00p.m.; closed Mondays. Lausanne history, including an audio-visual programme and a scale model of the city

Musée de l'Elysee
18 avenue de l'Elysee.
Open: 10.00a.m. to 6.00p.m.; Thursdays, 10.00a.m. to 9.00p.m.; closed Mondays.This museum is devoted to the history of photography, and the Association for Contemporary Photography has its headquarters here.

Medals Collection
Palais de Rumine 6.
Open: by appointment only, Mondays–Fridays, 10.00a.m. to 12.00p.m. Tel: (021) 233920.

Olympic Museum
18 avenue Ruchonnet.
Open: Sundays, Mondays, 2–6.00p.m., Tuesdays–Saturdays, 9.00a.m. to 12.00p.m. and 2–6.00p.m.
Exhibition showing the philosophy of the Olympic movement, and the history of the games.

The Pipe and Tobacco Articles Museum
7 rue de l'Academie.
Open: 9.00a.m. to 12.00p.m. and 2.00–6.00p.m.

*T*he artwork on the interior of the cathedral is famous, and this ceiling is at the main entrance.

One of the most interesting museums is at the **cathedral**.

Lausanne Cathedral

One of the most fascinating sights to see at the cathedral, and more to the point to hear, is the **crier**. He shouts the time from the towers of the cathedral on the hour, every hour, from 10.00 p.m. to 2.00 a.m. He is one of the last "watches" to carry out this duty, shouting from each side of the highest part of the cathedral.

The building, which had its 700th anniversary in 1975, is the finest Gothic cathedral in Switzerland, and a stroll around its interior is certainly impressive. If your legs are strong enough the effort to climb the towers is well

*M*uch of the
*stonework can be seen in close
up on the long climb to the top
of Lausanne cathedral.*

Bells and Cannons

Throughout the country there are home-made church and cathedral bells. Some, like the Schiller Bell at Schaffhausen, are famous large bells, others are the common bells found in the likes of Lausanne Cathedral. Most of the bell-casting industry was in Zurich, in the 15th through to the 19th centuries. The Fussli family had a total of 20 members of the family to produce over 1,000 bells for the northern and central parts of Switzerland. They were also involved in the cannon industry, and the oldest Fussli cannon found dates back to 1533. In this aspect of their work, the Fusslis made the in-line cannon for the fortifications of Zurich, but as this trade petered off in the 18th century, they turned their attention once again to the bells and smaller objects, such as soup dishes, pumps and door knockers.

worth it and although you may think you have reached the top when you arrive at the **bell tower**, this is not the case: each of the four **spires** has its own spiral staircase which takes you even higher.

Beware of being in the vicinity of the bells at any quarter of the hour: the noise is extremely loud when you are standing next to them. Once you reach the very top of the spires the view of the cathedral itself and of the whole of Lausanne is breathtaking. On a clear day you can see across Lac Léman to the Alps. There is a charge of about 2–3 SFr to go up the tower, and you should be aware of the height to which you are ascending—definitely not a place for vertigo sufferers!

Opening Times
Cathedral
Open: summer, 7.00a.m. to 7.00p.m.
Winter, 7.00a.m. to 5.30p.m.
On Sundays the cathedral is not open to the public until 11.30a.m.

Tower

Open: Mondays–Saturdays, 9.00–11.30a.m. and 1.30–5.30p.m.
In winter, the tower closes at 4.30p.m.

Daily services are held in the cathedral from 7.30–7.50a.m. and 12.00–12.20p.m. in addition to the Sunday morning service.

If you should like to see the restoration work being carried out on the cathedral, then groups of between 5–20 can see this on the first Tuesday in each month. Advance notice is required and the telephone number for reservations is (021) 447285.

The cathedral **museum** has details of the history of the building, as well as drawings and coins relating to the Lausanne diocese.

To get to the cathedral area, which includes the city's **château**—you can look down on it from the tower—the best way is to use the TPR tram system, which provides a very comprehensive service. You will need to take tram number 5 from the place de Gare to **Tunnel**. This stop is fairly obvious—there is an arched tunnel ahead of the tram stop.

If you are coming up from the quay at Ouchy, which is also where the main **tourist office** is situated, then you can either take the **funicular** to the railway station then tram number 5 or take tram number 2 to **St Francis** and then change to trams 5, 8 or 6, all of which go to Tunnel. It is a fair hike up to the cathedral from Ouchy or place de Gare, but if you do go by foot you can approach the cathedral from **place de la Riponne**, and then up the steps by **place Madelaine**.

The Château

Lausanne's castle is directly behind the cathedral, and it's worth going over to have a look whilst you are in the vicinity. It accommodates the cantonal centre of government, so there are no tours of the building. It does have a terrace, from which you have a good panoramic view of the town and which may satisfy those whose nerve gave out in the cathedral tower. The château dates from of the 14th and 15th centuries, and was formerly the residence of the Bishops of Lausanne. In this area, around the cathedral and château, there are all sorts of small galleries, and antique and art shops in the small cobbled lanes—a delight for those who enjoy browsing.

Other Sights of Lausanne

Just down the hill from the cathedral and the place de la Riponne, in the place de la Plaud, is the 17th-century **town hall**. This has the **fountain of justice** and a **clock**, which is not old (1964), but which has animated historical scenes that appear every hour from 9.00a.m. to 7.00p.m.

In the town centre there are a few interesting buildings, such as **St Francis' Church**. This is the changeover point for the trams if you are coming up from the lake, so you could have a look at this church on the way, or on the return journey. It was the sanctuary of the old Franciscan friary, and dates back to the 13th century. Restoration work has been carried out here recently, so the church should be looking good. The city is quite good for shops, and prices are more realistic than in Geneva or Zurich. There are probably fewer goldsmiths here,

but if you are interested in contemporary or traditional art, including photography, then Lausanne is a better place to find it than most cities. On Wednesdays and Saturdays there is the traditional **market** in the streets in the centre of the town.

The shopping area is in the upper middle part of the city, and between here and the station there are more shops. Further down than that is mainly terraced housing, hotels, and offices, so if you are looking to go down to Ouchy, then the funicular (*metro*) or the tram (number 2) are the best ways of getting there.

Ouchy

Ouchy is part of Lausanne, although strictly speaking it could be regarded as a separate village. This is the port area, and is one of the best on the whole of Lac Léman. In summer the gardens and flower beds are superb, and the place is a vibrant, exciting place to be. The continual coming and

The Château of Lausanne is a public building, and is situated just behind the cathedral.

going of the lake steamers makes it all the more interesting. Ouchy has been the scene for quite a few treaty signings, or at least some of its magnificent hotels have. The **Lausanne Palace** saw the Treaty of Lausanne, after the 1914–18 war. The most pleasant feature of Ouchy is the walk down the promenade past the Lausanne Palace, and the marina. From here you can look over the lake to the Alps, and to the sloping vineyards of the region.

The old back streets of Pully, near Lausanne, have remained unchanged for centuries.

188

Walking

The vineyards provide some of the nicest walking country of the canton of Vaud. One of the great things about vineyards is the intricate system of lanes which run between the various plantations. There is a series of sign-posted **vineyard walks**, suggested by the Vaudois Wines Office. They produce a booklet (*Guide du Vignobles Vaudois*) giving 22 recommended walks, detailing where you can stop off at various *pintes* to sample the wines. The guide is available from:

Vaudois Wines Office
6 ch de la Vauchere
Tel: (021) 296161.

The tourist offices may also have copies.

The routes are quite short (depending on how much time you spend drinking!). A typical one would last about two hours, and would go from **Lutry** to the east of Lausanne to **Savuit**, **Ligne**, **Montagny** and back to Lutry. This is a 3.7-km (2.3-mile) walk. There are longer walks of up to 12 km (7.5 miles) from **Vevey** to **Corseaux**, **St Saphorin**, **Rivaz** and **Espresses**. Walking is a great way to enjoy the Vaud countryside and to see many of the local villages.

Excursions

Of the two sides of Lausanne, the east side (towards **Pully**) is better for vineyard trips. Pully is an old village which has hardly changed over the centuries. You can get there from Lausanne by rail, or tram. The railway station is quite a way up the hill, whereas the tram (number 8) will take you directly to the port area. Pully was a Roman town and has a **Roman villa.**

Roman Villa Museum
place du Prieure.
Open: October–April 2–5.00p.m., Saturdays and Sundays.
April–October 2–5.00p.m. daily, except Mondays.

The Lake

From Pully, which is a lovely village to look around, you can go on around the lake, where there are plenty of small villages. The hillside behind is covered with neat rows of vines. They look their best from spring through to summer, and just before the grapes are picked in the autumn. In winter the area has a rather stark look, with rows and rows of regimented twigs lined up on the hills.

Some of the village hotels have lakeside pools, or if you're brave enough, platforms from which you can dive straight into the lake. On certain stretches you can also find limited areas of sand.

The lake is an irresistible attraction. There are countless ways of spending your time on the water, and the yachting and boating fraternity use it constantly. It is large enough to make the yachting interesting, and the wind can blow up quite a rough water. For those on smaller craft, such as sailboards and windsurfers, Lac Léman is not so easy, although this does nothing to deter the enthusiast.

Water Sport Activity Centres abound:

La Nautique, Ouchy. Tel: (021) 260023.

Vidy Sports Centre has facilities for sailing, windsurfing, motor boat and water skiing courses. Also rental of cruise boats, dinghies windsurf boards and multi-hulls. Open 9.00a.m. to 7.00p.m. daily. Tel: (021) 617 9000.

Place du Vieux Port, where you can take water skiing lessons from Barke Claus. Tel: (021) 260844.

Also at place du Vieux Port are Henri Loup, tel: (021) 262771, for motor boats and rowing and Jacques Marachel, tel: (021) 261465 or 203310, for motor boats and water skiing.

H eading into land, one of the old Lac Léman paddle steamers.

These facilities operate from March to October, 8.30a.m. to 8.00p.m.

For those of us who enjoy the water from a larger vessel, where a drink or two is served on the sunny deck while the old paddle steamer ploughs its way past the beautiful countryside, there are a few good excursions taking in half a day or a

191

whole day. All these cruises are run by the Compagne Générale de Navigation sur le Lac Léman, whose base is in the city. The address and telephone number are given in the Geneva section.

Cruises on the Lake

Upper Lake Cruise: Lausanne to Evian to St Gingolph to Chillon to Montreux to Lausanne.
Middle Lake Cruise: Lausanne to Rolle to Yvoire to Thonon to Evian to Lausanne.
Chillon Cruise: Lausanne to Montreux to Chillon to Lausanne.

There are also **dancing cruises**, **evening cruises** and all sorts of specials, details of which are available either from the tourist office or the company itself.

The upper and middle excursions cost around 25–30 SFr, but you could choose to return by train if you wanted a change of scenery.

As a centre for touring the lake Lausanne is excellent, as are the small villages on its shores. There are plenty of apartments, chalets, hotels and campsites in the area, so there should be plenty to choose from.

Accommodation

Hotels

In Lausanne, there are two hotels which deserve a special mention. For sheer grandness, the hotel **Beau-Rivage Palace** ranks as one of the finest in Europe, if not the world. Needless to say it's a five-star place, but it has the real elegance of a Victorian hotel, which many city hotels purport to have but lack. My only complaint was the bright yellow blinds which detract from the look of the building, but since I have not actually had the pleasure of staying there I should not really comment. In the same top-of-the-range category is the **Royal Savoy**, which is another magnificent turn-of-the-century building. This used to be the Swiss residence of the Spanish royal family and is again very elegant. These two hotels are special in Switzerland.

Back on realistic terms, there are some good places, although the prices tend to be on the high side. The town hotels are either rather basic in design or are of the new business type, which could be anywhere in the world. However, there are a few which could appeal. If historical guests are of interest, then Byron, whose writings from this area brought us *The Prisoner of Chillon*, stayed at the **Hotel d'Angleterre**. It has a lakeside position and is rated as a two-star, which is at the reasonable end of the market (100–155 SFr). Also in a good position, near the Ouchy marina, is the **Hotel Aulac**, but this is three-star, and so a bit more expensive at 150–200 SFr for a room. At the cheap end there is the one-star **Auberge de Rivax**, which will not win any awards for architectural design, but does cost considerably less. It is situated well down the shore, in **Lavaux**, some 13 km (8 miles) from the city.

Lausanne is not a cheap place to stay if you go by the tourist information brochure. You should remember though, that like Zurich, many of these lists are by no means exhaustive, and I have found on numerous occasions perfectly good hotels (with lower rates) that are not in the hotels list. It is well worth choosing a village and giving yourself some extra time to have a look around at all the accommodation available. If nothing else you will nearly always find a Hotel Bahnhof in a village where there is a rail service.

Youth Hostels

There are two in the area, one in Morges at avenue de Marcelin, and one in Lausanne itself at the chemin du Muguet, which is in the Ouchy area.

Camping

There are four sites in the region around Lausanne.

Lausanne Camping de Vidy: this is the nearest camping area to the city, and is almost in the suburbs. It is a top-quality five-star site, situated right next to the lake, off the Route du Lac, about 300 m (330 yds) past the Lausanne Sud roundabout. Tram route number 18 will take you to Vidy from Bel Air, which has connections to the railway station by trams 2, 1, 8 and 5. Open throughout the year.

The other sites are in the hills, a good situation especially for walking in the vineyards.

Bussigny La Venage: a three-star site which is just outside the village of Bussigny, on the river. There is a rail connection to Bussigny, as well as bus routes to the village.
Open: 1 April–31 October.

Cully Moratel: Cully is a lake village, to the east of Lausanne, and this three-star site is right on the shore. The village is just off the N9 autoroute, near

Villette, Grandvaux and Riex. There is a regional train which runs along the side of the lake to service all these villages.
Open: 1 March–30 September.

Corseaux—Vevey La Pichette: this small site is near the village of St Saphorin, and is also near the N9 and on the regional rail route. A three-star site.
Open: 1 April–30 September.

The boundaries of the cantons in this region are rather odd in that some of the places are in Vaud and some in Fribourg. The two are so similar in nature, apart from Lac Léman, that the difference between the two is almost unrecognizable. The area between the two cities is full of rolling countryside, and is very much castle country. The details of all the sights around Fribourg are in the section on Central Switzerland, but one castle which really borders the central and south-east is at **Oron**. The town is not of any real interest, but it has a typically romantic **château** very close to the railway station. A large sign will invite you to *Visitez le Château,* while you are sitting on your train from Fribourg to Lausanne. This is where the benefits of a Swiss Rail Pass come in since, if you did fancy a look at the château, you could get off the train, make your visit, and catch a later connection through to your destination.

Oron le Châtel

The château sits on a hill, giving it an air of superiority over the surrounding countryside. The castle goes back to 1190, so it is one of the oldest around,

and was a home for Bernese bailiffs for 250 years. Inside you can see the **apartments**, the fine 15th-century **wood ceilings** and 18th-century furniture. Also there are **dungeons**, cells and best of all, a **torture chamber**, which was cut from the rock.

Open: 9.00a.m. to 7.00p.m. daily, except Mondays.

Guided tours are available.

Châtel St Denis

Further to the east is another château town, Châtel St Denis, which is larger, and easier to find than Oron, but is not as attractive. It is not far from here down to the shores of Lac Léman and the large city of **Montreux**, and **Vevey**.

Montreux

Montreux has a reputation all of its own: it is almost all that Lausanne is not, to the extent that it can look slightly out of place in this area. Perhaps the coast of the Mediterranean would be a better place for it. Montreux has casinos, rock and jazz festivals, and is altogether a modern, up-tempo resort. The main autoroute goes

*C*hâteau Chillon was made famous by Lord Byron, but even without the Prisoner of Chillon the castle is a major landmark.

The Prisoner of Chillon

Byron wrote his poem about the misfortunes of François de Bonivard at the Anchor Inn at Ouchy on the opposite side of the lake from Chillon. Apparently he actually knew little of the facts about Bonivard's imprisonment from 1530 to 1536, so he added a few lines at a later date.

---

past the city on a higher level, so many travellers carry on to the Valais and the ski resorts. However, Montreux does have a beautiful **promenade** area with the sort of vegetation seen much further south, and at its eastern end, stands one of the most famous castles in Switzerland—**Château Chillon**.

Château Chillon

The castle, originally 9th century, has the perfect position, jutting out into the lake, and provides an ideal subject for artists and photographers. Visitors interested in the history of the castle will also enjoy the scene.

But the castle has a slightly more sinister history than the lyrical scene reflects, since it was used on several occasions as a state prison. Its most famous occupant was Francois de Bonivard, whose reformist views led to him being thrown in the dungeons for four years. It is said that he was chained to a pillar for those years until released by the Bernese in 1536. This is the story immortalized in the poem *The Prisoner of Chillon* by Byron.

You can take a guided tour of the castle, which will take you into the **great hall**, the **banqueting hall** and the **knights' hall**. These halls are all superbly decorated, and along with the

collections of arms, furniture and coins, it makes for a good day out.

Open: April–October 9.00a.m. to 6.00p.m.
October–April 9.00a.m. to 12.00p.m. and 2–5.00p.m..

Château Chillon marks almost the last of Switzerland's section of Lac Léman, and the autoroute N9 thunders on towards the highlands with some of the world's greatest ski resorts. There are some beautiful villages nearer than those around **Sion** and **Zermatt**, just an hour away from the lake, with some of the best skiing in the country. It's an expensive area, and one chosen by many famous people as "the" part of Switzerland to live in.

Around Montreux

The loop from **Aigle** on the N9 to **Château d'Oex** and back via **Gstaad** and **Les Diablerets** covers a very beautiful area, but you can count on spending that bit more than usual for even the simple things. However, if you want to mingle with the stars, especially in the high winter season, then you must expect to pay for it. Thankfully there is a small, still unspoilt, village that has kept some sense of proportion when it comes to prices, and which hosts one of the most spectacular events in the country's calendar; an event which, given good weather and snowy conditions, attracts competitors and spectators from all over the world. It takes place in the small village of **Château d'Oex** and is the Château d'Oex balloon festival.

The Château d'Oex Balloon Festival

This usually takes place in January, but the dates tend to change from year to year so you should check with the tourist office. You may have a friend in ballooning circles who would know, as this is a very famous "meet"—part of a global "Grand Prix" type competition.

Accommodation is quite difficult to find in and around the small village during the festival, since many of the available rooms get booked by the balloonists and their entourage of helpers. However, Château d'Oex is only a few hours' drive from Lausanne, and the rail links via Montreux mean you can get there very easily. The balloon festival

On a bright winter's day, the balloons from Château d'Oex create a memorable sight.

takes place over a three-day period, and you probably would not want to spend all three days there unless you are a keen follower of the sport.

This is one of the more colourful and spectacular scenes around, even for Switzerland. If the weather is clear, and it quite often is in this region in January, the competitors meet in the morning to decide on the day's competitions. This can be a frustrating time, especially for children who can't wait for the big balloons to appear, so you could be advised to delay your arrival until about 10.00a.m. because before then there's a lot of hustle and bustle, but little actually happening. Once the balloons start to be spread out on the snow, the scene becomes increasingly dramatic. Anyone who has been to see a balloon fiesta will appreciate the excitement generated as the bright, colourful monster balloons start to fill with hot air.

The arena at Château d'Oex is more or less the village green (which it isn't because it's covered in snow), and slowly the field is enlivened by the colourful spheres. This is where the helpers come in—to stop the balloon from going off on a journey of its own: it takes a good few people to weigh the basket down. Like thoroughbred horses before a race, the balloons pull on the ropes to take to the skies, and when they do Château d'Oex disappears under a mass of colour. From any point in the village or in the valley it is a spectacular scene. All sorts of races are held, and the programme gives some explanation as to how balloons *can* race against each other.

Once the main batch of balloons are airborne, and you can see them rising higher and higher until they are up amongst the peaks around the valley, the novelty balloons start to inflate. Elephants, cans of beer, and shoes have all appeared against the sunny skies in Château d'Oex. It's a sight that children and adults alike thoroughly enjoy. The

Amongst the mass take-off at the Château d'Oex balloon festival, a basket full of hopeful fliers manoeuvres its way skywards.

race and the competitors, who are by now gently floating around on the winds some 3,000 m (10,000 ft) up, have been forgotten. Not all the novelty balloons achieve perfect take-off, and I have witnessed the unforgettable sight of a very large rolled *Financial Times* wedged in a field on the slopes above the village. One of the delights of ballooning is the element of madness about it, and for the whole day four-wheel drive vehicles may be seen chasing around the valley, collecting unfortunates from hazardous landings, sometimes in the middle of a road, or half-way up a mountain. It's great fun, with a good atmosphere, and a day out which I would certainly recommend.

To get a really good view of the whole event stop at one of the lay-bys on the road down to the village, or take the cable car to La Braye.

Sports at Château d'Oex

The first **Alpine Ballooning Centre** was set up in Château d'Oex, so if you like the idea of a trip in a balloon, then this is the place to come, winter or summer. In fact the whole region is something of a sportsperson's paradise. The possibilities cover the usual sports such as swimming, golf, mountain biking, tennis, riding, and fishing, but as well as these you can try paragliding, parachuting, whitewater rafting or hydrospeeding. Hydro-speeding appears to be one of those sports for people who have tried everything else, and involves careering over whitewater rapids, hanging on to a large piece of bouyant plastic—safety helmets are provided! There is a kayak school for those who prefer the more conventional whitewater sports. Another unusual sport which has become popular is "canyoning", where you are given some training in caving before heading into the deep canyons and gorges of the area.

All of the above-mentioned adventure sports must be booked, and there is a schedule for various classes etc. For the most up-to-date information contact the Information Office, at:

Château d'Oex (Rivières et Aventures)
Office de Tourisme
CH–1837, Château d'Oex.
Tel: (029) 47788, fax: (029) 47789.

They will also be able to advise you on clothing, insurance and costs.

The tourist office in the village is very well organized even by Swiss standards, so if you want an element of arrangement about your visit, then you can book one of their packages covering particular "hobbies". There is an "adventure" package, which involves three days of taking part in many of the previously mentioned river sports, two days mountain biking and a few added extras like free admission to the swimming pool. The six arrangements are:

Ski lesson week
Cross-country skiing
Adventure
Hiking
Edelweiss.

The last is a sort of cultural week, spending time visiting various workshops, museums and the cheese cellar.

All the packages include welcome drinks, accommodation in a rated hotel (of your choice, from one- to four-star), at half-board terms, and of course all the facilities for your week's activity. It's the sort of package for those who would like to have some arrangements made for them, but who prefer to travel independently.

For the winter the downhill skier's needs are met by 69 lifts and 250 km (155 miles) of slopes, and for the cross-country skier there is a 28-km (17-mile) track between Château d'Oex and **Gsteig**, as well as training tracks in the village.

In all, Château d'Oex has one of the most comprehensive collections of sporting facilities in the country which, amazingly, seems to have had no effect on the size or the quality of the village: it remains a relatively unspoilt place. The proliferation of ski-lifts are spread over a fairly wide area, and on the higher slopes above the tree line, so they cannot be seen from the village.

Getting to Château d'Oex

This beautiful village is easily accessed by road or by rail. You can arrive at Geneva airport and be in the village within a couple of hours. Simply take the first train from the airport to **Montreux**, and then the **Oberland Express** up to Château d'Oex. There are various types of express from Montreux, such as the Panoramic Express and the Superpanoramic Express, which both have those wonderful observation cars at the rear, and although it is a private line, the Swiss Pass is valid. Some of these trains may be used only by first-class passengers, though, so it is worth checking before you get on the train. By road, turn off the N9 at Aigle and follow an easy series of bends up to the resort.

Accommodation in Château d'Oex

Compared with some of the more famous resorts, Château d'Oex is not too expensive, and is certainly cheaper than its neighbour, Gstaad. Its top

One of the small mountain villages near the swish resort of Gstaad.

hotel is La Rocaille which charges between 65 and 95 SFr per night. Middle of the range, and a nice-looking hotel, is the Richemont at 45–50 SFr and for a real cheapie it has to the simple but good value La Printenière which charges about 28 SFr per person per night. At the exchange rate of about 2.45 SFr to the pound, this works out at about £11 for bed and breakfast, so maybe Switzerland doesn't have to be that expensive, after all.

Camping

The campsite at Château d'Oex is down by the river, and is a neat little site with its own swimming pool. It is only 500 m (550 yds) from the village, and a three-star site. Take the turn-off by the bridge over the river, on the road to Col des Mosses.

Open: 1 May–30 September.

The valley in which Château d'Oex sits is a valley of intense activity, and although this village is quite unspoilt, the villages further down are often very busy. In all there are seven resorts in and around the valley of the River Saane. What makes the area so attractive is the ease in which you can travel around, by road or by rail. Unlike the high mountain resorts, where half the time is spent going up and down hairpin bends or through tunnels, this region connects with several other valleys, and in no time you can be in Gruyères or in the Simmental valley, on the way to Thun and Interlaken.

Skiing at Château d'Oex

The ski facilities relate to the whole area, and the 69 ski lifts are fairly well spread out over a wide area. This means that you could start off at **Rougemont** by taking the cable car to **La Videmanette**, ski down to **Rubeldorf**, just outside **Gstaad**, and then go up the opposite side of the valley to **Launne** or **Saanerschlochgrat**, and ski back down into **Saanenmoser**. There are plenty of ski buses in the region to get you back to your accommodation, so for the skier there is a greater range of possibilities here than in many resorts. For the summer the area offers the walker a tremendous range, although the temptations of the mountain restaurants may prove difficult to avoid. There are so many, it would be difficult to mention them all. Suffice to say that at almost every staging post on the 69 lifts there is a café, so even if you are not a skier then a trip into the mountains can be just as enjoyable an experience.

Cross-Country Skiing

For the cross-country enthusiast, this region is absolutely ideal. It has good long river valleys connecting the villages, so you can feel that your trip has some purpose, and isn't simply a journey around a set of tracks. The *langlauf* facilities offer the following routes:

Château d'Oex to Rougemont to Saanen to Gstaad: 15 km (9 miles). Gstaad to Chlosteterli to Feutersoey to Gsteig: 11 km (7 miles). Col des Mosses to La Lecherette to Col des Mosses: 6 km (3.7 miles).

There are also some smaller *langlauf* runs in **Schonried** and **Sperenmoos**, but the best of them is undoubtedly the first route, right along the valley, following the course of the River Saane.

This region is almost totally dedicated to sport in any form, and apart from the river pursuits, the downhill and cross-country ski runs, there is one other important feature of the area, and that is **curling**. The curling rink is near the main road on the way into Gstaad from Château d'Oex, and it is here that one of the most prestigious events is held in the world of curling— The Jackson Cup. Anyone interested in this event should contact the Gstaad tourist information office:

Gstaad Tourist Information
Vereinigung der berghagen von Gstaad und Umgebung
CH-3780 Gstaad.
Tel: (030) 45353, fax: (030) 46212.

This office will also be able to give you details of any other events happening in Gstaad or its environs. As an alternative to all the sport, there is a **cheese dairy** at **L'Etivaz**, not far from any of the villages of this area. L'Evitaz is one of the lesser known Swiss cheeses and demonstrations of the techniques for making the cheese are held.

Gstaad

At the heart of this super ski region is the famous village of Gstaad. It is home to film stars, authors and a certain ex-James Bond actor—Gstaad attracts the rich and the not so rich. Being the centre of things makes it

*V*ers l'Eglise is a small village in the Les Diablerets region. It is a good alternative to the big resorts around here.

particularly busy, and there are times when even the many tea rooms and cafés can't cope with all the people. What the chances are of sharing a table with a famous film star, I would not know, but I'm sure they must be around somewhere. Gstaad is very picturesque, and in the winter is a very typical Swiss village of chalets and fir trees with a mountain backdrop.

Accommodation in Gstaad

If you intend to stay in the area and make excursions to various places, then it is better to stay in the smaller villages rather than Gstaad, which is quite expensive. The hotels of Château d'Oex have been mentioned, but there are also good hotels at **Rougemont**: The Hotel Caprice (four-star), the Hotel Valrose (two-star), and the Hotel Viva (two-star). The very small villages have usually two or three hotels, so if you are looking for reasonably priced accommodation, try places like

L'Etivaz, which has the Hotel Chamois at about 30 SFr per night. Villages on the route from Château d'Oex round through Gstaad to Gsteig and the Diablerets are **Flenduz, Rougemont, Saanen** (Gstaad), **Grund, Feutersoey, Gsteig, Reusch, Vers l'Eglise** and **Le Sepey**.

You will need to experiment, by stopping off at a particular village and having a look at what is available. You can find some real bargains in some of the villages like Vers l'Eglise, which, incidentally, has its own small lift system.

Camping
Considering the type of landscape, there are fewer campsites than you might expect, but Vers l'Eglise has something to offer:

Vers l'Eglise la Murée: a three-star site on the River Grande Eau just on the edge of the village. The village is so small it would be impossible not to find the campsite.
Open throughout the year.

There are two other sites in the region, both at **Col des Mosses**, and there are also three more near Gstaad. Due to the odd boundaries imposed by mountain ranges, Gstaad comes under a different section to Château d'Oex. So the three Gstaad sites come into the **Bernese Oberland** section, as **Saanerland**.

Les Mosses la Toundra: the site is just off the road from Aigle to Château d'Oex, fairly close to the river, la Raverette. It's a simple two-star site. Open throughout the year.

Les Mosses Toundra-Cuizon: this site is right on the river, about 1 km (0.6 miles) out of the town, towards La Lecherette. This is an even simpler, one-star site, of which there are few. Open: 1 June–31 October.

In the Saanerland, there are:

Saanen Beim Kappeli: a two-star site on the outskirts of Saanen, on the Gstaad side.
Open: 1 December–31 October.

Gsteig b. Gstaad: another rarely found one-star site, between Les Diablerets and Gstaad.
Open: 16 July–16 September.

Gstaad Camping Bellerive: the only large four-star site in the area, to be found on the outskirts of the town, towards Gsteig.
Open throughout the year.

As a contrast to the type of holiday offered by the whole area in that triangle of Château d'Oex, Gstaad and Les Diablerets, there are "destination" resorts, which have specifically grown to cater for the summer and winter tourist. Such a place is **Leysin**, which has marketed itself as a resort supplying all the facilities you will need. The town is at the end of a road, effectively going nowhere, so it is totally unlike the other villages of the area, where you can drive from one to another.

Leysin
Due to its rather "end of the line" position Leysin was largely left alone for centuries, and it was only in the early 1800s that word spread that the

town was a much healthier place than some of the villages lower down. The first foreigner arrived for health reasons in 1873, and began a tourist stream which has yet to stop. The medical aspect of the town grew with clinics established around the turn of the century. An astonishing statistic regarding the population of the town is that in 1930, of the 5,698 people living in Leysin 3,000 of them were tuberculosis patients, and I can imagine that another 2,000 were there to look after them. Now the patients have turned into tourists, and some 7,000 visit the town each year. The healthy aspect of the town has not changed, so a holiday in this self-made resort should do you some good.

It is quite a big town, spread across a wide valley, but encircled by good-sized mountains. Ideal for a ski resort, and now big enough to entertain its clientele within the valley, summer and winter, it has established itself as a **convention centre**, with two American colleges in the town. This has led to hotels offering convention facilities, and to meet this side of the business, there is a **Holiday Inn** at Leysin. To keep its young executives happy when they are not slogging away on the latest marketing schemes, the town has unparalleled **sports facilities**. It is similar to Gstaad and Château d'Oex in that almost every sport is catered for, and a new **sporting club** has been opened to provide the indoor facilities. The sporting club offers four indoor tennis courts, five outdoor courts, squash courts, solarium, fitness rooms, golf practice, ice rink, mountain wall, football pitch, a restaurant and a games room. Out on the mountains there is

paragliding, climbing, mountain biking, horse riding and (of course) as much skiing as you can handle.

If you are looking for an authentic Swiss village, then Leysin is not really the place for you. It has everything for a really good holiday if you enjoy the outdoor life, sport and are after a healthy, invigorating time. If, on the other hand, you enjoy museums, old buildings and the like, then you will have to go down to Chillon and Lausanne for your entertainment. Maybe you could mix the two since Leysin is only 30 minutes by car from the N9 and about two hours from Geneva. There is a **cog railway** to the resort which runs from **Aigle**, on a narrow-gauge track. Trains leave from Aigle every hour, at about 8 minutes past, and go to the **Grand Hotel**. This was once one of the clinics (in 1892), but since 1956 it has been as a hotel.

Leysin is quite unusual for a Swiss mountain resort, but you have to admire the way in which the locals have turned a health resort into a general tourist centre within a relatively short space of time. But it has become a rather purpose-built resort, which has none of the flavour and atmosphere of the usual Swiss Alpine village.

In this respect, the hotels are the main culprits. Places like the Hotel Residence, the Vermont, the Beau Rival and the Holiday Inn show none of the character or feel for their environment. Even the Leysin Parc, which is gloriously furnished inside, looks like an apartment block from the outside.

Accommodation at Leysin

Both the Holiday inn and the Leysin Parc are four-star hotels, and I would

In the summer the mountain tops still have a good deal of snow, but with occasional bare patches as at the mid-way station for Mt Gelé.

guess that most of their guests are on paid courses. There are some hotels which are more in keeping with the Alps, and they are the Hotel Colina (three-star), the La Primevere (two-star) and La Paix (two-star).

Camping

Campers are catered for in the Camping de Leysin, Georges Cross, which is found on the road into the old part of the village, near the sports centre. Open throughout the year.

The Valais

From Des Alpes de Rivière, as the region around Château d'Oex and Gstaad calls itself, the route south goes into the most popular region of Switzerland: **Valais—Wallis**. This part of Switzerland is inundated with skiers from all over the world for at least three months of the year. From January through to the end of March thousands of package holiday skiers, plus the weekend trippers from

France and Germany come to the Valais to sample the high, guaranteed snow of the Alps. On the way down the N9 there is a small area worth looking at, which probably appeals more to the summer visitor, mainly because there is little to see in the winter.

Taking the turn off the autoroute at **Ollon** the road goes up to the village of **Villars sur Ollon**. There is also a rail connection to this small resort from **Bex**, a few kilometres further south. It is quite a quiet place, with good views down to the Rhône valley, some 1,000 m (3,300 ft) below. It also has a good compact lift system which takes you to the summit of **La Chamossaire** (2,113 m; 6,932 ft), a golf course and a swimming pool. Coming down the same route as the narrow gauge railway from Bex, there is a turn-off to

the **Pont de Nant**. If you have an interest in gardens and flowers this will appeal greatly: in the gardens there are over 2,000 types of Alpine plants, including some of the rare ones.

Eventually, after a good number of hairpins or, in the case of the train, tunnels, this small side road rejoins the main route down to **Martigny**. This large town sits at a junction, where routes from France, Italy and

Some of the neatest vineyards around are in Switzerland. The glacial waters are spreading towards Martigny Castle.

Switzerland meet. Many people carry on to the big resorts around **Sion**, at **Crans Montana**, and onto the roads leading to **Nendaz**, **La Fondaz**, **Zinal** and **Zermatt**. This is the real ski country, with a mass of lift systems, some of which join up to offer the skier unrivalled ski routes up and over the mountains.

But for those who take the southerly route, there is the village-come-town of **Verbier**. This is a resort that in winter attracts the skier who can use the **Mont Fort** system to go over to Nendaz and come back by the ski bus. In summer it offers high walking routes in spectacular scenery. But Verbier is a resort to stay in, rather than travel around from. After you have negotiated the 14 hairpin bends from the valley floor at **Sembracher**, you really have no desire to go anywhere else too

---

Irrigation in the Valais

Water in such a mountainous area as the Valais can prove to be a problem, or rather the inconsistent supply of it can be difficult. Throughout the Valais there are examples of the early answer to these problems, with the construction of channelled water to the places which needed the water. These were called *bisses*, and the troughs and channels would run along the mountainside, dropping very gradually. The source of the water would be the Rhône tributaries, which in the spring would fill the *bisses* to carry the water across country to the pastures. At one time there were 2,000 km (1,240 miles) of *bisses*, although most of them have now fallen into disrepair.

206

soon. In winter the PTT bus makes its way up the mountainside, but if all else fails there is a cable car to take you from the railway station at **Le Châble** up to the resort.

Verbier

The new town of Verbier is slightly higher than the original village, and you pass by the old **church** on the last leg of the journey. The town is already at a height of 1,500 m (4,900 ft) before you take any of the cable cars and chair-lifts to the peaks. Its position is good in some ways, providing winter tourists particularly with almost certain snow conditions, but its drawbacks are similar to all high-level resorts, in that it's not easy to have a look at the rest of the region. If you do want to take a trip to the **St Bernard pass**, maybe to see the famous dog kennels and the **monastery**, it will take you nearly an hour to reach the main road. Even using the gondola lift down to Le Châble means that you will have to take a train to the main station at Sembrancher.

On the positive side, Verbier has everything to satisfy the holidaymaker in terms of hotels, chalets, sports facilities, lift systems and walks. You can easily

*T*he last lap of the Mt Fort cable system takes the visitor across the summer skiing area.

spend your entire trip here, and in the winter use the extensive lift system to ski to areas on the other side of the mountains. Verbier is the proud owner of the largest cable car ("le Jumbo") in Switzerland, which is part of the Mont Fort summit system. Up here in summer there is a whole range of walks, taking the hiker well out into the high mountains, something which balances the travel aspect of actually reaching the town.

Things to do in Verbier

The town centre is quite an active place, with tennis courts, shops and hotels gathered around a central square. Further down, at the edge of the town, is a modern **sports centre**, with ice rink, superb heated swimming pool, sauna, solarium and squash. There is also a new 18-hole par 70 golf course. Hang gliding, paragliding, mountaineering courses, heliskiing and mountain biking make up a range of activities which can be equalled by a lot of resorts, but certainly not bettered. The emphasis is very much on the active holiday, whether you go to Verbier in summer or winter. In the in-between period, around early June, many of the facilities are having maintenance work done on them, so the cable cars and even the sports hall can be out of action for a few days. If you are planning a trip to any of the Swiss Alpine resorts at this time, it is worth checking just when they run their maintenance programme, so that you are not disappointed on arrival. It would be a great disappointment to a family going to Verbier when these check-overs are taking place, because so much depends on them for the full enjoyment of the holiday. Verbier is not the sort of place from which you can easily trot off to another village each day to compensate. The price of the holiday, in the case of a package, is often the pointer to some of the amenities being withdrawn, so beware of unrealistic bargains!

Skiing

Presuming that all is well on the cable cars, and it most definitely will be in

winter, the possibilities for mountain touring are tremendous. The first stages of the lifts out of Verbier go from the station about ten minutes' walk up the hill. This is also where the lift from Le Châble comes in, so those coming up from the valley will go straight on to the next stage. From there the gondola will take you to **Les Ruinettes**. The station for le Jumbo does not follow directly on from here, so there is a short walk or bus ride to the main station at **La Chaux**. The huge cable cars then take you on up to **Col des Gentianes**, and then another gondola to the summit of Mont Fort. From here, the world is your oyster, and you can ski to **Tortin** and on to **Siviez** (Super Nendaz), **Nendaz**, **Lac des Vaux**, and so on. The whole area takes in 320 km (200 miles) of ski runs, and within the four valleys there are some 84 lifts in the form of chairs, cableways, cabins and drag lifts. It is an ideal ski centre, and even in the summer there is skiing on the higher slopes of Mont Fort, and the runs to Tortin.

Verbier typifies the whole philosophy regarding skiing in Switzerland. It simply provides everything in one centre, and in this region there are a great number of resorts similar to Verbier. They all have superb facilities, they will get you on to the mountains as quickly and efficiently as possible, and if you don't want to spend your entire trip on the slopes or summer walking, there are sports centres for

*I*n the spring, the Swiss Alps are covered with colourful flowers, making walking in the area a real pleasure.

swimming and the like. The choice is almost overwhelming, and it would be difficult to say which resort is the best. I prefer Verbier to Crans Montana, mainly because there is more of a semblance of the old town still left. It has fewer high-rise apartment blocks, and it is marginally easier to get to.

For the cross-country skier there are some short circular trails in the four valleys at **Vichères**, near **Orsières**, around **Bruson**, at **Super Nendaz**, and a good distance run from **Thyon**.

Walking
For walkers there is the opportunity to take mountain side paths which may give glimpses of Ibex and Chamois, along with some of the most beautiful Alpine flora to be seen in the country.

Accommodation
For accommodation in Verbier there is also a tremendous choice. A great many people coming to the town have self-catering chalets. There are probably more in Verbier than many other resorts. They are built towards the back of the new part of the town, looking down on the village. The views can be stunning, looking right across at the high mountains above the Rhône valley. In the hotel list, there are some very good ones, in the centre of the village (again the new part).

The high grade hotels here are expensive, with rates for the four-star hotels running up to 425 SFr (the Rosalp and the Montpelier). Even the two-star hotels are somewhat pricey, with the Crystal and the Rosablanche both charging around 136 SFr for their cheapest rooms. These are high-season winter rates, but those rates are halved

*A*lpine chalets often *offer good secluded accommodation, with benefits for both the summer and winter visitors.*

in the summer period, which is from June onwards. The period at the beginning of June is to be avoided in Verbier for annual maintenance takes over. Of all the hotels in the area, the two-star Mont Gelé offers the best deal with rooms at around 60 SFr in summer and 100 SFr in winter The main reason for it being slightly cheaper is its position, which is just a bit out of the centre of things, near the Télécabine Medran.

Camping
Anyone hoping to camp in Verbier could be disappointed, since there are no official campsites. There are the mountain huts, which can be rented out, but these are obviously for the more rigorous, some would say "real",

camper. Those in search of the multi-facility four- or five-star site may have a problem, since the only organized site is down at Le Châble, and that is the one-star Le Châble St Marc. It is, however, open throughout the year.

Excursions from Verbier

There are two good excursions from Verbier, one of which does not require you to go down to the main road, but does need some careful driving. The trip is to one of the large **dams** in this region at **Lac de Mauvoison**. Only in summer can you use the road, which runs at a fairly high level from **Les Morgenes** to Verbier, but if the opportunity arises this non-metalled road does give some superb views down the valley to Le Châble. The alternative route to the dam is to drop down to Le Châble, cross the river and follow its course along the Val de Bagnes. The dam is hard to miss, since it blocks an entire ravine. There is one point on this road, at the valley floor, where the true size of the concrete barrage can be appreciated. There are also two **bridges** across the ravine, one of which is particularly old. This is a good spot for a picnic. At the dam, there is a restaurant, and from the car park a path leads to the reservoir. This dam is not as big as the neighbouring **Grand Dixence**, which is the largest in Europe, but it is still impressive.

*T*he St Bernard Hospice straddles the pass between Italy and Switzerland. The dogs still work on the mountains.

The other day trip from Verbier does involve going back down to the valley, and can only be done from July onwards. The **St Bernard Pass** is often still closed, even in June, so a visit to see the **hospice** is only possible for a few months of the year. This refuge for the cold and hungry still takes in travellers, and the famous **St Bernard dogs** continue their charitable work on the mountains. At the hospice there is a small **museum** detailing the history of the pass and the **monastery**, and you can also visit the **kennels**. The route up to the pass is easy enough, since you simply follow the signs for Italy from Sembrancher on the E27. The road over the pass splits from the tunnel road to take a series of steep bends up to the top at 2,469 m (8,147 ft). It is cold and icy up here, even in summer, so take some warm clothes, but it is well worth seeing this historic pass which has been the main entrance to Switzerland and the Alpine regions for centuries.

Verbier is one ski resort of a multitude in the valley running from **Martigny** through **Sion** to **Brig**. The mountain ranges either side of the Rhône are covered in lift systems, and there really is little to choose between them. Some will offer greater walking possibilities than others, with the opportunity to see some of the very high peaks such as the **Matterhorn** and the **Stockhorn**. But perhaps the greatest activity is seen in the section between Sion and **Sierre**, at **Crans** and **Montana**. Many skiers head for this high-level plateau, which, like many of the specialized resorts has been almost purpose-built to ensure the skier can almost fall out of the chalet or hotel and straight on to a well-prepared piste. Before heading into the hills, however, it is worth taking a look at **Sion**, instantly recognizable by the two **castles** perched atop craggy outcrops. These could be the only features of the town worth seeing, because the town has become something of a traffic jam.

Sion

The site on which Sion is built is around 2,000 years old, and has always been regarded as a place of strategic importance. The centre of the town is dominated by its two rocks, upon which are the **church** (*L'Eglise Notre Dame de Valere*) and **Tourbillon**, a ruin of a previous fortress. The church is 12th century, and is usually open for viewing. There is also a **museum** on the hilltop—the **Valere museum**—housing furniture, sculptures and religious artifacts. From the top of the Valere hill you can see down the Rhône valley towards Brig, and appreciate the strength of the position held by the Bishops of Sion, and how the town became the capital of the Valais.

From Sion there is a small road to the **Grand Dixence dam**, via **Vex**. At Vex there is a single track road going to the dam. If you have seen the **Mauvoison dam**, then Grand Dixence may not appeal, since it is very similar. However, as an excursion from Sion or one of the mountain resorts, it is interesting to see this the largest piece of Swiss civil engineering. It is impressive, with an 87-m (285-ft) high wall, and it has greatly increased the country's hydroelectric output. It is also the highest dam in Europe, taking its water from the glaciers of the Matterhorn via a series of tunnels.

Water Power

Switzerland cannot depend on fossil fuels for its power. It has invested heavily in a nuclear programme, but to supplement this, there is a strong hydroelectric industry, using the height and power of the Alpine waters to produce some large outputs of power. The two biggest hydroelectric stations are in the Bagnes valley at Grand Dixence and Mauvoisin. There are two more dams at the St Bernard Pass and Moiry, but these are smaller affairs. The Grand Dixence is 87 m (932 ft) tall, and even in 1935 had a capacity of 50 million cubic metres. It supplies two stations at Chandoline and Fionnay, and increased Switzerland's output by an annual 1,600 megawatts. Not far way, in the parallel valley, is the Mauvoisin Dam, which although not as great in size appears as a huge structure straddling the Bagnes Valley. This has an equally impressive quantity of water behind its walls, a massive 180 million cubic metres.

There is a road from Sion to the resorts at **Crans**, but most visitors leave the road at **Sierre** to head up to this intensive ski resort, which also includes the town of **Montana**. The two go together now, forming the general area of Crans Montana. The road winds up to 1,496 m (4,908 ft), and the chances are that, like Verbier, once you are up here a trip down to the valley does not seem a good idea.

Crans Montana

Set in forested hills these two towns merge to provide the ultimate sports complex—18-hole golf, lakes, ski trails and perfect ski conditions all add up to a resort ideal for those that have to be doing something on holiday. The trend towards activity holidays has increased over the past few years, so a place like Crans Montana certainly appeals to a large market. The advantages gained by the Swiss resort over similar places in France and Italy is the height—between 1,500 and 3,000 m (5,000–10,000 ft), and the confidence that the hotels and chalets are going to be of the best quality. A holiday in Crans Montana will not be cheap, but like all of Switzerland will be good value for money.

There are no rail connections to Crans, but there is a bus service for which the Swiss Pass is valid. The service goes from Sion and Sierre stations, and take about 45 minutes to an hour, depending on which village you're going to. Many visitors to the area are on package deals which include transfer from Geneva through to the resort, and I believe that this is the market for which Crans Montana is

intended. I do not think many independent travellers with a keen interest in Switzerland will be interested in the amenities offered by this plateau.

Accommodation

There is a wealth of accommodation available for the skier and the summer tourist. Whilst most of these places are taken up by groups, they will not turn the independent traveller away. The smartest hotel is at the golf club, where the Du Golf et des Sports is situated. This is a five-star hotel, next to both

*P*erhaps not the most obvious sport in the mountains, but many resorts double up their winter ski slopes as golf courses for the summer. This course is at Verbier.

of the 18-hole golf courses. There are a good number of the three-star category here as well, with quite reasonable prices for the sort of place it is. Most of them are in the central, newer part of the town, and in all honesty, Crans Montana has become something of a muddle of hotels and chalets. To pick out any from the rest is difficult.

Not so **Zermatt**, which has a history of mountaineering, and although it has an element of the intensive ski resort, has retained some of its character, partly because of the **Matterhorn** and the aura this mountain creates.

Zermatt

At Zermatt you can really claim to be in among the highest of the high, and as if to remind you, no matter which angle you choose, the mighty Matterhorn always appears as a background. The centre of the town has an old **church**, where there is a peaceful traffic-free atmosphere.

Getting There

Getting to Zermatt is easier than most of the high-level resorts, but not by car. For once, this is where the rail scores, and motorists must leave their cars at **Täsch**, the village at the end of the valley road. Coming from **Visp** and the main route 9, the road is only a second-class one, so you should take care, especially in high season. Either side of this road are the very high steep mountains of the **Mattertal**, with almost every one between 3,500 and 4,000 m (11,500–13,000 ft). At Täsch there is a large car park, but the rail service actually starts from Brig. There may be advantages to having the car at Täsch, but it is just as well to come

up from Visp or Brig if you intend staying for some time in Zermatt. The trains from Brig run hourly from 5.10a.m. to 8.23p.m., and from Täsch there are more local connections.

For those whose patience cannot run to waiting for a train, but whose wallet will run to using a helicopter, there is a heliport at Zermatt. The company operating the service is Air Zermatt: tel (028) 673487.

History of Zermatt

Zermatt's history comes from its association with the Matterhorn. This is where mountaineering, in the true sense, started with some rather bold escapades by the British climber Edward Whymper. He, along with three other British climbers and a guide, reached the summit of the mountain on 14 July 1865, but the descent saw the tragic death of two of his companions and the guide, and so gave the mountain its first victims. Since then, mountaineers have made the Matterhorn almost a point of pilgrimage, as year after year climbers from all over the world come to scale the peak. To see the history of the attempts on the mountain, there is an Alpine Museum, which also has reconstructions of mountain dwellers' houses.

What to do in Zermatt

Zermatt is another sporting paradise, and with the neighbouring glaciers skiing is possible summer or winter. But again, it is a place to stay, rather than tour from, even more so than Verbier or Crans Montana. There are some beautiful walks here, to places like **Schwarzsee**, the much-photographed lake with the Matterhorn in the background. In all there are 388 km (241 miles) of marked footpaths, some of which are on the higher levels. If you plan to take one of these walks you would be advised to let someone know where you are going, and be prepared for changes in temperature and weather. It can become quite unsettled in this region very quickly, so take some care; only experienced walkers should tackle the ridge walks.

In the village, if walking and climbing are too strenuous, there are innumerable swimming pools, although most of them belong to the hotels. There is, curiously, a salt-water swimming pool. In all there are 14 pools, saunas, solariums, squash courts, a fitness centre, mini-golf, and 17 tennis courts. Zermatt is well equipped for the summer months and has a wealth of skiing facilities for the winter. Being more enclosed than the four valleys or the wide plateaux, it cannot quite match up in terms of numbers, but there are 50 lifts of one kind or another and 230 km (143 miles) of ski runs, two natural ice rinks (frozen lakes), eight curling rinks and many cross-country trails.

Zermatt's Extensive Lift System

The main lift goes, not surprisingly, to the Matterhorn, or as close as you can get to it without putting crampons on. A trip up the **Klein Matterhorn** involves going to **Schwarzsee**, which may actually be nearer to the peak than the finishing point, on to **Trockener Steg**, and ultimately the Klein Matterhorn itself. At this point you are at 3,820 m (12,533 ft)—not bad considering that the mountain itself is only another 500 m (1,640 ft) above you. It is the highest cable station in Europe, and from here you walk through tunnels to the snowfields for summer skiing.

Another "highest" is the open rack railway (that is, it does not use tunnels) which goes to **Gornergrat**. From the station at **Riffelberg** there are stunning views of the Matterhorn, as well as **Monte Rosa**, which is the absolute centre of the Alpine structure. The rack railway connects with the **Stockhorn** cable system, so you can easily spend a day out on the mountains, enjoying the views, and, of course, the mountain restaurants. The **Gornergrat Bahn** goes from a station on the opposite side of the road to the arrivals point for trains from Brig. Next door to this station is the **information office**.

The third lift system out of Zermatt goes to **Unter Rothorn** and **Sunnega**. It is not as spectacular as the other two, but does have some good views of the whole Matterhorn range, and the **Ober Rothorn** at 3,415 m (11,204 ft).

Accommodation

If there is any doubt as to whether Zermatt can cope with its tourist invasion, then the 109 hotels (listed), should quell any fears. It is also a chalet and self-catering resort, and many people prefer this alternative. In Britain, Interhome of Twickenham have extensive lists of chalets for hire in Zermatt and other Alpine towns. The information office usually has lists of places for rent. Hotels in Zermatt can be as expensive as in Zurich and Geneva, probably because of the nature of the village—it is something of a captive market. There are some grand five-star places here, such as the Mount Cervin, costing in the high season 400–500 SFr. The best-looking hotel is the Alex Schlosshotel Tenne, which has a castle-like style to its architecture. It also has an indoor swimming pool, tennis courts and all the facilities of a hotel costing in the region of 400 SFr.

Fortunately, the majority of hostelries are in the three-star range, but these still cost around 200 SFr for a double room. The Garni hotels or pensions offer the best value and, as always if you are looking for a reasonable costing hotel, the Bahnhof is around 90 SFr for a double. I have lost count of the number of Hotels Bahnhof I have stayed at, but generally they are clean, with more often than not big rooms. This is due to the fact that most of the railway station hotels were constructed at the same time as the lines were laid, and in Switzerland this means the Victorian era. You therefore benefit from the Victorian-sized rooms.

Camping
There is a campsite in Zermatt, just outside the village between the heliport and the station. The site is non-classified and is called *Matterhorn*.
Open: 15 July–30 September.

Tourist Information
Information on activities and amenities in the village, along with the likely maintenance programme times can be obtained from:

Zermatt Tourist Office
Bahnhofplatz
CH-3920 Zermatt
Tel: (028) 661181; fax: (028) 661185.

Saas Fee
In direct competition to Zermatt, and almost in the same valley is the resort of Saas Fee. Instead of carrying on the main road at Stalden, 7 km (4 miles) from **Visp**, take the left fork towards **Eisten**, and follow the **Saaser Vispa river**. Saas Fee is at the end of the road, on a spur road from **Saas Grund**. This resort is the most aggressively marketed place in Switzerland. You can be on a station platform in Basel, or at a bus stop in the Appenzell, and I can guarantee that there will be a poster somewhere advertising the delights of Saas Fee. It clearly has competition in Zermatt, because it has no Matterhorn, but it has got some very high peaks, and in fact **Mt Dom** is marginally higher at 4,545 m (14,911 ft), but is not quite so obvious or accessible.

You could say, "Well here we go again", because Saas Fee boasts a whole host of attractions. The lifts go to the peak of the **Mittelallin** at 3,500 m (11,480 ft), and to reach this peak the town has invested in an underground metro service. This means year-round access to a difficult summit (or near to the summit). It is not very high, but it does offer summer and winter skiing on the glaciers. This tunnel for the metro means that Saas Fee can boast the world's **highest underground railway**, and the highest revolving restaurant in the world. Whether firsts and highests really attract any more visitors I'm not sure,

*T*he past few years have seen a tremendous increase in mountain biking. Most of the mountain trails are used by bikers slogging their way to the summit.

but when the competition is as fierce as it is between Alpine resorts, you have to have something to shout about.

Sports

In the sporting range, there is the Bielen Sports Centre, which offers a swimming pool, including a children's pool, Jacuzzi, steam bath, sauna, solarium, fitness room, massage and billiards room. There are tennis courts, ice skating (artificial) and curling, so you cannot fail to be entertained if you want an active holiday. The cross-country skiing opportunities are slightly restricted, as they are at Zermatt, and there are only two real routes. One is an 8-km (5-mile) circular route through the woods, the other a more challenging 25-km (15.5-mile) trail to **Mattmark**. There is a toboggan run from **Hannig Station** to **Waldeg** and down to the village.

For the downhill skier, the lifts spread out around the village, with the main **Mittelallin** being the longest and the highest. Smaller systems go to **Langfluh, Plattjen** and **Hannig**. In between these main lifts there are plenty of small drag and chair-lifts, so there is plenty of skiing to be had in this area.

Transport

Like Zermatt, Saas Fee has adopted a traffic-free centre, and it would seem that most Swiss villages are deciding to take up this policy. It is good for visitors in winter not to have to make their way through piled up wet slush on the way to the ski stations. It is so much better to be able to walk in relatively fresh snow; apart from this it enhances the sight of the village. Cars should therefore be left at one of the two big car parks at the edge of the village, whence a new cable car operates. This is an addition to the metro, and links up with the Mittelallin route at **Maste**. It is called the Alpine Express, and takes skiers directly from their cars up to the slopes without having to walk some distance to the original station.

If you are visiting the area for more than a day, and even for such a short period as half a day, it is well worth buying a day ticket, since the one-way fares on all these lifts are very expensive. There are usually special rates which are lower for non-skiers, so you do not have to pay a high price to simply enjoy the scenery and a cup of coffee. In Saas Fee the day ticket costs about 44 SFr, which gives you access to all 25 lifts. The one-way fare from Saas Fee to Mittelallin is about 34 SFr, so just by using it once on a return journey you have saved a bit of money.

Sights in the Village

In the **old village**, which is still at the centre of things in Saas Fee, there is a small **museum**, highlighting the lifestyles of the mountain people from the area. The valleys around Zermatt and Saas Fee were once isolated communities, with little communication with the outside world. Without the modern civil engineering techniques many of the village people would still be farming and living a much poorer life than they do today. Development may have gone too far in some places, but then most of us did not have to live there before.

As a reminder of the local costume there is an annual **procession** featuring traditional folklore, on 8 September, which is a pilgrimage to the **Hohen Steige Chapel**.

Accommodation

Hotels are as plentiful here as in all the bigger villages, and self-catering chalets are equally popular. The whole perimeter of the village is covered with chalets, with the hotels taking up most of the central positions.

To its credit, Saas Fee has kept its buildings in the traditional style of the Alps. There are few block and balcony hotels here, and the majority of them cater for the mid-range visitor. The highest grade hotels are four-star and in this category there are the Ambassador, the Walliserhof, the Beau-Site, the Metropol Grand and the Saaserhof. All except the last have their own swimming pools, which is good for the winter months.

In the three-star category there is the greatest range (24 hotels) to choose from. Some, like the Hotel Elite, are slightly out of the town, whilst the Hotel Burgener is almost directly on the slopes. Saas Fee also has a few *Garni* (Guesthouse) hotels, which are less expensive but can still be rated as four-star, and have their own pools. A good example of such a place is the Hotel La Collina.

Camping

The campsite is very centrally placed on the right of the road from **Saas Grund**. It is also very close to the parking areas. It is a non-classified site called Terminus.

Open: 19 July–11th September.

Tourist Information

The Saas Fee Tourist Information Office is at:

Tourist Office
CH-3906 Saas Fee.
Tel: (028) 571457; fax: (028) 591111.

Minor Roads of the Valais

It would be unfair to suggest that these are the only places worth going to in the Valais, either for a skiing trip or for a summer holiday. Verbier, Crans Montana, Zermatt and Saas Fee are the bigger resorts with the greatest range of facilities, geared to provide certain snow, with the maximum lift capacity. In many of the neighbouring countries, more recent years have led to disappointment over the lack of snow, and with no alternatives should the weather not be suitable. The big resorts mentioned have done their best to make sure that, particularly the winter, tourist does not leave without having had some form of activity to enjoy. As a balance to this, the smaller resorts such as **Leukerbad**, with its superb thermal baths, offer alternatives.

This small spa town developed a wide reputation as the place to go around the turn of the century, when it boasted 23 thermal **lime springs**. It is still regarded as an important health centre, and to this effect there is a **campsite** at Leukerbad which has **thermal baths** within its perimeters. It is a four-star site, and offers everything in the way of health and fitness for its visitors. It is open 1 May–31 October.

To reach Leukerbad you will first go through **Leuk**. This is an interesting town with two **castles**, built in a

Out in the mountains the flowers are a natural part of the wild scenery. Switzerland is trying hard to preserve this wild beauty of the mountains.

(7,546 ft) pass to **Kandersteg** and into the Bernese Oberland.

For the visitor who is genuinely not interested in the skiing and sporting aspect of the area, but still likes the Valais, one of the best places to travel to is the **Val d'Hérens**. Going from Sion, a minor road runs deep into this unspoilt valley, which to a great degree has retained much of the character of the Valais. The small villages of **Vex**, **Nax**, **Evolène** and **Les Haudères** are set in spectacular scenery, and here you will see the old wooden houses, decorated with flowers, as they have been for centuries. This is one of the most peaceful valleys in a region of activity, and is ideal for walkers and hikers who simply enjoy the mountains without any razzamatazz.

There is one particular area where there is no question as to how peaceful it is, and that is the **Lötschental Valley**. For those in search of the real old Switzerland, where you can imagine how life was before the ski-lift was invented, then this unspoilt part of the country will provide just that.

The Lötschental Valley

Lötschental was the most isolated valley of Switzerland until the 1950s, and even now it is not possible to take a car by road from **Goppenstein** through to **Kandersteg** on the way to Interlaken. This is an area where the mountains have won, and I think this is important in a country where every attempt has been made to circumnavigate, tunnel through or go over the mountains. Lötschental is surrounded by glaciers, which makes it a unique environment. In the valley there is a single road, ideal for walking, and

similar position to, and for much the same reasons as, those at Sion. The original site was founded in 515 for the **Abbey of St Maurice**, but was taken by the Bishops of Sion in 1138. Both are in commanding positions at another stronghold in the valley. The **castle of Vidonnes** is now the town hall, but the castle further on remains as a historic building.

One of the most spectacular walks in the country stems from the Leukerbad area, where the cable car ascends to the **Gemmi pass**. This walking route takes the hiker over the 2,300 m

I would encourage people to leave the car at **Kippel** and walk to the hamlet, **Guggistafel**, at the end of the valley. From this walk, you can begin to understand the harsh life of the Swiss farmers before the modern world impinged. The crops grown in this valley are barley, rye and potatoes, with some cattle farming, but the culture and lifestyles of the people of the Lötschental can be seen at the **Lötschentaler Museum** at Kippel. Although this museum is at the head of the valley, do not let this deter you from a walk down to Guggistafel. One of the more interesting **folklore festivals** is held in Kippel, with the men wearing bearskins and plumes for the event. It is the **Corpus Christi Procession**, held annually on the Sunday after Corpus Christi.

Camping in the Valais

Most visitors coming to this area of Switzerland use the high resorts for their accommodation, but the camper is left with little to choose from, especially in the big purpose-built places. Saas Fee and Zermatt are fortunate to have small basic sites, which will satisfy the trekkers and those needing only a pitch for their tent, but what of the serious four-star camper, possibly with the caravan or tourer? All of the sites for this area are down in the main valley, running along the length of the Rhône. Going from west to east:

Martigny el Capio: a three-star site, on the edge of **Martigny**. This is a large busy town, but the site is on the more peaceful side of the town near the river.
Open throughout the year.

Saxon le Grenier: situated between Martigny and Sion, this is a two-star site.
Open throughout the year.

Les Vernes les Roches: a three-star site higher up, above the Rhône, the nearest village is **Chamoson.**
Open: 1 April–31 October.

Vetroz Botza: a top-quality, multi-amenity, five-star site, offering everything including swimming pool, set amongst trees and cultivated landscape. Vetroz is just on the outskirts of **Sion**, near **Ardon**.
Open throughout the year.

Sion les Iles Sedunum: one of two sites in the main Sion area, this is a three-star site.
Open: 1 May–30 October.

Sion Bramois Valcentre: another three-star site for Sion, in a quiet picturesque setting.
Open throughout the year.

Granges Robinson: Granges is about 5 km (3 miles) out of **Sion**, and is found on the southern side of the Rhône. Stay on the main 62 road, not the autoroute, as there is no turn off the motorway. A three-star site.
Open: 1 March–31 December.

Sierre Salgesch: a four-star site, close to the resort of **Sierre** and the mountains of Crans Montana.
Open: 1 January–31 October.

In the mountain regions, south of the valley towards **Arolla** there is a number of small villages along the road. This is a particularly good area for mountain sites.

Nax: a four-star site, with swimming pool and superb views over the mountains. Nax is a very small village, on a minor road, near **Granges**. Detailed guidance may be needed to find it! Open: 1 May–30 September.

Vex Val d'Hérens: a four-star site, at the village of **Vex**. This is the first village on the minor road out of Sion. Open throughout the year.

Evolène: a simpler three-star site, in the village of **Evolène**. This is further up the Val d'Herens, and is easy to find.
Open throughout the year.

Les Haudres Molignon: at the very end of the minor road into this valley, this is a three-star site.
Open throughout the year.

Arolla Petit Praz: catering more for the hiker and backpacker, this is a one-star site, well into the mountains.

From Goppenstein the road meets with the Rhône valley, and from here the main route runs through to **Brig**, and on through another, more peaceful and serene valley. Before going into this area, it is worth mentioning a special attraction, especially for those with an interest in rail travel. Recently an enterprising businessman resurrected the old service from **Zermatt** to **St Moritz**. It uses all the high-level routes and tunnels to make its way through some of the most spectacular scenery that can be seen from a train.

The Glacier Express

The route begins in Zermatt, and in a way connects two similar places, for both this Alpine village and the high-altitude resort of the Engadine have always attracted the rich and famous. Some of the carriages are re-creations of the originals, and by offering first-class meals and service, the Glacier Express has brought back some of the glossy romanticism of rail travel. The full route takes passengers from Zermatt out into the Rhône valley, to Brig and the **Oberwald pass**. It then drops down from **Andermatt** towards **Disentis**, an old spa town, and round to **Chur**. From here it takes the superbly scenic route through to **Davos** and **St Moritz**.

The journey could be made using regular SBB services, but the attraction of this train is, as with The Venice Simplon Express, the atmosphere created. The service is in the hands of a private company, and is apparently a great success. The trip takes a total of seven and a half hours, which is very good, since it would probably take at least that time to drive. It uses 91 tunnels and 291 bridges, its highest point is on the **Oberalp pass** at 2,033 m (6,670 ft); you are getting the very best of the Swiss' unique ability to take a train almost anywhere.

For reservations and information contact:

Schweizerische Speiswagen-Gesellschaft CH-7000 Chur.
Tel: (081) 221425; fax: (081) 245275.

Local tourist offices usually have some information, as do the main city ones such as Bern and Zurich.

From Brig to Chur

At Brig, the turn-off to Italy goes towards the **Simplon Pass** and this scenic route across the border is often used in preference to the **St Gothard Tunnel**. The road climbs steeply to the top of the pass (2,005 m; 6,578 ft) and runs into Italy at **Gondo**. This is a summer route; like all the passes in this region it is closed in winter. However, there is a rail service through the tunnel, which takes cars from Brig through to **Bertonio**. To stay in Switzerland, and to move through another language barrier to the **Grimsel** and **Furka**

The perfect Swiss scene on the hills near Neiderwal.

Passes, you follow the Rhône. Brig is something of a bottleneck for motor traffic, so the rail traveller has some advantages here.

Brig

The town of Brig is another important strategic centre, which has developed over the years. Ideally placed between the valleys of the Rhône and the Saltine, it owes a lot to a single family—the Stockalpers. Kasper von Stockalper lived for most of the 17th century, and in his time made a personal fortune out of the position Brig offered. His trade was moving salt between Italy and Switzerland, a business which he protected with an armed guard of 70 men. Eventually he fled to Italy, the target of some very jealous countrymen. He later returned to Brig,

where he died in 1691, but sadly he never had the opportunity to finish his **castle**, which can still be seen. The **Stockalper Palace** can be recognized by the three domes atop the towers. The palace was constructed between 1658 and 1678, but Fernanda von Stockalper built another residence in 1727. This now houses the local history **museum** for the town.

Brig to Oberwald

The road between Brig and Oberwald shows delightful countryside. This is another strong agricultural area, which has benefited from some high mountains to provide ski areas and summer resorts. The great advantages gained by the small villages along the Rhône is their accessibility. After Brig, there are several resorts worthy of a visit. None of the villages has particularly big ski areas, although the **Reideralp** and the **Bettmeralp** are around the 2,000-m (6,560-ft) mark and the **Eggishorn** is close to 3,000 m (9,840 ft). This last mountain provides the biggest of the ski-lift systems from **Fiesch**. This whole region is part of the very old Switzerland, and you are coming close to the Romansch-speaking regions. If you are travelling from Chur then the difference in the dialect is noticeable in this part of the country. Opposite Fiesch, on a small road off the main route, is the village of **Ernen**, which is full of old wooden buildings dating back to the 15th century. This village was one of the principal centres for the area at one time, but it is now a typical example of the style of housing in this area. All along this valley, which for drivers is thankfully straight, village after village, hugs

the gentle sides. If you travel in this region in spring, when the fields are full of the small yellow fields, you could be forgiven for expecting Julie Andrews to appear with the Von Trapp children in tow. It's that part of Switzerland, almost too perfect to be true, where the chapel spire is at *just* the correct position in relation to the mountains behind.

St Maurice

On one of the great walks across the Alps, from the Grisons to Lac Léman, there are several small villages dating back centuries. One such village is St Maurice, a former important Roman military base. The abbey there is the oldest north of the Alps, and the monastery was founded in 515. The King of Burgundy believed in the Byzantine tradition of continual psalm reading, but despite this devotion the monastery fell into decline in the 10th century. The abbey's treasury contains some remarkable artifacts including chalices, Roman cups and a casket made by Burgundian craftsmen.

A leisurely journey through this part of the country can be a great tonic, and it is almost a disappointment to reach **Oberwald** and the distinctly more difficult time ahead. This route from Brig to Chur can take a long time, and you will have to negotiate six high-level roads (up and down), which can be very tiring. The **Furka** is the highest, but all of the three passes you traverse involve some steep, winding roads and you should allow plenty of time. This problem is solved in winter because the passes are closed, so you have to go round, via Interlaken, or use the car-rail services to go through to the other side.

This rail service through the mountains departs from **Oberwald**, and by using it you avoid the stress of the Furka pass road. Unfortunately, this means you also miss the opportunity to see the source of the mighty River Rhône, at the **Rhône glacier**.

The Rhône Glacier

Glaciers can seem disappointing, in that they are usually rather nasty looking collections of dirty ice. The Rhône glacier is no exception, but is still worth seeing, and for a small fee you can go inside the glacier, where the ice is pure and clean. The road up to the glacier is long and full of hairpins.

For a few francs you can walk into the Rhône glacier. There are a few cut-outs in the ice so you can look out from the middle of the glacier.

225

*T*he Rhône glacier can be seen from the road approaching from Brig, and there are quite a few stopping places for cars nearer the mass of ice.

There are nearly always some road improvements being carried out, since the road suffers from all manner of damage during the winter. The winter up here does not finish until well into May, so this trip is very much a summer one.

way down the hillside. Geographically, this point is one of the most important parts of Europe, since the Furka is almost at the exact centre of the Alps. This glacier feeds the waters of both the Rhône and the Rhine, as well as the rivers of the Ticino. Eventually these waters will run into the Mediterranean via the Camargue, the North Sea via Rotterdam and the Adriatic via Venice. When put in this context, the scene becomes quite awe-inspiring. The glacier is very accessible, and you can go to the very edge of the ice flows. To either side of the road going up the mountain, there are lay-bys where you can stop to take photographs. At the very top of the pass there is a shop, selling souvenirs, a hotel (appropriately named the Hotel Belvedere), and an access point to the glacier.

It costs about 3 SFr for a ticket to go and explore the innards of the glacier, but as with so many of these types of attractions, there is a tacky side. Not content with letting people admire and enjoy the novelty of being inside a glacier, surrounded by rather ghostly blue ice, the tunnel which has been built leads directly to a man offering to take your photograph—with a suitably decked-out sledge. The scene may change from year to year, but this sort of commercialism will destroy the atmosphere for many people. Your children, however, may like this aspect of the trip. At various points in the glacier you can look out to the descending ice flow.

The glacier is a remarkable sight, and a good stopping point in either direction. The advantage of coming from the west is that you are able to enjoy

The top of the Furka pass is at 2,431 m (nearly 8,000 ft) but you can see the glacier from well down the road if approaching it from Brig and the west. The glacier strides a wide gully, and from it the waters of the river Rhône can be seen trickling their

a sight of the glacier as you approach it; coming from Chur and Disentis means that you only see the glacier when you turn the last bend at the top of the pass. If you do not have your own transport, there are plenty of excursions in the summer, from Brig and Chur especially, but also from many other cities in the country.

Andermatt

After the Rhône Glacier the road drops dramatically into an altogether too short a stretch before heading up again into the **Oberalp Pass**. For many drivers, the sight of another set of bends is not at all welcome. However, there is nowhere else to go, although at **Andermatt** you have the choice of heading north to **Lucerne**. Andermatt is quite a nice town, with plenty of restaurants and hotels available for a meal or a welcome drink. The town has been a centre for travellers in all directions for many years, and there are references to the old stagecoaches (*diligences*) which used to make the same journey over the Furka some 115 years ago—the journey from Brig to Andermatt would take over 12 hours for the 92-km (57-mile) trip. As a crossroads of the country Andermatt remains a fairly easy-going town, and the winter attractions include a sk-lift system up to the **Gemsstock** mountain at 2,961 m (9,715 ft). The rail services tend to bypass Andermatt on the north–south route, using the **St Gotthard tunnel**. However, if you wanted to specifically come to the town, perhaps to take a trip up to the glacier, there is a rail service from **Goschenen**. This is a private rack railway, and the journey only takes 15 minutes. On the

west–east route all the trains stop at Andermatt going from Brig to Chur and vice versa. Travellers using the roads from the south, from Italy and the Ticino region of Switzerland, should realize that up until the end of May all the passes into the Valais, will be closed. The **Simplon**, the **Nufenen**, the **St Gothard**, the **Furka** and the **Susten Pass**, are not generally

accessible until early June. This means either taking a long route around through Lucerne, or going by train, in which case the only real option is the Simplon connection from **Bertonio**.

From the St Gothard Pass eastwards takes you into the **Ticino** and the **Engadine**—very much south-east Switzerland, which is covered in Chapter 7. Here you will encounter

*S*mall villages like Selva are the ones untouched by the tourist industry. They have remained an agricultural community.

another language, another culture, and the remains of the oldest Swiss language of them all—*Romansch*.

There is Some Gentle Heckling, but Usually the Proceedings are Orderly

At Appenzell and Glarus the last remaining examples of the *Landsgemeinde*—the open air parliament—can be found. Zurich, home of the world's bankers, can surprise with trips out on the Zürichsee, while the gentle hills of the Appenzell provide a soothing relief to the most commercial city of the country. At Stein am Rhein there is an open-air art gallery in the city centre, and not far along are the mighty Rhine Falls. It is another example of the great diversity found throughout the country.

Zurich

Zurich is without doubt the busiest city in Switzerland. It may not be the political centre, but commercially it is way ahead of any other city—and it shows. The rush and bustle of any large commercial centre is here, with its people toing and froing with little regard for the rest of humanity. It does have its attractions, however, hidden

Zurich in summer can be a very pleasant city, helped largely by the expanse of water, the Zürichsee.

away behind the smart shops, which most people cannot afford to buy from. It's worth paying a visit to **Jelmolis** (a department store), where it's easy to feel under-dressed compared with the assistants. All that glitters is not gold, however (although in Zurich there's a fair chance that it is), and there are some affordable items—such as the doner kebabs on sale outside the store.

On the positive side, Zurich has a large **lake** and a **quay**, which in winter is downright miserable, but in summer brightens up considerably. These, along with a few notable buildings and the **Swiss National Museum** (which is well worth a visit), are its saving

231

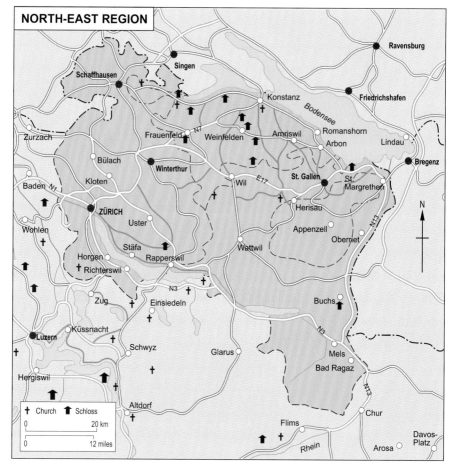

NORTH-EAST REGION

Map legend:
+ Church ▲ Schloss
0 — 20 km
0 — 12 miles

M ap of north-east Switzerland.

graces. You could live a life of luxury in any of the splendid hotels along the Belle Rive, but if do I think it hardly likely that you would be reading this guide book.

Zurich is a good place to look at, to sample, and then move on. If you are planning a couple of days, for business or pleasure, it's worth staying in one of its many suburban villages, especially those along the northern shores. You then have the choice of travelling into the city by bus, train or, best of all, by boat.

Transport

The northern side of the lake, that is where route 17 skirts the lake through **Zollikon**, **Kusnacht**, **Erlenbach** and **Herrliberg** (the villages continue along this road right through to **Rapperswil**, but at 24 km (15 miles) from the city, this is probably too far away to stay) is Zurich commuter country, and you will guess by the size of the mansions at

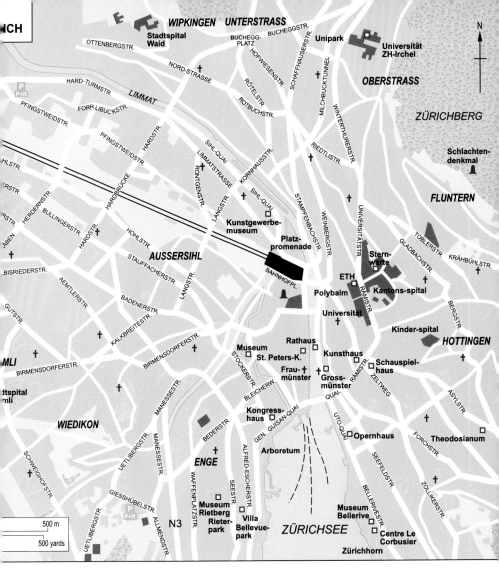

*T*own plan of Zurich.

the lakeside and in the hills that most of the cars on the road are Mercedes, Jaguars or Porsches.

There are three good reasons for not taking a car into Zurich. One is to save yourself the embarrassment of trying to park your hired Fiat Panda between the Ferrari and the Lambourghini. The second is that Zurich is full of underpasses and tunnels, which ought to be avoided. The worst example is on the road into the city on the N11 from St Gallen, where there are three tunnels to choose from—the middle one being a car park! The last problem is possibly the most hazardous—trams. There *are* ways of avoiding them in a car, but you have to be very aware of the rules, especially where the tram joins a single car lane.

233

If you have a car you would be advised to join the many commuters, and go by train or boat to the city. The train has the more frequent service and from a larger station such as Kusnacht, the schedule has at least one train per hour. One of the novelties is the double-deck carriages used on this line—by some clever design work they have managed to create two floors for each carriage and these bright, clean trains must make it almost a pleasure to commute to work. The fare is the same as for the boat.

The boat takes a little longer, about 30 minutes, but if there's a chance of breathing some decent air in Zurich, it must surely be on the lake. Again, from Kusnacht there are two early sailings, for the commuter traffic, and then there is a gap until 10.35a.m. For stages further down the shore, such as **Herrliberg**, the first sailings are not until after 11.00a.m. If this is the case

then you could go in by train and come back by boat. The Kusnacht service leaves Zurich from landing stage 3, usually on the hour, and the quay is situated opposite the point at which the Bahnhofstrasse joins the Burhile Platz, the **Schifflande Bahnhofstrasse**.

The trams are the best way to move around the city, although most of the sites are within walking distance. If you want to go from the Haupbahnhof to the quayside quickly, then tram number 11 is useful. The tickets are on a zone system, and the lowest local ticket will take you to most places. There is an annual rise in price, but at the time of writing it is 1.70 SFr. You

The trams in Zurich are by far the best way to move around the city, but beware of them if you are driving!

T he Landsmuseum, the Swiss National Museum, is certainly one of Zurich's most attractive buildings. It reflects the various styles of architecture to be found in the country, both inside and out.

could choose to buy a day ticket for the trams, if you think you'll be using them a lot.

Museums

By far the most interesting feature of Zurich is the **Landsmuseum** (The Swiss National Museum).

Landsmuseum
Museumstrasse.
Open: Tuesdays–Sundays, 10.00a.m. to 5.00p.m.

The museum is easy to find along from the railway station, and if you arrive by rail you will find it by coming out of the side of the station at the platform (*gleiss*) 17 end. The whole museum is housed in a **château** building, which has always belonged to the city of Zurich. It was constructed in 1892 as a reproduction of a castle for the purposes of housing the city's historical wealth. It has also re-created or used styles of room architecture from the various cantons of Switzerland.

The museum is split into five floors, and follows the history of the country from pre-historic and Roman times through the history of the confederation. There is a certain amount of trumpet-blowing, especially when it comes to the glory of the confederate armies. It does suffer from a slightly dry approach, when most museums are trying to breathe life into their exhibits.

One of the most interesting displays is the hall devoted to **arms and armour**. Swiss armaments in medieval times were legendary, and they not only hired out their soldiers to the various armies of Europe, but also made the weapons. The most obvious and famous was the **crossbow**, but some of the **swords** on display are staggering. How they were used is beyond me, and the variations adopted in the art of slicing someone's head off are endless. Breathing life into the use of such weapons would prove difficult, so they are safely placed behind glass. Another interesting part of this series of exhibits of war is the **model layout** of the **Battle of Morat**, which features the optimistic Duke of Burgundy—after his pounding at Grandson he regrouped his army to lay siege on Morat, and this model shows how the glorious confederates came, in the nick of time, to defeat his attempts to create a new empire in Switzerland. The layout shows just how many men were used in these affairs, thus accounting for the massive death tolls of war.

Other areas show stone-age, bronze-age and iron-age artifacts, the Romans in Helvetia (the original name for Switzerland), 16th-century Renaissance, 17th-century Baroque, through Napoleonic times to the modern era. Special exhibits are displayed on a temporary basis. General points of information in most of the display cases are in four languages: German, French, Italian and English, but information on individual artifacts is in German only, which can be annoying. In one section I thought that I had come across an example of an early Roman satellite dish, but there was nothing to confirm my discovery!

A useful guide book is for sale (one book per language) at the bag and coat depository next to the café. This is on the ground floor, near to the main entrance.

There are two other museums in Zurich:

Porcelain and Faience Museum
Munsterhof 20.
Open: Tuesdays–Fridays, 10.00a.m. to 12.00p.m. and 2.00–5.00p.m.
Saturdays, 10.00a.m. to 12.00p.m. and 2.00–4.00p.m.
Sundays, 10.00a.m. to 12.00p.m. and 2.00–5.00p.m.

This is an off-shoot of the National Museum, and is in the **Guildhale**, near the **Fraumunster** and the **Munster Bridge**. It houses collections of fine porcelain from the 18th century, and the settings are in beautiful rococo-style rooms.

Museum of Domestic Living
Barengasse 20–22.
Open: Tuesdays–Fridays, 10.00a.m. to 12.00p.m. and 2.00–5.00p.m.
Saturdays, 10.00a.m. to 12.00p.m. and 2.00–4.00p.m.
Sundays, 10.00a.m. to 12.00p.m. and 2.00–5.00p.m.
If you are interested in how people lived in days gone by you will find this museum particularly fascinating. The two buildings showing the exhibits were moved here from a point about 60 km (37 miles) away and then re-stored. Inside there are rooms showing the lifestyle of Zurich people through the centuries.

O pen air cafés bring an atmosphere of relaxation to the normally frantic city of Zurich.

Other Buildings of Interest
The main buildings of interest in the city are the **cathedral** at Munsterplatz and **St Peter's**, which is probably in the most interesting part of Zurich. Coming off the Bahnhofstrasse at In Gassen, or any of the streets around here, will take you into the narrow passageways of **old Zurich**. On the other side of the River Limmat the area from Gross Munster ot Central, by way of Munstergrasse, Hirschen platz and Niederhofstrasse is also part of old Zurich.

The Lake Side
The city is much improved by its lake position, and there are not too many cities of this size where you can hire a

*O*n the River Limmat at Zurich the pleasure boats give the city the feel of a summer resort.

pedalo and head out into open waters. In this respect Zurich is something of an anomaly. After pounding the streets you can come over the bridge by the cathedral and find hundreds of boats to hire. Motor boats, rowing boats and pedalos are moored outside ice-cream huts, giving it a summer resort atmosphere. This part of the city is beautiful on a sunny day, but the whole scene takes on the drab appearance of an unused fairground in winter.

Nightlife
You may think that, being a large city, the noise and bustle would continue into the night. This is not so. Zurich is quiet—not exactly empty, but certainly not lively—in the evenings. Unlike Basel and Bern where there is a good atmosphere, Zurich seems to simply peter out at night. Perhaps the people who make Zurich tick cannot do what they are best at—making money—out of hours.

Atlantis in Zürichsee
Around 4500 BC settlers in this area lived in stilt houses on the lake shore. These villages were dotted around the lake, and there are thought to have been around 34 settlements. This would account for many of the artifacts found in the depths of the Zürichsee by underwater archaeologists, who also believe there may have been a village at the deepest part of the lake some 6,500 years ago.

Accommodation

My preference is to stay out of the city in the suburbs, but if you do want to stay in the centre there is certainly plenty of choice. At the top end, if you want to enjoy five-star treatment, the two best-looking hotels are on the Belle Rive: the **Eden au Lac**, and next door the **Belle Rive au Lac**. There is not much to choose between them except the odd 100 SFr. Have all your credit cards ready—these will cost you between 400 and 500 SFr per night for a double room.

There is a multitude of three-star establishments, costing around 150 SFr for a double room. Zurich is expensive, and if you do go for the cheaper hotels you are not going to get the equivalent of a country hotel—in fact, some of the two- and one-star hotels look decidedly seedy and you will still be paying about 100 SFr. In the three-star range a favourite is the **Hotel Franziskarer**, which is very much in the heart of things, on Neiderdorfstrasse. Just out of town, near the university buildings, there are a number of hotels: **Hotel Bristol**, Strampfenbachstrasse (three-star) and **The Rutile** (three-star), Zahringerstrasse.

To take up my point about suburban hotels, I can recommend a guesthouse hotel in **Herrliberg**. It has no stars, but serves excellent food and costs around 120 SFr for a double room. It is the **Gusthof Rebe** (Grape Hotel) and is situated in the village. It is signposted on the main route 17. From Herrliberg you can go to **Kusnacht** for a more regular rail connection, or wait for the boat later in the morning—whatever, it certainly beats the problems of the city.

A further advantage to staying down at this part of the lake for those with cars is that when you want to leave the Zurich area southwards you do not need to drive through the city to get to the other side. From Herrliberg, for instance, it is a ten-minute drive to the car ferry at **Meilen**. The ferry, which takes everything from bicycles to buses, goes over to **Horgen** on the opposite bank. It is a very regular service, running every 15 minutes, and the cost for a car is about 7 SFr for a one-way journey.

Youth Hostel
Zurich-Wollishofen
Mutschellerstrasse 114.
Tel: (01) 4823544.

Camping
Zurich Seebucht: this is the closest you will get to Zurich in a tent, but it is a good site, on the Zürichsee. It is a four-star site on the See Strasse, just past the Wollishofen Quay.
Open: 1 May–30 September.

Hausen Turlersee: this is slightly further out into the hills but it is not too far from Zurich. However, it could be a difficult journey into the city compared with the previous entry. A two-star site on a small lake.
Open: 1 April–31 October.

Around Zurich
The area within the triangle of Zurich, Basel and Bern contains Switzerland's major concentration of motorways, and it is not very difficult to travel from one city to the other quickly. There are a number of small attractions in this region but most people,

especially the locals, are usually simply moving from one major city centre to another.

Some way out of Zurich, but certainly within the distance of a day trip, is the **Wildegg Castle**. This has been taken into the jurisdiction of the National Museum and is an impressive site on the hill overlooking the Aare valley. The castle was constructed in the 13th century, and follows the style of this type of building throughout northern Switzerland. High, flat walls with a steep roof were obviously a good design for defence. Inside the castle there are rooms arranged in the settings of a Bernese family from the 17th to the 19th century.

The only other town in this region, which is really bordering on central Switzerland, is **Solothurn**.

Solothurn

This is a fairly large industrial town that most tourists pass by on their way to Neuchâtel, Geneva and Lausanne, which is a pity because it has a lot of character. If you are staying in the town, or stopping off on your way to another region, you will see some interesting sights. The town is closely attached to the **River Aare**, and strides the river as it turns to head for **Lake Biel**. The northern bank has the older section of the town, with its 17th-century walls still intact. Within the walls are the **Jesuit church** (also 17th-century) and the **Cathedral of St Ursas**. Solothurn has a small centre and **old town** which would not take very long to explore. One of the most interesting museums here is the **Arsenal** (*Altes Zeughaus*), although the German tank comes as something of a surprise, on

the ground floor. In the narrow streets are the now-familiar flowers and shuttered windows, which make a colourful sight in summer. Over on the other side of the river (go by way of the **Kreuzackerbrücke**), is Solothurn's most famous landmark, **Krummturn**. This twisted **tower** is in gardens at the riverside, and those coming into the town by rail from Biel will get a good view of the tower by taking a seat at the right of the carriage.

There are three other museums: the **museum of fine arts** and the **natural**

history **museum** are of some interest, but the **Blumstein museum** is good, and since it is set in a park could make a pleasant day out. The Blumstein is marked as *Schloss Blumstein* and is found on the outskirts of the town on the **Untere Steingrubenstrasse**.

The Glarnerland

This is an area easily missed by visitors going from Zurich to the Engadine through Chur. It is something of a

*A*t the Glarus open parliament the whole community of the canton meet to decide on local issues.

backwater in tourist terms, yet has some lovely scenery with high, steep-sided valleys, a few ski-lift systems for the winter, and plenty of good walking in the summer. Prices tend to be lower here, with hotel costs about half of those in the Engadine and the Valais.

241

At the centre of the Glarnerland is the good-sized town of **Glarus** which is probably more well-known for the yearly *Landsgemeinde*—the public open-air parliament.

Coming from Zurich the turn-off to the valley and Glarus is at **Zeigelbrücke**. Surprisingly, Glarus is signposted on the motorway from just outside Zurich, so drivers will have no difficulty in finding it. Glarus is about 15 km (9 miles) from the turn-off and really, apart from the road up to the **Obersee**, this town is the first one of any interest.

Glarus

Although a fairly large light-industrial town, the centre is quite small, so it is no distance to walk from the railway station to the town square. It is here that the proceedings begin for the annual debate on cantonal affairs, on the first Sunday in May.

The Landsgemeinde

Glarus is one of only three cantons (the others are Appenzell Inner and Outer, so it really is only two towns) which still hold a public parliament. It is a serious and well-respected event, full of the pomp and ceremony practised by officials in all countries. Switzerland is no more traditional in this respect than Britain or USA, but it is good to see such things happen at a local level. The town councillors arrive to salutes and a brass band at 9.00a.m. and solemnly walk in pairs through the doors of the town hall. Thirty minutes later they all come out again headed by a dignitary carrying the huge cantonal sword. The procession slowly makes its way to the **Landsgemeinde platz**, where a raised platform awaits the day's speakers. The town's population, plus visitors, sit on benches and stand on galleries around the centrepiece. It is an impressive sight, and even if you have trouble understanding the language it's very interesting to watch this spectacle of democracy in action.

Each issue is put forward by a number of speakers: it is not a debate, simply a variety of views by different people. On some issues there may be only two speakers, on others as many as five. The decisions are made by a show of raised hands, with experienced adjudicators assessing the numbers. There is some gentle heckling, but the proceedings are orderly and good humoured. There can be 10 or a dozen issues to be decided on, so the affair takes up the whole morning.

As with most Swiss politics, the decisions tend to stay on the conservative side, so although the views of say, a socialist, are put forward, they are unlikely to have much support. What is interesting is that the people who do support that view can be seen to do so when they raise their hands—it is one thing to have a ballot by putting a cross on a piece of paper, quite another to vote openly against your neighbour.

While this serious and proper affair is taking place, the rest of the streets take on a market appearance. Since 7.00a.m. the stallholders have been busy getting their wares ready for the thousands of visitors. Few of the items have any relevance to Switzerland, never mind Glarus: balloons, T-shirts, records and all the paraphernalia of the fairground is here, along with plenty of *wurst* salesmen. You can usually find some good things among the junk, and the normally very expensive wooden toys can be bought here relatively cheaply.

In all, the events of the day are probably quite a boost to a town which doesn't attract the casual visitor—the hotels are full and the street traders do good business. If you plan to pay a visit to the Landsgemeinde, book a room in advance, since accommodation is difficult to get on the day or the night before.

Accommodation

In Glarus itself there is a good choice of hotels, all within easy distance of the railway station. The most expensive is the Glarrerhof (three-star), but the two-star Stadhof or Rossili provide good, simple accommodation for around 50 SFr.

There is plenty of accommodation in the area in small villages or in the larger towns such as **Linthal**. If going to **Braunwald** the only way up is using the railway, which takes about six minutes from Linthal. The last train up is at 9.55p.m.

Camping

Campers, surprisingly, have little choice in the Garnerland, and two of the nearest sites to Glarus are some distance away on **Lake Klontal**. This is about a 30-minute drive from Glarus, but there are bus services. The two sites are at each end of this turquoise lake, which has dramatically steep sides:

Klontalesee Guntlenau: this is the first site you come to when travelling from Glarus. It is a non-classified site for tents only.
Open: 15 May–30 September.

Klongalersee Vorauen: at the opposite end of the lake, another non-classified site but available for caravans as well as tents.
Open: 15 May–30 September.

Elm

One of the most pleasant villages of the region is **Elm**. It is right at the end of a valley running south-east from **Schwanden**. On the way to Elm there are two smaller villages—**Engi** and **Matt**—and although a non-metalled road does run on to **Wichlen**, Elm is very much the end of the road. The town is surrounded by steep-sided mountains, which in Swiss terms are not very high at around 2,900 m (9,514 ft). Nevertheless, the scene is dramatic, with huddles of farm buildings on the lower slopes.

Walking

Around Elm there are some good walks over the mountains. From **Wichlen**, over the **Richetilipass**, there is a six-hour walk to **Linthal**. You can walk over to the Flims/Laax lift system via the **Panixerpass** or the **Segnespass**, but it would take you some time to return by public transport.

Accommodation

Elm has four hotels, one of which, the Sardona, purports to be four-star but, as with many of these chain hotels, the actual facilities are disappointing. Centred in the village are the Hotel Sonne, the Elmer and the Segnes, which charge more realistic prices, representing better value for money. If you are looking for a quiet holiday, then Elm offers just that.

The visit to Elm is very much a special journey, since you have to come back to route 17 to carry on up the valley. The road continues over the **Klausenpass** to **Altdorf** and the **Brummer**, but the rail services stop at Linthal. There is a line here which takes you up to **Brunuwald**, which has a reasonable lift system for the **Eggstock** (2,449 m; 8,035 ft). This is the largest lift system of the Glarnerland.

This region, taking in the valley of the **River Linth** and the lakes between Glarus and Schwyz is rarely visited; most people go from the big international airports at Zurich and Geneva to the Valais. As with rural France, there is a wealth of beautiful countryside, small villages and quiet roads in these backwaters of Switzerland, making them perfect stopping places-between the larger centres.

Liechtenstein

One place which does attract many visitors on the way to the high mountain resorts is **Liechtenstein**. Sandwiched between Switzerland and Austria, is it in Switzerland or not? There are no borders or frontiers, and although the principality does have its own flag, it is very much assisted in many ways by Switzerland. As a day out, or as a stopping point on the way to the south, **Vaduz**, the capital, is a pleasant town, dominated by the **Schloss Vaduz**.

There are eleven villages in Liechtenstein, each with their own crest; even the smallest, with its population of about 300, has one. The state describes itself as "the best of Europe in the

*T*he castle of the *Prince of Liechtenstein at Vaduz sits on the hills above the capital town.*

244

smallest package", and you cannot really disagree. It's picturesque, it has a good selection of attractions such as castles, swimming pools, mountains for hiking, and a fair degree of history.

The original site can be traced back to 4000 BC, but the country of Vaduz was formed in 1342. It then followed a similar pattern to Switzerland and has largely followed the doctrine of the Swiss, including the right to neutrality—not that its neighbours ever saw it as a serious threat. In political terms the major difference between here and Switzerland is the hereditary monarch, currently Prince Hans-Adams II.

For many non-Europeans the idea of a prince in a castle in a principality the size of Liechtenstein (population about 28,000) is too much to imagine. Vaduz is regularly included on tours, showing visitors from the Far East and the Americas that such a place does indeed exist. If you want a genuine Liechtenstein passport stamp, you can get one at the tourist information office in the centre of Vaduz.

Notwithstanding the slightly commercial aspect to the principality, it is a nice place to visit and there are some lesser-known parts.

Seven of the villages are to the north, where within a very small area there is good hiking, cycling and two indoor swimming pools.

Accommodation

Taking in the villages of **Eschen**, **Gamprin**, **Ruggell** and **Schellenberg** will provide you with all these attractions in a splendidly quiet and beautiful setting. Hotels are not around every corner, so a telephone call in advance may be prudent. The Eintrqucht and the Fernsicht at Eschen have nine rooms between them, whilst at **Nendeln** there are 32 rooms between the Hotels Engel, Landhaus and Schalses Weinstube. There is one hotel at each of the villages of **Berdern**, **Ruggell** and **Schellenberg**. There is camping at Gamprin, Berdern and at Triesen.

The area around **Triesen**, just south of Vaduz, does seem to be well set up for visitors, although to be fair the area of **Triesenberg** does take in five other hamlets including **Malban**. This village has made itself a winter ski resort situated at 1,600 m (5,249 ft). It has eight hotels and six lifts. Most of the runs are red category, which seems to suit most vacation skiers, and there is also a cross-country course and a toboggan run.

Vaduz

If your visit to the principality is just a one-day affair, a quick hop off the N13, then Vaduz is the most likely place to visit. It is easy to see the main street, get your passport stamped, send a postcard with those special stamps, and get on your way. However, there are some specialities:

The Postage Stamp Museum
Stadtle 37.
Liechtenstein has a history of producing interesting stamps and has thus created a small museum devoted to its philatelic development.

Liechtenstein National Museum
Stadtle 43.
Open: 1 May–31 October, 10.00a.m. to 12.00p.m. and 1.00–5.00p.m.
Closed Mondays.
1 November–30 April, 2.00–5.30p.m.

The museum's collection is entirely made up of items portraying the history of the state from prehistoric times to the present. Included is a collection of Liechtenstein coins, as well as firearms, some of which belong to the current prince.

Liechtenstein Wines

For some one-upmanship in wine circles you can reserve, in advance, a wine tasting session in the *Hofkellerai des reguerender Fursten von Liechtenstein* (or the wine cellars of the ruling Prince). The wine is from the private vineyards of the family, and to make a reservation you should contact:

Feudsftrasse 4
FL-9490 Vaduz.
Tel: (075) 21018.
Mark the envelope "Wine Tasting".

Out of Vaduz there is another wine cellar at **Nendeln**, not quite as royal, but they offer tasting of a range of 250 different European wines for 5–50 people. Reservation is necessary, from:

Schachles Weinstube
Churer Strasse 263
FL-9485 Nendeln.
Tel: (075) 34144.

Liechtenstein Pottery

Also in Nendeln you can see a pottery demonstration and you can buy ceramics made here. The pottery from Liechtenstein is particularly good, so it may be worth a trip here.

Schaedler Keramik AG, Nendeln
Open: Mondays–Fridays, 8.00a.m. to 12.00p.m. and 1.30–5.00p.m.

The Rhine provides the border between Switzerland and Liechtenstein, although there are no frontier posts. Back over on the Swiss side, the N13 motorway runs north to Germany and south to Chur and the Italian lakes. Travelling west via **Buchs** will take you into another of those unspoilt country areas, with two reasonably high mountain ranges. The other canton to hold a Landsgemeinde is in this region, at **Appenzell** and slightly further to the north the city of **St Gallen**.

The view from the road over the Rhine valley is outstanding. This road will take you into an area called **Churfirsten**, which comprises a valley with three villages, of which **Wildhaus** is the largest. Between this, and the other two villages of **Unterwasser** and **Alt St Johann**, there is good walking to be had in summer.

Churfirsten

Wildhaus

The village sits astride the main road, route 16, but takes in some of the outlying roads to provide access to the mountain lifts. The lifts go to the summit of **Gamserragg** via **Oberdorf**. Unusually, this is one ski area which does not have a lot of cafés and restaurants attached to its mountainside, which may be the reason for its appeal. The ski runs include a good number of the testing black variety, and cross-country skiing is well catered for with some high-level routes. The Gamserragg is 2,076 m (6,811 ft) high, so the snow levels could be a problem in bad years for this area.

Walking

For the summer there are walks throughout the region, which is full of soft undulating hillsides rather than steep mountainsides. I would think that the walking may be better than the skiing here, and once you are at the Oberdorf station of the lift there are some really good walks to the lake of **Voralpsee** and through forested areas at **Gupfenweld**. For the more seasoned walker (although this can also be enjoyed in parts) is the **Thurweg**. This is a 60-km (37-mile) walk using the River Thur as a route from **Wil** to Wildhaus. It is quite a gentle walk, much of it alongside the river, and the only real climb is from **Nesslaus** at 754 m (2,474 ft) up to Wildhaus at 1,090 m (3,576 ft). The suggested time for the walk is 17 hours.

On the route from the Wildhaus area to Appenzell, the pass goes through heavily forested hillsides.

Swimming

One attraction that I would not be all that keen to use is the outdoor swimming facility, which is actually a small lake. Often these lakes are described as swimming amenities but they are very basic. Take the turning to **Schonenboden** out of the village centre, past the small army barracks, and the lake is about 4 km (2½ miles) away. There is also a heated outdoor pool, and three indoor public pools.

The next village down the road, moving east to west, is **Unterwasser**.

Switzerland's Customs and Traditional Festivals

Switzerland is a traditional country. It often delves deep into its past , keeping alive customs and traditions many countries would forget. In an attempt to show how seriously Switzerland takes its history, the tourist office produces a list of the cultural traditions of the land. In an introductory passage, the message is: "If you understand our traditions and where they have come from, you will understand our country better". Quite rightly it is pointed out that so often, a festival is kept alive as a tourist attraction, giving it a commercial edge which can ruin the original reason for the event. This would seem to be less of the case in Switzerland, although while some fairs and festivals are commercial, many are village affairs with the most peculiar of backgrounds.

The events are spread over the calendar year, and occur throughout the country. A visitor can quite easily come across one of these processions or fairs without prior knowledge, making a holiday or visit that much more special. To help ensure this is the case, this is not a definitive guide to all the fairs and festivals of Switzerland, but more of a pointer to the kind of thing that you may come across, summer, winter, spring or autumn.

Christmas is an important time in Switzerland. Not because there is a mass of shopping to buy, or a turkey to be eaten, but because in a great number of villages across the country, December features some very traditional events. Hallwil, in the Aargau canton has a few interesting events, well before the start of the Christmas season. A whip-cracking contest takes place in the last week of November or the first week of December. The classes of whip cracker are split into three age groups, with an equivalently long whip to crack. The length varies between 3 and 5 m (10 and 16 ft), and the judges adjudicate on the skill of each performance. This theme is carried on later in the month when boys between the ages of 12 and 14 see to the pursuit of St Nicholas by cracking their whips. On Christmas Eve and Christmas Day, the same boys, along with seven girls act out an old custom restricted to a small number of the village community. A Christmas child, veiled and dressed in white, visits families of the village, along with six companions. The *Wheinechtchind* (Christmas Child), greets all in silence, and distributes cakes to the tune of carols.

The programme of events in Hallwil continues on New Year's Eve, when village communities meet on the hill above the village at the bonfire. At 10 minutes to midnight eight men flail a threshing board, but stop just a few moments from midnight,. The threshing begins again with greater enthusiasm immediately after the sound of the New Year's bells. The point of all this is to cleanse the air of evil spirits for the New Year.

To complete the cycle, there is the Barzelitag on 2 January, when 15 unmarried adults run masked through the village. Split into two groups, the "Greens" symbolize spring and life, while the "Browns" represent winter and death.

This series of events in Hallwil is typical of the traditional calendar found in Switzerland at Christmas. At Kussnacht am Rigi, in the very heart of the country, you will find bishops' mitres of enormous proportions on 5 December.

Geneva has a winter custom not associated with the Christmas festivals. This is the Escalade, which re-creates

the scaling of the city ramparts on 11 and 12 December by French soldiers. It is an historical procession, and always features a person playing the character of Madame Royaume, who in defence of her city poured a pot of hot soup on a Savoy soldier.

The events of Laupen have been mentioned in the context of the pig

Strange-looking French horns rise above the crowds at the Basel Fasnacht, probably the biggest of Swiss festivals. Be prepared to have plenty of stamina if you decide to visit, as it goes on for 72 hours!

bladder beating, and this Bernese town celebrates the New Year in this fashion. Curious it certainly is, and up until now I have found no real explanation for this slightly odd behaviour. The "broom" men waving their poles of juniper branches, and the "bladder" men carry out their pranks purely for the fun of it. Its history is not that long since it would seem to have started in the early 19th century. It was clearly so much fun for the participants that they had to carry it on!

In Basel, the forerunner to the Fasnacht takes place early in the year. This is the Vogel Gryff, and takes place on the River Rhine. Always facing Kleinbasel, a masked figure carries an uprooted pine tree. With him on the boat are two drummers, two cannoneers, and flag bearers. At the Middle Bridge, the figure is met by two strange creatures, one a dancing lion, the other a bird with a particularly nasty beak. At noon the three figures dance alone on the bridge, symbolizing the old societies.

The valley of Lötschental is in itself an historic part of Switzerland, and on the Thursday before Shrove Tuesday there is a carnival featuring grotesque masks. This is one carnival which may have succumbed to the tourist industry in so much as the masks have become souvenir items. However, the carnival does go back some time, and the reason for the event is to scare away evil spirits from the valley. The spirits would live in the chimneys, and once scared away would fly from their homes covered in soot.

At this time of year Switzerland is in full swing, in terms of festivals and carnivals, and it is likely that a visitor could easily stumble on some procession or other. In the Ticino there is an Italian-based carnival—The Rice Carnival—and in Zug there is a torchlight procession which coincides with the events in Basel.

The Basel Fasnacht has been mentioned in some detail, but if there is a chance to see this oddity of Swiss life on one of the three days and nights, then it is well worth going to see.

Once the winter and Christmas and New Year events are gone, the spring and Easter festivals take place. On Good Friday, in the small town of Romont, there is the 15th-century custom called the *Pleureuses*. It is a Christian custom whereby a funeral procession of mourners dressed in veiled black outfits sombrely proceed through the streets. It is a solemn affair, which may not be that appealing to the general onlooker. *Pleureuses* means "weepers".

On a slightly lighter note, May Day heralds the coming of spring, and it is celebrated across the country.

In the spring in the Valais, there are cow fights. If mention of this activity is about to bring out the anti-cruelty to animals lobby, then it has to be said that this is a purely natural phenomenon. Cows of the Hérens breed organize themselves into a hierarchy, and the choice of which cow fights which is left entirely to the animals themselves. The purpose is to choose a queen cow, who will lead the rest of the herd up to the meadows. Whether this is an actual event or custom is doubtful, but it is something to look out for when in the Valais at this time of year.

Some of the events only take place every other year, or even every three years. Such an event takes place in St Gall. The Kinderfest is held in 1992, but not again until 1995. It is a children's festival, and is held on the parade-ground in the city.

The 1 August is an important day in Switzerland, being the celebratory day of the beginnings of the confederation. 1991 saw the 700th birthday of the country, and although it featured pomp, ceremony and fireworks, it did create some tension among the various national groups of the country. It is as good a day as any to be in Geneva, or any of the big lake-side towns, because if nothing else there is likely to be a good firework display.

The wine regions show their flags in the autumn, for this is harvest time. Lugano, Neuchâtel and Schaffhausen all have their harvest festivals. The events take on the customary processions of floats and bright costumes. Of them all the Lugano Vintage Festival on the first weekend of October is likely to be the best in the country.

Finally, as the winter approaches, there has to be one of those odd traditions, which does have its reasons, although they may not be too obvious. To celebrate the end of the harvest, Sursee engages in a *Gansabhauet,* or a knocking down of a goose. The bird is already dead, but it is hung feet down on a platform outside the town hall. Competitors dressed in a purple robe, a mask in the shape of a sun and blindfolded are invited to knock the unfortunate goose down, with a blunt sabre. One attempt is allowed, and the participants are usually young boys. In between the thrilling sight of these strangely dressed boys hurling their sabres at a dead goose, there are children's contests, such as sack races, and ugly mask competitions. It sounds like fun for all the family.

Whichever time of year you happen to be in Switzerland, there is a good chance that there will be a festival, or procession of some kind happening. It is unlikely to be advertised, since most of these events are really for the locals. Visitors will be welcome, but the traditions of the country will not be forsaken to make these tourist attractions, which makes the finding of such a custom all the more pleasurable.

The confetti rains down on players and watchers alike during Basel's festival.

Unterwasser

This is a smaller place altogether, with some reasonable hotels to offer. The main lift goes from here to the summit of **Mt Chasserug** (2,262 m; 7,421 ft), with a stop at **Iltios** on the way.

Alt St Johann

The last in this threesome of villages is Alt St Johann, which is at the end of the valley. Smaller again than the others, it is generally a quieter place, with a small lift up to **Selemart**. One of the attractions here is to go up to a level on the mountainside at one village, walk on the same level across to one of the other stations, and come back down to that village. If you enjoy walking, but not necessarily hill climbs, then this area is ideal. The more ambitious walker can walk the ridges on the northern side and move onto the **Santis** lift system, taking you into the Appenzell district.

Accommodation

Like so many of the smaller, quieter areas, it is significantly cheaper to stay in the valley. Hotel rooms can cost as little as 50 SFr for a double room, and for skiers a seven-day pass for the whole area is around 175 SFr; this gives you access to 15 ski-lifts plus the cable car, the chair-lifts and the funicular railway.

The hotels vary from the Sporthotel, such as the Toggenburg at Wildhaus, to the small Hotel Waldi with costs from 100 SFr to 160 SFr per night. **Wildhaus** has the best choice of accommodation with the aforementioned Toggenburg, the Hotel Sonne and the wonderfully named Friedegg being worth a try. In **Unterwasser**, the largest

of the hotels, the Hotel Santis, is at the bend of the road, just before the village. Just before the hill down into Unterwasser is the Waldi, which is good, clean and inexpensive. At **Alt St Johann** there is a more imposing hotel, the Schweizehof, but it is still quite reasonable. Higher up, at the **Selemitt** station, there is an 80-room *gusthaus*, which is useful for skiers or hikers.

Camping

There are two sites in this valley, one at each end:

Wildhaus Schafbergblick: this is at the eastern entrance to the valley at Wildhaus. It is on the lift side of the road as you come towards Wildhaus village, almost opposite the PTT stop. It is a non-classified site.
Open throughout the year.

Alt St Johann Eidgenossen: this is also a non-classified site, 2–3 km (1¼–2 miles) out of the village. It is next to a PTT stop on the road junction where the road runs into the village.
Open throughout the year.

Although these are both non-classified sites they are very close to all the village amenities so there is no need to go without anything—including a swim.

The Schwalgalp Pass

Further along the road at another **St Johann** (**Neu**), you can go over the **Schwalgalp Pass** and into Appenzell—one of the oldest, original Swiss cantons.

The journey over the pass is delightful, passing thickly forested hillsides and by the side of the river which brings life up on **Mount Stockberg.** It is an easy drive and mountain bikers would enjoy the journey. This area is used as a training ground for the army post at Wildhaus, and it is not unusual to see a young soldier in a woollen cape huddled by a smoky fire.

At the top of the pass a right fork will take you to the **Santis Mountain** lift system. To say it is a bit out of the way of things would be an understatement, and the only reason I can see for there being anything on the mountain at all is the fact that it is the highest point in the area, at just over 2,500 m (8,202 ft). It is a rocky, unattractive peak, but for day trips from St Gallen it is probably a good day out.

On the way down, looking right, you will see a sliced-off hillside: the forest grows to the very edge of a cliff about halfway up the mountainside, as though a knife has literally sliced a piece off.

This road takes you into **Umasch,** where there is a well-signposted route to Appenzell. If you are on public transport you will have to use the PTT service to Umasch, but from there a local service will take you to Appenzell. This little railway meanders across the road, over fields and through forests on its way to Appenzell. It is a lovely sight to see the red train in amongst some of the greenest countryside anywhere in the world.

The Appenzell

If rolling, soft green hills are your thoughts of an ideal scene, the Appenzell is just the place for you. The rugged glory of the Alps may be one Switzerland; this should be regarded as just as typical. From Umasch on through to the town of Appenzell it is all fields, cows and peace. Anyone with a heart problem or high blood pressure should come here—it is very soothing.

Appenzell is a particularly artistic town, and the chemist shop—the Drogerie *—has a splendid collection of herbal drawings on its façade.*

Appenzell

Like Glarus, the town holds its cantonal Landsgemeinde every year. It is slightly different in that there are two Appenzell cantons, inner and outer, so the public meeting moves from the town square to the country meeting place from year to year. The system is the same though, and while Glarus waits until May, Appenzell holds its Landsgemeinde on the last Sunday in April.

With the amount of farming in this region it is not surprising that the spread of the town is quite large. But it does have a picturesque and colourful **village centre** dating back centuries. In this part of the world the image of cow appears on just about everything—it is the focal point for local industry in the production of cheese and milk, it appears on buildings, clothes, leatherware and in paintings. The peasant art of the Appenzell is not particularly to my liking, but then I am not an authority on Swiss art. What I do like, however, is the **decorative work** on some of the buildings in the main street. The lower *drogerie* (chemist) has superb paintings of herbs on the front of its building. This main street also has a terrific collection of shop signs: for the *drogerie*, the goldsmith, the odd hotel and so on. It is a small, tight street, so the effect of these signs is even more eye-catching. In the main square are some of the oldest houses and buildings in the town.

History

To find out more about the Appenzell culture and its history it is worth making a visit to **Stein**, which is only about 2 km (1¼ miles) out of Appenzell.

Appenzeller Volkskunde Museum (Folklore Museum).

Open: January–March, Sundays, 10.00a.m. to 5.00p.m.
April–October, Sundays, 10.00a.m. to 6.00p.m. Tuesdays–Saturdays, 10.00a.m. to 12.00p.m. and 1.30–5.00p.m. Closed Mondays.
November–December, Tuesdays–Saturdays, 1.30–5.00p.m. Closed Mondays.

The museum is set among beautiful gardens and open fields, and goes into the working of the dairy farmers, their cows and their art. There are some good working demonstrations of cheese making, weaving and embroidery sections. The dress of the Appenzell women is quite distinctive, and if you were to witness the Landsgemeinde you would see the traditional dress of the region. You would also see all the men wearing their swords, which is one difference to the event at Glarus. The museum gives a good understanding of life in the green valleys of the Appenzell, and possibly shows why the cow is such a prominent feature of life here.

Next to the museum there is a demonstration dairy. Similar to the one in Gruyères, it gives a run down on the cheese-making process, and has a shop and restaurant should you like the sample the produce.

Museums in Appenzell

In the town of Appenzell there are a few museums showing local crafts and culture, although the one at Stein is by far the best. Another way of seeing the local arts and crafts is to browse in the shops in the main street.

Heuriatmuseum
Open: July–November 2.00–4.00p.m.

Retorios Mech Musik Museum
Situated between the Postplatz and the Bahnhof, this is a private museum of wood carving and furniture at the **Blauen House**, **Weissadstrasse**. This is by the river on the opposite bank to the parking area.

Out From Appenzell

Appenzell is a good centre because of its position, but in the town there are also tennis courts, indoor and outdoor swimming pools and mini-golf. Add those to the excellent walking and cycling possibilities and you have the basis for a healthy holiday—provided you don't over-indulge in the produce of the Appenzell cow.

From the station there are connections to railways as well as a number of chair-lifts and cable cars running into the hills and mountains. Going south-west towards **Urnash** the local railway, the Appenzaller Bahnhon SB, links up with the cable car at **Jakobsbad** to go to the top of **Kronberg** (1,663 m; 5,456 ft). If you go east into the steeper mountains you can go up to **Holer Kaser** (1,795 m; 5,889 ft). This trip involves taking the train to **Weisbad**, the bus to **Brulisau**, and then a cable car up to the mountain top. From here you can look over the flat valley to **Feldkirch** and the Austrian Alps. Another cable car trip in this area is to the **Ebenalp**, which is a good starting point for walks to **Seealpsee**.

Accommodation in Appenzell

Most visitors like to stay in or near the village, as it has the best atmosphere.

There is a good number of hotels in this area, considering its size. The most obvious, by colour and position, is the Hotel Santis. It is in the **Landsgemeinde platz** so is very much at the centre of things, but it is quite expensive. Also in the main square almost opposite the Santis is the Hotel Appenzell, which is not quite as expensive. In the main street (*Hauptgasse*) there are the Lowen and the Krone, of which the latter is a chain hotel. The rest of the hotels are spread out around the village, and the cheapest of the group is the Pension Union in Gringelstrasse which offers accommodation at about one-third of the cost of the Santis. If you are coming to see the Landsgemeinde you must book your rooms well in advance—it is a more spectacular event than its counterpart in Glarus and Appenzell is a smaller town, so accommodation is scarce. Also bear in mind that the event happens in this town centre every two years—there will be gatherings in the town in 1992, 1994, 1996 and so on.

Outside Appenzell quite a few of the villages have hotels and guest houses, although costs are not much lower than in the main town. There are hotels at **Glen** (The Baren, Pension Chalet Erika), **Hasten** (The Rossli and higher up the hillside The Leermansteig), **Brulisau** (The Krone and The Rossli), **Schwende** (The Alpenblick, The Edelweiss, Frote Aussicht), **Weissbad** (The Weissbadbruke, The Gemste, Kurhaus Bio Sara [a health centre] and the Loosmuhile), **Wasserauen** (The Alpenrose, The Bahnhof).

In this region of north-east Switzerland one area tends to run into another, unlike the high Alpine villages where you are very much restricted by the high mountains. This is more touring country and having been in, say, the Wildhaus and Appenzell districts, you can add a city trip to your itinerary by a visit to **St Gallen**.

St Gallen

This is a city that on the face of it has little to offer, but inside the hard shell is a cultural nut of the highest order— The St Gallen **cathedral** and **library**.

The rest of the city is a busy commercial centre, but at the very heart of it is a small village-like section called

*T*he site of St Gallen was founded in the 7th century by the Irish monk Gallus.

the **Klosterwiertal**. These are the signs to look out for, because although the twin spires of the cathedral can be seen from a distance, it can be quite difficult to find your way through the maze of streets to get into the cathedral area. The cathedral, the churches, and the houses make up what was once a small village community centred around the **monastery** which dates back to the 8th century.

The Cathedral

The monk who began this development, an Irishman named Gallus, started it off in 612. The abbey continued to grow as a cultural and religious centre for the next 1,200 years, and it wasn't until 1805 that the building ceased to be a monastery. In the last part of its life as an abbey, the building was decorated with the most fantastic Baroque art, all of which remains today.

It is one of those sights which takes your breath away. No photographs can quite do justice to the splendour of the ceiling decoration and stucco plasterwork. It is a monumental piece of art and history that, given the opportunity, you should not miss.

Abbey Library

Alongside the cathedral is the abbey library. It was constructed at about the same time as the cathedral **towers** were added. The unique aspect of the library is its collection of manuscripts— 130,000 volumes and manuscripts dating back to the 1600s, as well as some of the very early documents relating to the history of St Gall from the 8th to the 12th centuries. The library is situated on the side of the cathedral, and

The magnificent Baroque interior of St Gallen cathedral.

around the cathedral perimeter there are maps showing the exact layout of the Klosterwiertal. The cathedral is always open, but the library has the following opening times:

April: Mondays–Saturdays, 9.00a.m. to 12.00p.m. and 2.00–5.00p.m. Closed Sundays.
May: Mondays–Saturdays, 9.00a.m. to 12.00p.m. and 2.00–5.00p.m. Sundays, 10.30a.m. to 12.00p.m.
June–August: Mondays–Saturdays, 9.00a.m. to 12.00p.m. and 2.00–5.00p.m. Sundays, 10.30a.m. to 12.00p.m. and 2.00–4.00p.m.
September–October: Mondays–Saturdays, 9.00a.m. to 12.00p.m. and 2.00–5.00p.m. Sundays, 10.30a.m. to 12.00p.m.
November: closed all month.
December: Tuesdays–Saturdays, 9.00a.m. to 12.00p.m. and 2.00–4.00p.m. Closed Sundays and Mondays.

All around this central "park" are historic buildings, many of which are antique shops, cafés and art studios. It is difficult to associate the city with the old town, as they are so unalike. Apart from the old town, St Gallen has few sites. It has plenty of shops, and the **Markplatz** area is quite interesting.

Museums
There are several museums all on the same street, the **Museumstrasse**. The most notable of these is the **textile museum**. If you have not seen any of the local (Appenzell) linen and embroidery then this museum is worth a visit. It is situated just off the **Obergraben**.

*O*n the old house and buildings surrounding the cathedral at St Gallen, there are some fine frescoes.

258

Textile Museum
Open: Mondays–Saturdays, 10.00a.m.
to 12.00p.m. and 2.00–5.00p.m.

Historical Museum
Museumstrasse 50.
Open: Mondays–Saturdays, 10.00a.m.
to 12.00p.m. and 2.00–5.00p.m.
Sundays, 10.00a.m. to 5.00p.m.
This museum shows local history and
has temporary demonstrations of glass-
ware painting techniques.

Natar Museum
Museumstrasse 32.
Open: Mondays–Saturdays, 10.00a.m.
to 12.00p.m. and 2.00–5.00p.m.
This museum has sections on cartog-
raphy, optics and holography.

Kuntsmuseum
Museumstrasse 32.
Open: Mondays–Saturdays, 10.00a.m.
to 12.00p.m. and 2.00–5.00p.m.
Sundays, 10.00a.m. to 5.00p.m.

Accommodation
St Gallen is probably a good day trip
if you are touring or staying in the
Appenzell, but if you have to stay
here, then there are plenty of hotels to
choose from.

The hotels are fairly typical of those
found in a large city, with a profusion
of four-star business establishments.
With the rolling hills of the Appenzell
on your doorstep it would seem unlikely that you would want to stay
here, however the hotels which may
appeal are near the cathedral, one of
which is almost opposite the abbey
library. This is the Hotel Schwaren,
and round the corner from there is the
Hotel Im Portner.

The Bodensee

On this diverse tour of the north-east,
you could now move into the **Bodensee**. This area between St Gallen, Rorsach, Romanshorn and Kreuzlingen is
low, not very interesting farmland.

Lake Bodensee
Lake Bodensee (or Konstanz) is shared
with Germany, and is a large expanse
of water. You can still see concrete
bunkers looking across to the other
side, when Switzerland was only too
aware of the threat from its neighbour.
It must have been a worrying time,
waiting for the invasion that never
came.

This area is excellent for cycling and
camping. There are plenty of campsites
right along the shores of Bodensee,
with plenty of quiet, flat roads for
leisurely biking. The area is easy going,
and well off the tourist route. If a trip
into Germany appeals to you, a ferry
service will take you from **Romanshorn**
to **Friedrichshafen**, or you can cross by
road at **Kreuzlingen** into **Konstanz**—
another split city. The German side is
actually more interesting, having the
greater part of the **old town**, but allow
some time to come back into Switzerland—the Swiss frontier guards are as
keen here as anywhere else in the
country.

Camping
The campsites along this shoreline of
the Bodensee are:

Altenrhein Idyll: a two-star site near
the village of Rorsach, which is only
just in Switzerland.
Open: 1 May–30 September.

Arbon Buchhorn: another lake position for the four-star site at the village of Arbon.
Open: April–21 October.

Egnach Wiedehorn: a four-star site on the lake at the mid-point between Rorsach and Kreuzlingen.
Open: 1 April–31 October.

Uttwil Royal: a three-star site near the village of Keswil.
Open throughout the year.

Uttwil Strandbad: at the same place as the previous entry, this is a non-classified site.
Open: 1 April–30 September.

Altnau Ruderbaum: a two-star site, not far out of Kreuzlingen.
Open: 1 April–31 October.

From Kreuzlingen, Switzerland stretches into German territory. But this area is one of Switzerland's backwaters, a finger of land which cuts into the Germanic quarter, creating its own culture and lifestyle. This is the area of **Schaffhausen**, wine and oriel windows on every corner. It's a delightful part of the country, great for cycling, with big attractions such as the **Rhine Falls** and **Stein am Rhein**. Not many tourists come to this corner of Switzerland.

Before leaving the Konstanz and Kreuzlingen region, should you have some time to spare for a good lunch or an overnight stop, I would recommend a trip down to the river at **Gottlieben**. It is signposted off the main route 13, although there are some turns to get to the river. The village is small, very quiet, on the banks of the Rhine, and has the most glorious inn you could

ever wish to see—the **Hotel Dragon**. It dates back to the 17th century, and has the most elaborate green domes above its oriel windows. Even if you only look into this old inn it is worth seeing, and just around the corner there is a small promenade bordering the Rhine. The river at this point is slowly edging its way towards the huge lake of **Konstanz**. The whole village, and there is not a great deal of it, is full of character, so even away from the riverside it can be pleasant to stroll around.

The **architecture** in this region is very unusual for Switzerland. Most of the houses are half-timbered, which in Britain would mean the Tudor period.

Further along the Rhine is one of the most richly decorated towns anywhere in Switzerland.

Stein am Rhein

You can reach Stein am Rhein by river boat from **Schaffhausen**; from the southern side it can be reached from the main route 13. It is on the northern bank of the river and only just in Switzerland. It is almost unique in that its historic art is there for all to see, and has been so for nearly 470 years. The **town square** is the main attraction, for here the buildings (which include houses, public buildings and an inn) are covered in **frescoes** which make "ornate" seem an understatement.

One of the backwaters of Switzerland is the small village of Gottlieben, with one of the most attractive inns in the region—The Dragon.

From the middle of the cobbled square there is the **Sonne Inn** and the **Roter Oschen** with façades originating from 1446, although the decoration was not complete until 1615. The façades were painted to interpret the name of the particular house, so the scene on the Roter Oschen relates to "The House of the Red Ox". The **town hall** has stained glass from the 16th century, while another façade, just by the town hall, is one of the most famous buildings—the **Zum Weissen Adler** (the White Eagle). The hotels in the square have all been operating since medieval times, so it would seem apt to stay at one of these historic buildings, if only for one night. The Adler has good rooms for around 75 SFr per person, though many of them are in a modern annexe at the rear of the hotel.

Stein has another historic attraction. The **Abbey of St George** originates from the 11th century and has pillars with dates like 1026 on them. It is a quiet place, but worth a visit for those interested in the history of this area. It is the best preserved German Benedictine monastery and occupies a splendid position right on the banks of the Rhine, just as the river flows into the **Untersee**. Inside there is a collection of **carved woodwork**, paintings and frescoes from the Gothic period.

Many of the towns of this area date from medieval times, and similar façades can be seen in some of the villages along the river. None of them matches the "open-air art gallery" of Stein am Rhein, but it is an interesting area. The largest town in this region, and a good base from which to tour, is **Schaffhausen**.

*T*he Munot Fortress at Schaffhausen still accommodates
the watchman who calls for the town gates to be closed at 9.00p.m.

Schaffhausen

The most striking feature of Schaff-hausen is the peculiar building in the old quarters. It towers over the whole town and from its high position, dominates the river. This is the **Munot Fortress**, and although it is by no means the only interesting feature, it is certainly the most obvious.

The Munot Fortress was built in 1564 but was not finished until 1585. Its design, a tower above a circular battlement wall, follows an idea of Albrecht Durer. From the circular **keep** you can see the river and most of the surrounding countryside. The keep is occupied by the watchman and his family, and it is still his duty to ring a bell at 9.00p.m. This used to announce the time for last orders at the inns, and for the town gates to be closed. It is doubtful if anyone takes much notice now, at least not at 9.00p.m! Directly below the Munot are **vineyards**, which symmetrically stretch away down to the streets and the river. The Munot and the fortifications are open to the public, and you can climb the stone **spiral staircase** inside the tower.

The rest of the old town of Schaff-hausen is one of those medieval experiences, with a similar feel to Bern and Fribourg. Tall old **terraced buildings** line the squares and courtyards, where there are water **fountains** and **statues**. It is a superbly kept town centre, with a style of its own. The use of the oriel window is very much in evidence in Schaffhausen, and most corner buildings have these ornate features. If you arrive in Schaffhausen by rail, it is a short walk down into the old town by way of the **Lozenges**,

Oriel windows are a common sight in Schaffhausen, where the rich merchants of the area built their attractive houses.

almost opposite the railway station. The Hotel Bahnhof is on the right. Once in the cobbled streets you can walk down the **Verkehrsburo**, where the information office is located. After that it is simply a matter of wandering through the old passages and streets. Try to see the house on **Vordergasse**, the **Zum Ritter** which has the best of the house frescoes on its façade. These were completed by a famous local man, Tobias Stimmer, in 1570.

The **St Johannes Kirche (St John's Church)** is famous for its acoustics, and a Bach festival is held here every three years. Schaffhausen was a wealthy

Whimsical Windows
There are more than 170 oriel windows in Schaffhausen; it was regarded as something of a status symbol to have one. Many private houses have their own, with rather overdone names such as "Satisfaction" and "Delicious Nook". Apparently the local tax office was named "The Fountain of Joy", something which the local population hardly agreed with!

town, which is obvious from the decorative art throughout the town, but the less extravagant residents of Schaffhausen lived in the nearby **monastery**.

*W*ine is an important part of life in the Schaffhausen region, and this old wine press is in the monastery.

The All Saints Monastery
This is situated alongside the **Munsterplatz**. The monastery is also a museum, the **Allerheiligen**, where much of the local history is kept. It also houses

a very large bell, the **Schillers Bell**, which sits in a courtyard near the centre of the abbey. This inspired the *Ballad of the Bell*. Typically there is a small herb garden in the monastery, and also within the complex there is a music school, so the old building is still an active one.

The market place, which holds a market on Saturday and Tuesday mornings (very good for flowers), is close to All Saints, and from there it is a short walk down to the **quay** and the pleasure boats to Stein am Rhein.

Boat Trips

It is about 20 km (12½ miles) from Schaffhausen to Stein, but cruising on the Rhine can be a very pleasant experience. Snacks and drinks are served on the boats, and once you have reached Stein you have a couple of hours to enjoy this unique medieval town. The boat takes about one and a half hours to reach the old town, and leaves late in the morning. It returns to Schaffhausen in the afternoon.

The Rhine Falls

The other big attraction for visitors to this area are the **Rhine Falls**. These falls are publicized as "the largest waterfalls in Europe", but this claim is slightly misleading. They may be the largest in volume of water, but I am sure most people think of a waterfall in terms of height and the Rhine Falls are quite small. If the subject is given some thought, there is no way the river Rhine *could* suddenly produce a spectacular mountainside waterfall. However, there are some good aspects of the trip out to the falls, largely depending on which side you visit, since

from one side there is a viewing platform and from the other a boat out to the middle of the falls. It is well worth trying to do both, since the boat ride is quite exciting.

The falls are near **Neuhausen** which is about 20 minutes from Schaffhausen, heading downstream towards Zurich. On the left side of the river, the southern side, is the **Laufen Castle**. There is a car park, and the entrance to the falls is through the castle so there is a small entrance fee. From here the path goes down to the river. The path is quite steep, and often wet, so those who may have difficulty may be wise to give this viewpoint a miss. Once down at the river's edge a concrete platform juts out into the river, actually under the overhanging rocks. To say you get a taste of the power of the falls from here would be an understatement. The flow rate is 700 cubic metres (25,000 cubic feet) per second, which is what is meant by "the largest waterfall in Europe". It is certainly impressive, and once you are in this position the temptation to go out on one of the small craft to the middle island of the falls can be very great. This short boat ride goes from the opposite bank, but you can take another boat over there or you can walk across the bridge upstream, or drive around.

On this side, the northern bank, there is a more commercial air to the scene, with a café, souvenir shop, and flat-bottomed boats to take you out into the river. Some 2 million visitors come to see the Rhine Falls each year, so do not be surprised to find a queue. The trip costs around 6 SFr, and is, thankfully, a return journey. The destination is a small quay at the very

The Rhine Falls is a raging torrent of water, and the best place to get the feel of the power of the falls is from the platform on the northern bank of the river. Take a raincoat because you will get wet!

centre of the falls, on an outcrop of rock with a surprising amount of vegetation on it. You can climb the steps to the top of the rock and gaze out at the onrushing water. There can be few waterfalls where you can stand in the middle and not get wet. The Swiss flag stands proudly on the top of this rock, and from a distance there seems to be an air of defiance to the scene. The boat will come back for you as it

brings in more of the adventurous. It is very convenient that this rock has provided a pool of still water for the boats to manoeuvre in, but it is also illustrative of the Swiss ability to make the most of their natural resources.

Walking

The region around Schaffhausen is wine country. From the Munot, with its vineyard sloping down to the river, out to the very edge of Swiss territory, there are acres of land used for the grape. As in Germany, the hills along the side of the Rhine are also used for vineyards and this area is Switzerland's largest producer of wine.

This flat, low land means good cycling and walking and as in some of the other areas of the country the vineyards offer the opportunity to wander from village to village with ease.

The web of roads which stretches from Schaffhausen is covered by the PTT bus service, so you do not have to have a car. The services are not all PTT, but include the local ASS, VBSch and the German DB, and if you want to use all these services you can get a group ticket for about 10 SFr. This gives you the opportunity to use the buses at will and also use the connections for your walks. For example, a two and a half-hour walk from **Siblingen** (which is about 7 km; 4⅓ miles from Schaffhausen), to **Hemmental** takes in some lovely countryside—you can take one bus to Siblingen, go for your walk, and then take a return bus from Hemmental. This route will take you through the small village of **Randenturm**, at 790 m (2,591 ft) a high spot in the area, down to **Winklacker** and Hemmental.

Bright Yellow Buses

The bright yellow buses of the Postal Service are a common sight in Switzerland, particularly where there are few railways. Often the choice in winter will be either the cable car or the PTT bus, and remarkably there are few services which do not operate throughout the year. Excursion guides are available from the PTT, with routes for hiking or touring using the service. In all there are 633 routes, which at 8,000 km (5,000 miles) is more than the federal railways network. In total over 70 million travellers use the PTT buses each year. The guides are 3 SFr each, cover all the main areas, although some are linked together such as Engadine and Ticino, Appenzell and Toggenburg, and are available from post offices or by post from Finanzdienste PTT, 3030 Bern.

There is a whole variety of walks in this region, but for the best of the vineyard areas the place to head for is **Hallau**. This is the most intensive wine-producing region of Schaffhauserland, and the entire hillside is covered in grape vines. Even the **church clock** has a grape at each end of its hands. From Hallau the permutations are endless for wandering at your leisure among the carefully laid out vineyards. From the higher points you can look across the hills to the other villages of **Oberhallau**, **Wilchingen** and **Neunkirch**. Obviously a good time to come to this region is around the autumn, when the vines are being picked and there is plenty going on. As a refreshing alternative to short walks, a superb track runs alongside the Rhine in the direction of **Stein am Rhein**. In autumn this walk is particularly good, with the vineyards on the left and the Rhine to your right. Many of the local residents use this pathway which is flat, easy going, and very picturesque.

Accommodation

Villages such as Hallau will have inns, and in this less-visited corner of Switzerland prices are very reasonable. Schaffhausen and Stein am Rhein are more expensive, but there is more going on there.

In central **Schaffhausen** many of the hotels are for business use, so those like the Bahnhof will be in the medium price range, without any great character. A double room here costs about 120 SFr, even though the hotel is rated as three-star. Slightly more expensive, but in the middle of the old town and full of character, is the Kronhof, and for a cheaper alternative with some of

the local flavour there is the Hotel Steinbock, which at about 65 SFr (no breakfast) is a good deal.

At **Stein am Rhein** the most obvious place to want to stay at is the Hotel Adler, in the main square. This is a three-star hotel costing around 160 SFr for a double room. Most of the rooms are in the newer part, at the rear of the hotel. Most of the hotels in Stein are slightly more expensive, with the cheapest being the Ilge at about 100 SFr for a double room.

Out in the villages it is a different story, with some of the small inns costing as little as 65 SFr for a double room. Most of the hotels are in the 100 SFr range, and typically the one at **Neunkirch**, the Hotel Schweizerbund, is around this price. The **Rhine Falls** has the Hotel Belvedere, which justifiably claims a brilliant view of the falls. However, for the privilege of having this view you must expect to pay about 190 SFr for a double room. The

*T*he grape even appears on the face of the clock at Oberhallau.

two cheaper alternatives, but without the benefit of the view, are the Edelweiss and the Lowenbrau.

Camping
For campers this is a slightly difficult area, since all the sites are straggled along the Rhine towards **Konstanz**. There are no sites in this small area, west of Schaffhausen, so those on cycling trips will have to consider the small inns rather than campsites.

From Kreuzlingen
Kreuzlingen Fischerhaus: as the name would suggest, this is on the side of Lake Konstanz, very close to the towns of Kreuzlingen and Konstanz. A three-star site.
Open: 31 March–31 October.

The next sites are well up the Rhine, near the Stein Am Rhein region:

Mammern Guldifuss: a four-star site close to the Untersee, just outside the village on the Kreuzlingen side.
Open: 1 April–31 October.

Eschenz Huttenberg: another four-star site on the southern side of the Rhine very close to Stein am Rhein.
Open throughout the year.

Kaltenbach: very close to the last site, but just along the road by a few hundred metres. A three-star site.
Open: 1 April–31 October.

Wagenhausen: this is a four-star site almost opposite Stein am Rhein.
Open: 1 April–31 October.

Stein am Rhein Grenzstein: this an ideal site for touring the area, and within the town of Stein am Rhein. A four-star site.
Open throughout the year.

Diessenhofen Laui: situated between Schaffhausen and Stein Am Rhein, this three-star site is right on the river.

Schaffhausen Strandbad Rheinwessen: this non-classified site is the nearest to the town on the river and in a shaded position.
Open: 1 May–20 September.

In the autumn both locals and visitors enjoy a walk along the Rhine from Schaffhausen.

Your Chambre, *which became a* Zimmer, *is now a* Camera

Home of the Romansch culture, the region borders Italy and has absorbed much of its way of life. Italy is over the St Gothard and San Bernardino passes, but slightly further north are the swish resorts of Klosters, Davos and St Moritz. This is where your franc buys less, unless you look for the small villages of the Engadine Valley. Switerland's National Park is left alone here. Oddities like the horse racing on ice at St Moritz make for a good day out, but once you are beyond those high passes or long tunnels, its Italy, and time to turn your attention to pizza and pasta.

The south-east of Switzerland covers the area from **Chur** down to the Italian borders, and includes some of the richest, and some of the poorest, landscapes of the country. In the northern parts, in the **Engadine**, there is the showbiz style of **St Moritz**, while down past the **St Gothard Tunnel** the **Ticino** has harsh, rough mountains around the lakes of **Locarno** and **Maggiore**.

*T*he rail journey from Chur to St Moritz passes through small Engadine villages such as Preda. For those looking for a quieter ski resort, this village is ideal.

The Surselva Valley

Your first glimpse of the eastern side of Switzerland when coming from the west is of the soft rolling lands around Disentis. In this valley, which is really a continuation of the type of scenery seen between Brig and Andermatt, the skiing attraction continues, but without the intensity of the Valais. There is a greater concern with agriculture here, and only a few towns which have opted to go for the tourist market.

The two major areas in this, the Surselva Valley, are **Disentis** and **Flims/ Laax**. The latter is a big sports area which includes some of the best white-water rafting in the country. Further down the valley is Disentis. It is a splendid sight as you come off the

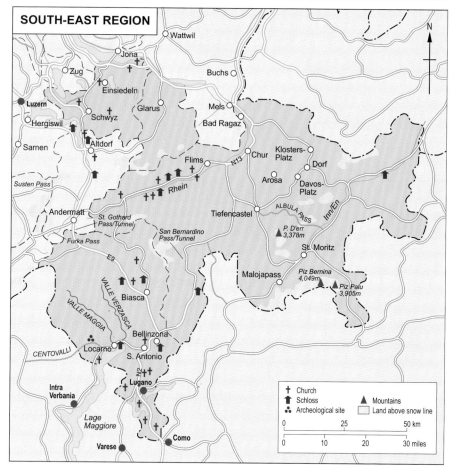

SOUTH-EAST REGION

Wattwil
Jona
Zug
Buchs
Einsiedeln
Luzern
Glarus
Mels
Hergiswil
Schwyz
Bad Ragaz
Sarnen
Altdorf
Flims
N13
Chur
Klosters-Platz
Dorf
Susten Pass
Arosa
Davos-Platz
Rhein
Andermatt
St. Gothard Pass/Tunnel
Tiefencastel
ALBULA PASS
Inn/En
San Bernardino Pass/Tunnel
P. D'err
3,378m
Furka Pass
St. Moritz
E9
Malojapass
Piz Bernina
4,049m
VALLE VERZASCA
Biasca
Piz Palu
3,905m
VALLE MAGGIA
Bellinzona
CENTOVALLI
Locarno
S. Antonio
Intra
Verbania
Lugano
Lage Maggiore
Como
Varese

† Church
🛡 Schloss
⁛ Archeological site
▲ Mountains
☐ Land above snow line

0   25   50 km
0   10   20   30 miles

M ap of south-east Switzerland.

Oberalp Pass down into the town, as you know that (for some time at least) you have seen your last hairpin bend.

Disentis

If you have an ear for the dialects of Switzerland, this may be the first time you will have heard the *Romansch* tongue. This is the only region of the country where there is a chance that the majority of the people speak the oldest language in Europe, and Disentis is regarded as something of a centre for the speaking of Romansch. But Disentis is probably more famous as a spa town, and the home of the Benedictine **monastery**.

The Abbey of St Martin

This is still very active today, and is used as a school by the monks. It dates back to the 8th century, although much of the interior decoration is Baroque. The rebuilding took place in 1712, and the inside of the abbey is well worth a visit.

Skiing

There have been efforts to cater for the winter tourist at the town, and there is a lift to take skiers to the surrounding mountains, the top heights being a very respectable 3,000 m (9,843 ft). Between the main town and **Sedrun** there are three lift systems.

Routes From Disentis

At Disentis you can carry straight on to **Laax** and **Flims**, and ultimately **Chur** or head south, over the **Lukmanier Pass**, to the **Ticino**. This is one of the passes which is closed in winter but, since it is not at too great a height, it could be open as early as March. Oddly, this is a road-only route, with a distinct lack of a railway line. There does not seem to be any good reason for this, since just about every other part of the country has a train. The small villages along the way are proof that you are moving towards Italy, and the language moves away from the harsh Romansch.

The most interesting villages are after the pass summit, at 1,914 m (6,280 ft). The road then drops down to **Camperio**, before producing some

*T*he architecture of the churches changes gradually to a more Italian flavour in the Flims/Laax region.

startling turns to skirt **Olivone** and on to the larger village at **Lottigna**, where there is a 15th-century **bailiff's house**, now the **Blenio museum**. This is a regional museum, showing local craftwork, tools and a good arms collection. From here the road goes on to **Malvaglia** and rejoins the main route from St Gotthard at **Biasca**. This road (and the pass) is really an excursion route, since there could be no other good reason for using it. If your journey is from Chur you will use the San Bernardino Pass, and if coming from Lucerne or Zurich you will use the St Gothard Pass.

Back at Disentis the main road (route 19) continues east, and the style of the churches and houses changes from onion domes to lofty spires, and the whole architectural scene begins to look vaguely Italian until you reach Flims, where it reverts to Alpine again.

Flims/Laax

Flims and Laax are two villages which have almost joined together on the main road. The winter attractions at the two towns are well advertised, and there has been considerable investment in the area to bring in the winter tourists. From both towns, and the areas in between, there are lifts up to a variety of peaks, all around the 2,500–3,000 m (8,200–9,840 ft) mark. It has about eight major lifts, from

which the skiing areas run around the slopes of **Fil de Cassons**, **Crap Masegn** and **Vorab**. But perhaps the major attraction in Flims and Laax is the **water sports**.

Water Sports

The largest white-water rafting company in Europe (Euro Raft) has it base here, at a complex of Sportshotel, shops and restaurants. From very close to this spot you can enjoy a breath-

W̲hite-water rafting can be done at a number of locations across the country, but the course at Flims/Laax was one of the first.

taking trip down the ravines and gorges of the **Rhein Anteriur** river. It is a well-organized affair, with plenty of rafts available. Although it is best to book in advance, it is sometimes possible to take the trip at the last minute. Wetsuits can be hired at extra cost, since wearing them is not obligatory, but the safety aspect is looked after by the company, who provide helmets and life-jackets. The best way to enjoy the rafting, which is open to anyone who would like to try it, is to book for a whole day. You can then feel your way in the morning and really enjoy it on your second go in the afternoon. One of the best times to go is around late May and early June, when the river is running particularly fast. The complex where the company is based is approximately between the two towns. Going from Laax the turning is on the left, and is marked as the Sports Centre. Euro Raft are towards the rear of the complex and almost opposite one of the big sports hotels. The kayaks and rafts are usually on trailers nearby, so it is easy to find. At the end of each run, a coach will bring the wet, but happy, participants back to the complex. Information about white-water rafting is available from:

M. Chezière
Euro Raft
Flims Laax Tourist Office
CH-7032
Switzerland.

Accommodation
There are two hotels which specialize in sports holidays. The Sportshotel Rancho has rooms as well as self-catering accommodation and features swimming, fitness, a games room as well as golf, tennis and water and ski sports.

From Flims, the road splits to go to Chur or turns left towards the N13 and Bellinzona.

East Switzerland and the Engadine

By far the best route through to the Engadine is from Zurich, along the N3 and then the N13 autoroutes. The rail journey follows a similar path, with **Chur** being the major junction for onward travel to **Klosters** or **St Moritz**.

Chur

For this reason, Chur (pronounced "coir"), has become quite a large town, although it does have some of the attractions seen in the smaller villages of the area. It is the administrative capital of the **Grisons** canton, with a 12th-century Gothic and Romanesque **cathedral**. There is also the **old town** and two museums: the **Rhaetic museum** and the **Fine Arts museum**. Rhaetic appears in several places, and the local rail system linking Chur with St Moritz is the Rhaetian Railway. These red trains provide one of most scenic rides in Switzerland, and given the choice I would always opt for the train journey from Chur to St Moritz.

The connection with the main intercity train to and from Zurich is perfect so, although you have to change at Chur, the journey from Zurich to St Moritz can be made in about three and three-quarter hours. Most of this time is spent edging through the mountainous region east of Chur, as the train climbs slowly to **Thusis** and **Tiefencastel**. In the winter, it can only be described as chocolate-box scenery, as you pass through some of the deepest ravines possible. The really exciting views start after Thusis, and if you have a right-hand view there are some terrific sights out of the window—try to look down into the gorge at **Furstenabrücke**. It is not far from Thusis to St Moritz, as the train climbs into the mountains, and it is very spectacular. On the way up, most of the best views are from the right-hand side of the train, and eventually you reach Tiefencastel.

From here the train carries on through tunnel after tunnel, and it's interesting to see the same scene several times from different heights as the track winds its way up the mountainside. The valleys in this region are very much on their own and there is an atmosphere of Shangri La in some of them. Mountains either side and steep passes at each end mean a total reliance on the rail services for part of the year. Along this route there is a number of small villages, with small ski centres and basic lift systems. Nothing is very grand, and not for the first time you get the impression that this is where many Swiss people spend their weekends and holiday breaks.

Two of the prettiest villages are at **Naz** and **Preda**, just before the **Albula Pass**. Much of this end of the trip is spent going in and out of tunnels, with just glimpses of the high mountains, but it really is the most fantastic scenery. Cars, by the way, are transported on through the pass on the train in the winter, since it is closed until May. The only alternative is the **Julier Pass** from **Tiefencastel**, but this too can cause problems in winter.

The line comes down from the Albula Pass and into **Bever**. You are now in the heart of the Engadine valley, and only a short distance from the town of **St Moritz** which marks the end of the journey.

St Moritz

Of all the villages, towns and cities of Switzerland that I have visited, I have to say that St Moritz is *not* my favourite. In conversation with a Swiss television presenter I found that she too found the place slightly distasteful: "this is not Switzerland" she said. Yet for many people who have not visited the country the image of this rich and famous resort typifies all that they know to be Swiss—how untrue: in my travels in the rest of the country I have yet to find anywhere quite like St Moritz. It is unique and not, in my opinion, for the best reasons.

Its history points to a strong British influence, and you can still feel the presence of the aristocracy here, in the form of the **cresta run** and the big hotels. "Decadent" continued my TV friend, pointing to the number of fur coats which floated up and down the high street, covering large men with fat cigars and painted women with dark glasses. It *is* that sort of place, but I am now sure that St Moritz and the people who stay there are living in some sort of time warp. The ridiculousness of St Moritz, I think, is illustrated by the Cadillacs that collect guests from the railway station or the airport. The sight of one of these monster cars trying to turn through narrow mountain lanes in the snow is absurd.

Horse Races

In its favour St Moritz quite rightly claims to have the greatest number of hours of sunshine in Switzerland, along with the best snow record in the country. This combination of sun and snow guarantees that the visitors will flock here every year. There is an event in St

Horse racing on ice is one of the highlights of the winter season in St Moritz. The races are short but fast.

Moritz that is worth seeing, although I would recommend that you stay out of town, if only to save yourself high prices for basic hotel rooms. The **St Moritz Horse Race** is held three times a year—on ice. The frozen lake provides the track, and for all the world, when the punters arrive (again sporting too many furs and too many gold accessories for my liking) you could well be at Ascot. Race days at St Moritz are good fun, and even some of the horses seem to enjoy it.

Horse racing in the town began back in 1906, when 12 horses and a mule ran the first race, which was supposed to be on the lake. It was deemed as too dangerous, so they put it off until the following year, when Professor Heim of Zurich decreed that "a heavily equipped cavalry regiment could drill at a gallop without danger". The race in that year, January 1907, involved 14 horses, but no mule, and featured the idea of **skikjoring**. The races were suspended for various wars in 1915 and 1940, and there have been odd occasions when the temperature has been too high. But in most years the lake starts to freeze in December, and as soon as it is 10 cm (4 in) thick, preparations begin. By the end of January the ice is 30–50 cm (12–20 in) thick, and is considered able to withstand anything. Certainly, when you are walking through the car park, the crowded stands and watching the races you forget that you are standing on a frozen expanse of water.

All the usual business of a fully blown race meeting is put together for the St Moritz races, and apart from the unusual sight of a Snow Cat preparing the track it's much the same scene as at any course in the world. The betting is curious in that no odds are declared, and you simply bet on a number for a win or a place. This, along with the neat rows of betting booths takes some of the atmosphere away, but the races themselves are short and exciting. It is difficult to tell whether the horses do actually like the snow—certainly, in the paddock, some of them look a bit miserable, possibly hoping they would be entered for a race down in Marseilles quite soon. Apart from the regular races there is the **skikjoring**, with the "riders" on skis, and **trotting**, which is the old horse-and-chariot-type race. The skikjoring races are the biggest, both in length and in prize money, and there are also some important cups and trophies to be won.

A trip to the races at St Moritz is a good day out, and on a bright sunny day in February it can be very pleasant to eat *wurst* (sausage), along with a good helping of *gluwein* (hot spiced wine), between races. There are usually three meetings a year, all of them in February. Entry fees vary, ranging from a seat in the main stand through to a standing position on the rails. Of

*W*inter sports in Switzerland come no faster or exciting than the two- and four-man bob.

course, you can just watch from further down the course for nothing, but then you miss out on the *wurst* and *gluwein*.

The other two big sporting events in the town are centred around the **cresta run** and the **bobsleigh** course. If you want to listen to the inane drivel of an expatriate Brit who is still living in the

The flat and long Engadine valley features the annual cross-country ski marathon and even as the morning light creeps into the valley, marathon skiers can be seen training on the course.

1920s then the cresta run is ideal. If you would rather see some exciting Swiss sporting action, then the two- and four-man bobsleigh events are really good.

Skiing

Skiing is what the majority of the visitors come for: certain snow, hours of blinding sunshine (be sure to have some good sunglasses with you) and exceptionally well-kept pistes. From the centre of town you can be up on the high slopes within half an hour, and on the first station at **Corviglia** in ten minutes. This station has the added attraction of horse-drawn carriages to take you on to the main slopes, and a

restaurant. You can walk the ten minutes up the hill to the ski slopes. **Pt Nair** is the main summit at 3,057 m (10,030 ft), and is reached on the funicular after the change at Corviglia. February and March are very busy months in St Moritz, so there can be some waiting involved. It would seem that most of Europe comes to town in February, especially if the snow has not been too good in the other resorts.

Cross-Country Skiing
One of the biggest events of this area is the Engadine marathon, which is a cross-country ski competition. For weeks, and even months, skiers can be seen up and down the trail training for

the big event which takes place in March. It is a tremendous sight to see thousands of cross-country skiers begin the marathon. The course is over 40 km (25 miles), and information on this, and all the other sporting events of the Engadine, can be obtained from:

St Moritz Tourist Office
CH-7500 St Moritz.
Tel: (082) 33147; fax: (082) 32952.

If you enjoy cross-country skiing the Engadine is a very active area, as the marathon just mentioned suggests. Each year over 1 million SFr is spent on the upkeep of the 120 km (74 miles) of trails of the area. As there is no

charge for using these trails, you can show your appreciation for the work, and of course to help pay for it, by buying the stickers for sale in the tourist offices. The sticker depicts the Swiss working community, and has the badge of the Engadine Loipen Leben Cross Country Club. Details can be obtained from:

Upper Engadine Tourist Office
CH-7504 Pontresina.
Tel: (082) 66573.

Around The Town

The town was at one time probably quite nice. Now it is built up, with odd things like traffic lights and car parks. Alpine villages were never intended to end up like this, and you can only wonder at how some of the buildings were ever agreed to. Down by the lake there are some remnants of the village, although there is also a group of apartment blocks, presumably for the local workforce. Also in the lower end of the town is the large heated indoor swimming pool, and the St Moritz ice hockey pitch. Anyone who enjoys team sport would thoroughly enjoy an evening at an ice hockey game. In Switzerland there are about four leagues, offering a wide variety of skills. In St Moritz the team is about average, and most of the games are between local towns. This is due to the difficulties of getting to matches in winter, and I have been at games which have started after ten in the evening because of the opposition being stuck on a high pass. If the opportunity arises it is well worth going to see this display of skill mixed with gratuitous violence!

Accommodation

Hotels in St Moritz are ridiculously expensive, and I have found only one that I would regard as a reasonable deal. This is the Hotel Corvatsch, and it is down by the bus stop from the main town. It is also close to the racecourse/lake, so many of the trainers and jockeys drink here after the races. It has a big open restaurant, and the family that run the hotel is helpful and friendly. The prices here are not bad, at around 100 SFr for a double room. Elsewhere in the town, and especially up in the main centre, the prices are as high as the mountains, and not really worth it. The Hotel Soldanella is good, with a superb dining room and good-size bedrooms. This is a three-star hotel at about 140 SFr per person (they price the rooms per person in St Moritz), while in the very centre of the town the Hotel Albana should be avoided—it just is not worth spending 160 SFr each on a box room. This is another group-owned hotel, proving yet again that you are better off with family-owned places.

Given the choice, I would recommend staying out of town. There are some lovely villages in the Engadine valley, where the costs are considerably less. If you want (or need) to come into St Moritz, there are very good bus and rail services up and down the valley, so travelling is not a problem.

Zuoz

Zuoz is about 30-minutes' train ride out of St Moritz, and once there you can forget all the hype and glamour of the bigger town. It is a quiet, small, very picturesque village, with one of the best hotels I have had the pleasure

The town centre at Zuoz is true to the style of the Engadine. Other villages featuring the distinctive style of houses are Zernez and Guarda.

to stay in. Zuoz is situated on the **River Inn**, not far from the national park. It is a very typical Engadine village, agricultural by nature, and full of the old-style farmhouses unique to this area. These houses are worth looking at, since most in Zuoz date back to the mid 1500s. The **village square** and the hotels and houses near the main street show the type of huge farmhouse where the family and their cattle would live. The Crusch Alva Inn, on the main

square has the coat of arms of the town, and just opposite there is a superb hotel in which you will get the true feeling of the Engadine farmhouse. This is the **Hotel Klarer**, which was (some 400 years ago) a real working farmhouse. It was, apparently, the home of a quite wealthy family, shown by the fact that they had two floors of accommodation—the ground floor was used for the farm work, which included the housing of animals and hay. The Hotel Klarer is now a beautifully furnished modest hotel which has kept much of the character of the original building. The doors of the bedrooms are arched pine, and throughout the house there are antique furnishings and decorations. A double room here costs 140–200 SFr, but you will feel that it

*E*arly morning in Zuoz, and the heat of the sun begins to tell on the night's snow.

is worth it. Less expensive rooms can be had at the Steinbock, but generally the hotels in Zuoz all charge about the same rates. The Castell-Zuoz is the most expensive.

Silvaplana

Other villages and towns which would appeal to visitors to the region lie to the south of the main town. The biggest of these is **Silvaplana** at the head of another lake. The lakes of the valley are at their best in the summer, mainly because you can see that they *are* in fact lakes, and not race tracks.

Silvaplana in the winter is the base for the lifts up to **Piz Corvatsch**. From here you can ski down to smaller villages, and the whole network of ski-lifts, trains and ski buses is very impressive. It should be said that, compared with other resorts, St Moritz and the accompanying mountains have some of the best skiing in the world. It is also some of the most difficult, so if you want a challenge, then this is the place to come. Even the easy runs around these mountains can be quite tricky, so it is not the ideal place for a raw beginner.

Preda

A good family alternative to all this skiing can be found nearby, on one of the longest and best toboggan runs you are likely to find. It goes down to **Preda**, from a point higher up in the Albula pass. The chances are that if you go on the run at the weekend you will find it quite busy, with families from all over the region. These are local people more often than not, who come for a day out with the children to this hidden valley. Preda itself is a picturesque village, with some impressive **frescoes** on the **tower** of the church. Nearby is the small ski-lift, and whereas you may have a fully equipped café or restaurant in the big resorts, this ski area has a simple caravan. It sells all the usual things, and I can recommend their *wursts*. You can find out the details of the run from the railway stations at **Bever**, **Samedan**, or Preda.

Air Access to The Engadine

For visitors who do not like the idea of a two-hour train ride, albeit through some spectacular scenery, there is an air service to the Engadine. The route is operated by Air Engiadina from the airfield at **Samedan**, near St Moritz, to **Zurich Kloten**. The aircraft are the 18-seater *Jetstream*, and the service runs at weekends (on Friday and Sunday). There are plans to make it a daily service in the high-season winter months, and more ambitious plans include flights from Zurich to Eindhoven and Antwerp. For information on routes and times call:

Air Engiadina
Bassedorf.
Tel: (01) 8364600; fax: (01) 8365377.

Glisenti Travel Agency
St Moritz.
Tel: (082) 37008.

National Park

From St Moritz and the Ober Engadine it is not far into Italy, by travelling south or via the **national park** towards Bormio and Caterina. Most of the national park belongs in the Italian sector, but between the road from **Samedan** to **Zernez** (another well-kept Engadinian village) and the border, there is the Swiss part of the park. It seems odd to have or need a park of this size, since most of the highlands of the Valais, the Jura and the Engadine could be regarded as national parks. In most countries this is how they would be regarded. However, this area of the country has been set aside as an area of outstanding beauty, where the human factor has been reduced to the absolute minimum. It could be seen as Switzerland's attempt to keep this area of their country in a natural state—which means leaving the woodlands as they ought to be, not how tourists would like them to be. It is wild Switzerland, and not only are cars forbidden but also all walkers must keep to the paths. It covers about 16,188 ha (40,000 acres) of woodland, and within the park there are wild deer, Ibex, Chamois and Marmots. In the summer there are guided tours through the park, with information particularly on the flora and fauna.

All along this eastern edge of Switzerland, the borders follow the natural line of the mountains, with the more northern part being very close to the Austrian border. At **Zernez** and **Susch** there are routes via the **Ofen pass** into Italy and going through **Schuls** and the **Unter Engadine valley** will take you to Austria and the Tyrol. There are bus and train services from St Moritz, via Zernez and Schuls, through to Munich.

Klosters and Davos

These towns have something of a reputation. Both are charming old villages, although **Davos** is actually made up of two places: Davos Platz and Davos Dorf. Just outside of the town, which spreads along the valley floor, is **Davos See**. It is only a small lake, but is well equipped for water sports in the summer. Davos also has Europe's largest skating rink, which along with the ski area at **Weissfluhjoch** and the **Parsenn** make it a good winter resort. It is a fairly expensive part of Switzerland, although its neighbour at **Klosters** probably has some effect on that.

Klosters has become synonymous with the British royal family. Possibly, at one time, Prince Charles and his close friends skied here without much fuss; now, however, each and every time the royal party arrives, so do the masses of camera-sporting newspaper reporters. Clearly, this is not the time to try and find a room in Klosters, since the entourage probably had the whole town booked up a year in advance. Most of the remaining times of the year will find this picturesque village very pleasant. It too uses the Parsenn slopes and it is easy to connect between Klosters and Davos using the lift system.

Touring
From here the road returns to Chur, via **Landquart**. One of the best tours to be made, either by rail or by road, is from Chur to the Engadine by way of the **Julier** or the **Albula** passes, down the valley to **Zuoz** and **Zernez**, into **Davos** and **Klosters** and back to **Chur**.

Arosa
Set right in the centre of this circular route is a town that has somewhat desperately announced itself as "the place to go". Specializing in winter sports, the one-time small village of Arosa is very much at the end of a line, with nowhere to go. You come here to ski, and that is about it. The attraction of a large ski centre on the main route from Zurich means that much of its clientele is from that city. At weekends, the normally soberly clad bankers of Zurich don their most outrageous ski attire, and head for the likes of Arosa. As a consequence of its rather remote position, it is a less crowded resort. It has an extensive lift system, reaching up to the **Weisshorn** at 2,653 m (8,704 ft), and from here there are magnificent views over the **Grisons** and the small lakes and rivers (in the summer).

Camping in The Engadine
Camping is good in this region, with most of the sites being down near the river, at the valley base.

Arosa Kurverein Arosa: this is a high mountain site near the town of Arosa. It is a three-star site.
Open throughout the year.

*T*he frescoes of this region, decorating both houses and churches were done by a technique called sgraffito.

Chur Camp Au: a five-star site with excellent amenities, close to the river, Chur and Haldenstein.
Open throughout the year.

Churwalden Pradefenz: another good site with plenty of facilities on the minor road from Chur to Tiefencastel. A four-star site.
Open throughout the year.

Lenz b/Lenzerheide St Cassien: also along the minor road to Tiefencastel, this is a four-star site situated between Lenzerheide and Lantsch.
Open throughout the year.

Lenzerheide Gravas: a non-classified site closer to the village.
Open throughout the year.

Lantsch–Lenz Sozas: the last site on this road from Chur and another non-classified site.
Open throughout the year.

Thusis Viamala: the main route through to the valleys of the Graubunden or the Grisons goes via Thusis and there is a site just outside the town. It is a four-star site very close to the town and set in a forested area.
Open: 1 May–30 September.

Savognin Nadro-Camping: another four-star site well into the high-sided valleys from Tiefencastel between Cunter and Savognin. This is a small ski resort and there is a lift up to about 2,500 m (8,200 ft).
Open throughout the year.

Over on the route up to the Albula Pass, there are:

Filisur Isla: a small non-classified site in the village of Filisur between Tiefencastel and Preda.
Open throughout the year.

Silvaplana: a five-star site in the town just away from St Moritz. It is at the lake side and all the amenities of the site and the area are close at hand.
Open: 1 June–31 September.

Pontresina Morteratsch Plauns: a four-star site, on the road from St Moritz to Morteratsch. This is moving down towards the Italian border and the Bernina pass.
Open: 1 July–14 October.

St Moritz Olypiaschanz: this is a non-classified site in St Moritz about ten-minutes' walk from the old centre and the swimming pool and ice rink. It is also convenient for the bus routes.
Open: 4 July–12 September.

Towards Zernez and the Upper Engadine valley there are several camping possibilities:

Zuoz Madulain Polenta: a small non-classified site in a superb part of the valley. The site is between the two towns on the hillside.
Open: 1 July–30 September.

Cinuos Chel Chapella: a non-classified, basic site on the road from Zuoz to Zernez.
Open: 2 June–30 September.

Zernez Cul: a four-star site at the picturesque village of Zernez. The site is near the River Inn, in a secluded spot.
Open: 15 May–30 September.

Susch Muglinas: a non-classified site a few kilometres from Zernez. Very convenient for the road over to Davos and routes through to Austria.
Open: 15 June–15 September.

Sur En Camping Sur En: a superb riverside site, on the Inn, but slightly off the main routes.
Open throughout the year.

Davos Dorf Farich: the only campsite in Davos. It's a non-classified site, situated between the two villages.
Open: 20 May–2 October.

The Ticino building is almost everything that other Swiss designs are not. Rough, small, store houses and churches adorn this Italian region.

The Ticino

After the glorious sunshine of the Engadine valleys, and the rich living encountered in the villages of the region, you may suffer a slight culture shock if you then head directly into the Ticino. **Lugano** and **Locarno** are certainly *chic* resorts, complete with palmed promenades and casinos. But out in the country it is a very different story, with deep wild ravines, plenty of old stone cottage buildings and an entirely more Italian feel to it. Your *chambre*, which became a *zimmer* is now a *camera*. Before you arrive in the atmospheric and beautiful Ticino, you will have to come through one of the tunnels. The train is no problem, since it will arrive, as do all Swiss trains, on time and with the minimum amount of effort. If however, you are driving, the **San Bernardino tunnel** is a better route to take than the **St Gothard**; not only is it considerably shorter, it is also less prone to delays than the Gothard, which can, when there are road works on the approach roads, become an 8- or 10-km (5- or 10-mile) traffic jam. It is also one of the longer tunnels at 16.9 km (10½ miles), so those who feel claustrophobic in such places are probably advised to avoid it. Coming from Zurich the shorter route is to go via **Schwyz** and **Altdorf**.

After you come out of one of these tunnels, you will remark how much the scenery has changed. The high snow-clad mountains have been replaced by wooded hillsides and, particularly on the San Bernardino road, the valley route down to **Bellinzona** is adorned with churches, perched on outcrops of rock. The scene is similar on the road

---

Architectural Walks in the Ticino

For those interested in architecture of all periods, the cities of the Ticino offer marked tours. The collection of walking maps, along with some quite useful information on the particular city or town, is available from the tourist offices in Bellinzona, Lugano and Locarno. There are eight maps in the pack, with each map opening up to show the buildings you will see. It is primarily a tour of modern architecture, certainly of the 20th century. On the reverse of the map sheet there are comments about the buildings of the area. Some are more ecstatic than others, and I quote "here on the slopes of Monte Verita, where mysterious magic waves are released, still dance the shadows of those restless Russians, Germans and Scandinavians who, at the turn of the century, rediscovered their lost Eden..." Lost Edens can be found in Ascona.

---

from the St Gothard pass, with the Italian influence getting stronger as you move south. Remember that if you are driving in the early part of the year, you will have no option but to use the tunnels, because the passes will be closed.

The **Val Mesolcina** from San Bernardino and the **Valle Leventinga** from Gothard are both busy routes. Traffic from Germany and Italy uses these roads constantly to travel between the two countries, so you should make some allowance—spending a holiday in a traffic jam, is nobody's idea of fun. The first major town of the Ticino is **Bellinzona**. It is from here that you choose to go to either of the two lakes—right takes you on to **Lugano**, left to **Locarno**, and the picturesque lake of Maggiore.

Bellinzona

Bellinzona, for all that it is a major junction, has some interesting sights in the forms of its **town walls** and **castles**, which you can see from the approach into the town.

The three castles are named **Uri, Schwyz** and **Unterwalden** after the three forest cantons which started the Swiss confederation. The same sense of unity did not quite exist down here, where there was a greater allegiance to the Italian lifestyle. However, the names stuck, as did the administration from the country on the other side of the high mountains. The castles were erected between the 13th and 15th centuries and they make an impressive sight on the horizon of the town. The castles make for an interesting short detour, possibly as a stopping place *en route* to the south.

The **Uri** (or **Castello Grand**) is the oldest of the three, and can be seen from some distance. The **Schwyz** was restored in 1903, and houses an archaeological and historical **museum**. The third castle, the **Unterwalden**, also has a museum, mainly of the local scenes of Ticino.

Bellinzona has little else to attract the visitor, since it is primarily an industrial and business town. To see the real delights of the Ticino, carry on to Lugano or, if you prefer mountains, Locarno. There is a distinct difference between the two towns, with Lugano being the larger, busier and arguably more active. It is a great place to visit, especially in the summer, when the promenades and the open-air cafés are all open and the city is in full swing.

Lugano

The town owes a lot to its very close neighbours over the water in Italy. It has much of the Italian style of things, not only in its architecture, but also in its character and its people. It is some way down from the railway station into the centre of the town, but once you are there you will find plenty of things to do and to see.

Arriving By Air

The alternative to travelling here by road or rail is to use the excellent service operated by Crossair. Lugano is one of its main bases, and there is some merit in being able to fly from one of the more northerly cities to the south. There are non-stop flights from Bern, Geneva, Zurich and Basel. The Basel flight is only once a day, but the other cities have five or six flights daily. From the business point of view, it must be almost vital to have an air connection with the Ticino, because of the road conditions in winter, and the (vague) possibility of a train being late. Flight time from Zurich and Bern is 45 minutes, and an hour from Geneva. Lugano also has international connections to Nice, Florence, Rome and Barcelona. The airport is about 20 minutes away from the town, with a regional bus connection. For reservations or information on the services call:

Crossair
Postfach
CH-4030 Basel Flughafen.
Tel: (061) 3253525.

Crossair
Aeroporto Lugano
CH-6982 Agno.
Tel: (091) 505001.

Lugano is an artistic city and even the town hall features some fine work in the main entrance.

History

The history of the town relates very closely to the Italians, as you would expect. Initially a Roman town, it has been under the jurisdiction of a number of powerful forces. In the 1400s the Bishop of Como had some power, but eventually the Swiss took a greater interest in the running of this important centre for trade, although it was not until 1803 that Ticino joined the Swiss confederation. The opening of the St Gothard railway made communication with the centres of Bern and Zurich much easier. This helped a great deal in the progress of the town as a tourist destination, a factor which still holds true today.

Inside Lugano

The dominating point of Lugano is the lake and, like Lucerne, it is made all the more attractive by the inlets and bays created by the mountains. In many ways Lugano could be regarded as the ideal resort. It has the lake attractions, with all the water sports to go with it, mountains up to 2,000 m

*T*he Villa Giana *(Civica) is in a lush park alongside the lake. In summer it is particularly colourful, but even as early as March the park is full of flowers.*

(6,560 ft), cultural events and a good nightlife. And it has this dual personality—the character of the Italians with the organization of the Swiss. Whether this is an ideal combination is open to argument, but it does have something going for it.

The town is centred around the narrow streets and squares of **Piazza Riforma**, **Via Canova** and **Via Vegezzi**. In this area, there are morning flower and vegetable markets, small arty shops as well as the more day-to-day stores. Just down from this shopping area, which is pedestrians only, there is the **Riva V Vela**, the **Piazza Rezzonico** and the promenades. Within this small area there are some splendid Italian buildings, and none better than the **municipal building**. Either side of it are fountains and flower beds. It is from near here that the Lugano steamers leave for trips around the lake and regular services to the other resorts on Lake Lugano. The walk down the

promenade towards the **Parco Civico** is superb, with trees and flowers looking particularly good, even as early as February. It has a warm, Mediterranean feel to it, but without the heavy heat often found there. At the Parco Civico, which is also called the Parco Ciani, there is the **Villa Ciani**. The villa is currently undergoing restoration, and the park is well worth a visit. Full of the most beautiful lawns and flower beds imaginable, this is a very relaxing place to spend some time. Lugano is the sort of town which does not really need to place buildings, either religious or secular, as monuments. They are there to be enjoyed as places of interest, but also as working places. This is evident throughout Switzerland, and the number of town halls which in themselves would be museums in many countries is innumerable.

Museums

Lugano has quite a few museums, which house particular collections:

Villa Favorita Gallery

Castagnola.
Open: April–October, Tuesdays–Sundays, 10.00a.m. to 5.00p.m.
This museum is some way from Lugano, but set in amongst trees and close to the lake. It is about a 20-minute walk to reach it, or you can take trolleybus number 1. The museum holds one of the biggest private collections of art in the world, especially European art from the 13th to the 18th centuries.

Canton Art Museum

Via Canova 10.
Open: Wednesdays–Saturdays, 10.00a.m. to 12.00p.m. and 2.00–6.00p.m., Tuesdays and Sundays, 2.00–6.00p.m.
This museum is almost in the centre of the town, just off the Piazza Riforma. It includes work by local artists in its collection as well as 19th and 20th-century art from Europe.

Customs House Museum

Cantine di Gandria.
Open: April–October, 1.30–5.30p.m.
It is a long walk, although a pleasant one, to this museum in the nearby village of Gandria. Most visitors get here by boat or bus. The museum, which came under the control of the National Museum in Zurich in 1970, shows the history of the Swiss Customs. This outpost of the service is an ideal example of how Switzerland has managed to protect its borders, no matter where they are. The museum shows a guard room, offices and the home-like aspects of the customs service. Reference is also made to the more current problems of drugs and precious metals.

Parks

For all its museums, the aspect of Lugano I particularly like is the mixture of old Italian mansions with lush parkland. Set among the exotic plants, there are villas, sculptures and fountains. Apart from the Parco Civico, there is the **Parco Tassino**, which is higher up the hill towards the railway. This park has the **Villa Tassino**, and a children's play area. The gardens along the **Paradiso** have an open-air **museum of sculptures**, and at the other end of the bay there is another park on the **Viale Castagnola**, with tennis courts, a lido and a small harbour.

*T*he high, steep sides of the lake add to the visual drama on an excursion to this area.

Getting Around

To make life a little easier in Lugano, it being a hilly sort of town, there are four funicular railways around the bay. Two of them serve the railway stations, but going from the western end at Paradiso, the services are:

Paradiso–Monte San Salvadore (912 m; 997 yds)
Piazza Luini–Parco Tassino
Piazza Cioccarro–Stazione (main railway station)
Casserate–Monte Bre (933 m; 1,020 yds).

The last of these gives a superb panorama over Lugano and the western side of the lake. From here you could almost feel you were in Rio on the Sugar Loaf Mountain.

The Lake

Out on the lake there are many things to do, and for the water enthusiast this is probably the best lake in Switzerland. With minimal rainfall, plenty of sunshine and a less-open aspect than lakes Léman and Neuchâtel, Lake Lugano is ideal for water sports such as windsurfing, yachting, diving, water-skiing or just swimming. To **sail**, your motor boat or yacht has to have temporary licence plates. These are available from:

The Malcantone Tourist Office
Agno Piazzale Stazione
Ticino, Switzerland.
Open: Tuesdays–Fridays, 9.30a.m. to 12.00p.m. and 4.00–6.00p.m.

You will also need a licence for **fishing**; this is valid for 10 days and is available from either of the local tourist offices. There are two in Lugano, one at the railway station and the main one down by the promenade on the Riva Giocondo Albertolli. It is about five-minutes' walk from the municipal building at the centre of town.

For **swimmers** there is a wealth of pools, as well as the beach at the lido. This is the area towards Castagnola, through the Parco Civica. There is an entrance fee to this area, which includes the use of a common changing room. Within this park there are also heated pools and children's pools. This is the sort of place where you could easily spend a day—the pools, by the way, are only heated in spring and autumn. The other swimming pools are at Paradiso, Hotel du Lac, Bissone, Valgersa, Mezzovico, Agno, Sessa and Bogno. Quite a few of the hotels also have their own indoor pools, but there would seem to be enough of them around to satisfy most people.

For those seeking some **therapeutic treatment** from their swimming there are sea-water pools at the Hotel Eden du Lac and the Hotel Villa Margherita. Both are open to non-residents from 8.00a.m. to 8.00p.m.

Sports on the Lake

The activity sports on the lake have been mentioned, but to give some more detail, they are:

Rowing: there are five clubs, although it is not clear as to whether you can hire the boats.
Motor boats: there are plenty of hire points on the promenade area. A boat hire cost can vary so you'll get the best deal by negotiating.

*T*he excursion boats based at Lugano offer a variety of trips both around the lake and to Italian towns. The shortest is just an hour, but it is possible to make a whole day of it.

Underwater diving: Lugano Sub-Aqua Club. Tel: (091) 210550.

Water Skiing: Club Nautico Lugano (Tel: 686139), Club Sci Nautico Ceresio (Tel: 541221), Hotel du Lac (Tel: 541921), Lido Tropical, Agno (Tel: 593118). Costs are about 150 SFr per hour.

Sailing: Circola Velico Lao di Lugano (Tel: 510975), open 1.30–5.00p.m. Lido Tropical, Agno (Tel: 593118). Costs about 30 SFr per hour with a maximum of two or four people, depending on the craft.

Windsurfing: Club Nautico Lugano (Tel: 686139), Scualo Windsurf Lido (Tel: 514041), Hotel du Lac (Tel: 541921), Hotel Lago di Lugano, Bissone (Tel: 688591), Caslano Surf (Tel: 712525). Costs around 15–30 SFr per hour, tuition in the sport costs extra.

Boat Trips

There are plenty of trips to be made from Lugano. All the excursions go from the promenade area at **Riva Vela** and **Riva Albertolli**. Since none of these boats operate as service routes or as a public transport system, your Swiss Pass qualifies only for a half-price deal. Essentially they are tourist excursions, although some of them could be used to go to Gandria, for instance. The vessels are operated by the Societa Navigazione Del Lago Di Lugano,Tel: (091) 515223, from whom up-to-date prices can be obtained.

The various cruises are generally half- or full-day trips.

Suggested Trips

Riviera: Lugano to Porlezza (Italy), with a one-hour stay in the town. This trip calls at **Gandria**, **Oria**, **San Mamete**, and on the way back Osteno. **Porlezza** has a Saturday market, which could be interesting. The sailing leaves Lugano Central at 2.40p.m., or from the pier at Paradiso 10 minutes earlier. **Morning cruise:** departs 10.00a.m.. from the main pier and calls at Paradiso on the way. It then travels to the western parts of the lake, staying in Swiss waters, but only just. Towns on the trip include **Melide**, from where you can take a cable car to **Carona**, and **Morcote**. Meals are served and the boat returns to Lugano at noon.

Midday cruise: this follows much the same route as the morning trip, but goes into Italy at **Porto Ceresio**, and calls in at a few ports on the southern part of the lake. There are two departures, the evening one being the **Sunset cruise**: meals are served in the restaurant, with a choice of menus. The midday departure is at 11.50 a.m., and the evening one 6.20 p.m. The excursion lasts about two hours.

Grand scenic cruise: this goes round the entire lake, but stays in the Swiss sector by skirting the northern shores on its way up to **Agno**. The journey takes two and a half hours and there is a commentary (in four languages) about the sights as they pass by. The departure is at 2.35p.m. and there are meals available in the restaurant.

The one-hour trip could be regarded as a service since it calls in at some of the smaller villages on the shores around the town. It stops at Paradiso, Casserate, Castagnola and Gandria.

The sailings only operate from April to October, and can be cancelled in bad weather.

If the idea of sailing around the lake on a few occasions appeals then it would be well worth buying a short-term sailing pass. They come in a variety of types: 1–7 days unlimited travel; 2–3 days unlimited travel; a single day, valid for any day within a 12-month period. Two trips would cover your costs.

Excursions From Lugano

Further afield from Lugano there are some good mountain excursions. **Mount Bre** and **San Salvadore** are both good vantage points and from the top of Mount Bre there are walks across to **Mount Boglia** and **Alpe Bolla**, both of which are slightly higher than Bre. You can also walk down to **Castagnola** or to **Gandria**.

Mount Lema is one of the highest mountains in the area at 1,624 m (5,328 ft) and from the summit you can see across the Valais Alps and the Grisons. The cable car operates from the small village of **Seggiovia**. Another mountain of similar size, at 1,704 m

*T*he valleys of the Ticino are dotted with clusters of stone cottages.

(5,591 ft) is **Mount Generosa**. On this there is a cog wheel railway running to the top, which gives good views over the three **lakes** of **Como**, **Lugano** and **Maggiore**. To take the railway, head south along the N2 to **Mendrisio**. Using public transport the best way is to take the boat to **Capolago**, and then the railway to the summit. Leaving Lugano at 10.00a.m. will have you on the mountain at 11.40a.m..

Both San Salvadore and Bre have rail routes to their summits which run every 15 minutes during the summer. There are also self-service cafés and picnic areas on the mountain tops.

There are so many places in the valleys that day excursions from the town make it an ideal base. Some of the churches and the old Ticino villages are really beautiful places to visit, while some of them are quite famous. At **Ponte Capriasca**, there is a copy of Leonardo da Vinci's *Last Supper*. The copy was made in 1547.

To the east of the town, towards the Italian border, there are plenty of places to visit, such as **Villa**, **Sonvico**, **Piandera** and **Certara**. At **Tesserete**, in the lower part of the valley, there are the the hillside villages at **Bigorio**. It is lovely country to explore, and there is no doubt that you will find some where fewer tourists go.

Across the valley, one of the most picturesque villages is **Arosia**, from where you can take the minor road to the Mt Lema cable car.

Flowers

One aspect which delights most visitors to this region, is the glorious floral wealth of the town. The time to see the best of Lugano's colour is between January and April. Christmas Roses, winter Jasmine, Forsythia, Mimosa, Camellias, Magnolias, Japonica, Azaleas, Rhododendrons and Cherry trees flower over the four-month period.

Cultural Events

Lugano is also a place for festivals and cultural events, to the extent that it even produces a leaflet detailing the events for each month. The most spectacular one is the **Lugano Festival**, held in August. There are musical festivals on a regular basis, and the styles vary from jazz and rock to classical and organ recitals. From April to September there are concerts nearly every week, featuring international artists. The leaflet available from the tourist office will give the information for the whole summer.

Accommodation

The variety of accommodation in Lugano is staggering. It has been developing as an all-year-round resort for over a century, so to a certain extent the tourist industry has become a major factor in the economy of the town.

Hotels

At the very top of the lists you will find no fewer than four five-star hotels, which are all around the 400 SFr mark. The hotels are the Hotel Eden, Principe Leopoldo, Splendide Royal and the Villa Castagnola. In the centre of the town there are plenty of good hotels with views over the lake.

One of the best value places is down at Castagnola. It's only about a ten-minute walk from the centre, so is nicely situated out of the town without being too far away. This is the Hotel Aniro, a three-star hotel, where you can have the benefits of a big, older hotel which was once a retreat of a Russian duke. Although there are not many of them left now (Russian dukes, that is) the hotel has retained a good atmosphere and a friendly service. It has a lovely position above the lake and the prices are very reasonable at around 130 SFr for a double in the high season.

Lugano is a less expensive resort than you might think, and if you are looking for a real bargain, then some of the inns/pensions give very good value. The Kipfer, which is in a street not far out of the town, is a classified inn, so it has to reach a reasonable (Swiss) standard, and the prices are the same in high or low season at about 25 SFr for a single or 50 SFr for a double. Switzerland does not have to be expensive, since this converts to roughly £10 per person.

Camping

The camping, as you would expect, is very attached to the lake, although there are a few sites up in the hills. If anything there are more sites towards the Locarno area, but the first listed is closest to Lugano. **Agno** has a few sites, about 8 km (5 miles) from the town. However, remember that Agno is where the airport is situated. Although it is not a large airport, used by the smaller aircraft of Crossair, the noise may become annoying if you are there for a while.

Agnuzzo Piodella di Agnuzzo: a four-star site in the region of the peninsula, about 20 minutes from Lugano.
Open: April–September.

Agno Tropical: only a two-star site, but it is close to the lakeside and has plenty of amenities close by.
Open: April–15 October.

Agno Golfo del Sole: a slightly higher grade site, on the lakeside.
Open until 30 October.

Agno Molinazzo: next to the water. A three-star site.
Open: 1 April–31 October.

Agno La Palma: another three-star site, with similar facilities to the others.
Open: April–October.

Agno Europampo: a higher grade site than the rest, right at the lakeside.
Open: 1 April–31 October.

All you need for a peaceful day's fishing can be found on the flat waters of Lake Maggiore, at Locarno.

Locarno

The other big centre, and equally well situated for both touring and as a centre is the town of **Locarno**. It is not as big as Lugano and does not have the same general aura, but it has a lot of style, and is near some of the wildest countryside of the Ticino. You reach Locarno by much the same route as Lugano, except that from **Bellinzona** take the right fork. The rail service to Locarno is as good as for Lugano, except that you change at Bellinzona. There are fewer direct routes to the town, and no international services going on to Italy.

The town is within a bay on **Lake Maggiore**, which Locarno shares to a great extent with Italy. The lake provides some of the activity in Locarno, but there is a quieter feel about this town. The **promenade** area and the town centre are quite small, and to walk from the centre to the very outskirts at Via Navegna takes only about 20 minutes. This walk is particularly easy going and relaxing, along a lane which few cars are allowed to use; those belonging to residents along the shore of the lake. Otherwise it is for pedestrians and cycles only.

Locarno is an excellent town for lovers of the outdoors who are perhaps less interested in water sport activities. Walking, cycling, and camping are at their best in this region of the Ticino.

Cycling

There is a lot of cycling in the town, and it would be good to hire a bike at the railway station for a day and follow the routes laid out in the cycling map provided by the tourist office.

Lake Excursions

The lake has a number of excursion vessels, and there are some direct service boats to Italy. The services run from the quays at the very centre of the promenade area. It would be difficult to miss them, but they are about opposite the Piazza Grande and the Rondinella hotel. The vessels are operated by Navigazione Lago Maggiore, Locarno, Tel: (093) 311865, Fax: (093) 313024, who have a mixture of old-style boats and hydrofoils. The routes generally go south into Italian waters, and anything past **Brissago** will be in Italy. This means that on most of the excursions you will need to take your passport with you, if only to come back into Switzerland.

On the regular services there are boats leaving Locarno throughout the day, starting at 8.25a.m. for **Brissago**

Maggiore to the Castles

So popular is cycling here that the tourist office have made a special plan/map for the tracks from **Bellinzona** to **Ascona**. It uses all the smaller lanes and keeps well away from the main roads and highways. The route is just under 32 km (20 miles), and although it is called "From Maggiore to the Castles" which refers to the three **castles** at Bellinzona, it is more likely that visitors would use only sections of it. The route signs are the standard Swiss white on dark red, with the cycle motif, and the route goes through some lovely small villages. Probably the most popular section is from one side of Locarno across to Ascona. This is about 14 km (8½ miles), and for most of the journey skirts the lake shore.

Like Lugano the flowers bloom early in Locarno, and one of the best places to view them is on the long promenade walk.

and 6.10a.m. for **Magadino,** on the opposite shores of the lake. The service to Italy leaves from 8.50a.m., and there are five sailings in the morning to **Stresa**, with just three in the afternoon. The fastest is the hydrofoil trip at 11.00a.m., which arrives in **Arona** at 12.55p.m..

For the pleasure trips, there are a number of round trips that take in some of the lakeside resorts and the small islands of the lake. **Isole di Brissago** is an island, lying south of Ascona, that is famed for its vegetation

and botanical park. The trip leaves Locarno at 9.15a.m., arriving at Isole di Brissago at 12.10p.m.. You can stay on the island for three hours and take the boat back at 3.45p.m., or to go over to **Isole Bella**, which takes another 40 minutes. The return boat arrives in Locarno at 6.30p.m., so this is a good day out, especially for those interested in gardens and botany, as well as a very pleasant boat ride.

There is an excursion trip across to **Luino**, on the southern side, which serves an Italian lunch. This is one of the old-style boats, with an equally old-style restaurant.

The Sights of Locarno

In the town there are a few old Italian buildings, set in wonderful parkland. They are quite spread out, but it is such a small town that an afternoon walk would take you to most of the sights. A good place to start is at the top of the hill, at **Madonna del Sasso**, which is also the terminus of the **funicular railway**. This is a 16th-century **church**, which has had a few additions in terms of its decoration. The frescoes and stucco work belong to the 17th-century, and there are some grand **religious paintings**, going back to the 1500s. From this high point of the town you have a panoramic view over the lake. It is only a short walk from here, down the winding **Via Monti della Trinita**, to the cluster of old buildings in the centre of the old town. The first is the 17th-century **church** of St Antonia, then further down is the **municipal building** and the **Castello Visconti**. This castle, again 15th century, has a **museum** of archaeology, with Roman and Romanesque findings. The castle itself is probably of greater interest, as are some of the unmentioned villas and castle-like buildings along the Villa Riva, on the way to Via Nevagna. In all it is a pleasant town to walk around, although for some strange reason there have been some recent additions to the town that owe little to Ticinese architecture.

In nearby **Ascona**, there are more interesting buildings, especially the **Collegio Papio**, which has 15th-century **frescoes** of some note.

The area between Ascona and Locarno has a good park, which includes tennis courts, an 18-hole golf course and a campsite. Unfortunately, this is also where the airstrip is located. However, it is unlikely that aircraft noise would bother you much, since Locarno airport is used even less than its neighbour over at Agno. Just over the Maggia River is the lido, more parkland and a walk to the centre of the town. Locarno's size is one of its great attractions; it is easy and relaxing to move from one area to another, usually along a picturesque promenade.

Out of Locarno

To get into the hills directly from Locarno you can take the funicular up to **Madonna del Sasso**, the cable car to the summit of **Cardada**, and subsequently the chair-lift to the top of **Cinetta**, at 1,617 m (5,305 ft). This is a good day out. To really enjoy the mountains, but not necessarily from a summit, there are the wild Ticino valleys nearby.

Forests of Switzerland

One of the most obvious features of the highlands of Switzerland is the enormous amount of forest: from about 1,500 m to 2,200 m (4,920 ft to 7,220 ft), effectively between the top of the agricultural land to the point where the mountain pasture begins. There are four main species of conifer in the Alpine regions, making up the vast majority of Switzerland's forest land. They are the Norway Spruce found on the north-facing slopes, along with the Spruce or Fir tree. In the Valais and the Grisons, the Larch is very prevalent, found on the higher, lighter slopes of the mountains. This is the only conifer to shed its leaves in winter and because of its lighter nature, the larch woods are good places for picnics. The curved branches seen in some of the forests are those of the Arolla Pine, which makes up the fourth species of conifer in the forest of Switzerland.

Valleys of Ticino

For keen walkers the valleys around Locarno are superb. There are three small roads which lead up into the deep gorges and ravines. One in particular attracts a lot of visitors because of its **bridge**, and for this reason it can become somewhat overcrowded. This is the **Val Verzasca**, and the road for this valley actually comes out of the small village of **Gordola**. It is well signposted, and there are PTT bus services going up and down the road all day. In the summer months, driving along this road can become something of a nightmare, especially on the stretches where it narrows to single car width. Some drivers will try anything to get through, and nationality doesn't come into it. However, the early part of the road is winding, and on the way up or later, on the way back, it's worth stopping to look at the huge dam wall of the **Sassello Hydro-electric Station**. Once you have reached the top of this road, you will see exactly what the dam is holding back—an impressive scene from the road. If you are really interested in this construction, then you can visit the station, and walk along the dam wall.

The road levels off from here, and some of the old Ticinese villages appear on the hillsides. Throughout these valleys there are rows of really old stone cottages and buildings which look as though they could collapse at

*O*f the two lakes in the region, Lake Maggiore, and Locarno offer a more relaxing atmosphere.

any moment, yet they have been there for many years. These villages are sometimes close to the road; others, like **Corripo**, sit perched on the edge of something—it is difficult to tell what. Whatever the size of the village the common factor is always the church. No matter if the village is hanging on to the most delicate precipice on the side on the mountain, the church will be there to remind you that you are very close to the holy ways of Italy. As you travel up through the valley, Corripo is on the left, although if you are driving it is easier to leave the car and walk up to this mountain village.

Val Verzasca

The main attraction of Verzasca is a curious double-arched **bridge**, across the river at **Ponti del Salti**. Most cars and coaches stop here, and it is remarkable that the bridge is still looking as good as it is, considering the numbers of tourists it takes. It is very narrow, with a low wall, so keep an eye on small children. Under the bridge is the most perfect aquamarine water, of considerable depth. At this point the river has slowed, and this has created a pool of deep water, where divers occasionally practise. The other feature of this place is the **geological formations** in the river. It is possible to get down to these smooth rocks, which sit in the centre of the river, almost as far as the small village nearby. There is a path by the side of the river, from where you can take a closer look at the grey boulders, and see the real depth of the water. It is a fascinating natural attraction, which seems to have suffered little from the thousands who visit the bridge every

Ponti del Salti is a favourite spot for visitors, and while the bridge is one attraction, the smooth eroded rock formations provide another.

year. Many tourists, especially those on the coaches, travel no further than Ponti del Sasso, but it is worth carrying on up the road, which goes on for another 14 km (8½ miles), through more of the Ticino villages of stone.

Some of the villages are well up together, and there is clearly a market

on how to book these places later in this section.

Eventually this road ends at **Sonogno**, but not before passing some raw scenery, with raging rivers, waterfalls, and remote mountain hamlets. This is a wonderful place for walkers, and again the organizational abilities of the Swiss come to the fore. As in all the regions of the country, there are the yellow *wanderweg* signs, showing the names of the villages and the estimated time for the walk. In some ways it is better to leave any transport you have back at Locarno, because you can take the bus to one part of the valley, walk alongside the river to another part and return on the bus. It is fine, easy walking country, where you can take a picnic by the river and feel well out of the way of things. In Switzerland you don't necessarily have to climb a mountain to be away from the crowd.

Maggio

It would be difficult to say which valley is more attractive than the other. Verzasca is probably the most popular; once past the arched bridges of **Ponti del Sasso** you are out in the wilds, but **Maggio**, the next valley along, west of Verzasca, also has its attractions. The road along the Maggio valley is considerably longer than the Verzasca, and at the very end there is a small track to a mountain **lake**. At **Cevio**, where the road splits to go to **Fusio** and to **Bosco Gurin** there are some beautiful **wall paintings** on the old buildings and a **museum** of Ticinese art. At a further turn-off, at **Bignasco**, the road goes to **Bavona**, where there is a cable car to take visitors to the

for converted cottages in this area. Many of the old places are now let as holiday accommodation, and it must be one of the most attractive areas to take a self-catering cottage in Switzerland. The prices can be high, and the accommodation can get booked up very quickly—there are more details

*D*eep into the Ticino, the River Verzasca provides the
route for walkers, cyclists and motorists to Sonogno.

heights of the **Robei** at 1,856 m (6,089 ft). It is but a short distance between this mountain and the **Nufen pass**. The mountain walk from this summit goes up to one of the most idyllic lakes to be found, **Lake Cristallina**. This is at a height of 2,568 m (8,425 ft), and from here the hiker can drop down into the Val Ticino, and the small villages of Ossasco and Fontana. This is a summer walk to remember, and it must beat driving up the N2.

The Centovalli

The last of the three valleys is the one you might use to travel through to **Domodossola**, in Italy, as a short cut across to Brig. It includes a separate valley which cuts away from the main road, and this is the **Pedemonte/Onsernone** region. This way will get you on to the main route for the Simplon pass, or the rail link to Brig from Bertonio. This valley, which you may like to explore from Locarno, reaches **Moneto**, before transferring to Italian soil. This is the **Centovalli**, and it is scattered with small mountain villages and Roman churches. It has a small lift from the village of **Intragna** up to **Costa Calezzo**. At the very end of the Swiss portion of the road, there is a very small **lake** and a track up to the hill village of **Bordei**. The Onsernone valley has a less dramatic look to it, and the hill villages look less dilapidated than some of the others in the Ticino. The valley at **Mosogno** is

*T*he Ticino stone *cottages are now being renovated to provide good accommodation for visitors to the area.*

very scenic, with towered churches sitting on terraced hillsides. The road heads north-west to end at **Vergaletto**. These roads are very narrow, although there is a PTT bus service here. **Russo** is a lovely old town, and it is from here that you can take the right fork to head up to Vergaletto. This is the most remote route of the Ticino valleys within reach of motor transport.

Accommodation in the Valleys

To stay in this area, rather than visit from Locarno, must appeal to those whose love is for walking and the mountains. There are campsites in **Gordevio** and **Avegno**, but what a pleasure it would be to have one of those rustic cottages in a Ticino village. The information for these places can be difficult to come by, and it does take some effort to find all the details. The best places to start looking are the mountain tourist offices:

Valle Maggia Information Office
CH-6673 Ticino
Switzerland.
Tel: (093) 871885.

Tenero e Valle Verzasca Information
 Office
CH-6598 Tenero
Switzerland.
Tel: (093) 671661.

You could also try the organizers of the mountain huts and cabins:

Villa Turrita
Casella Postale 1441
CH-6501 Bellinzona
Switzerland.
Tel: (092) 257056.

Finally, try the Locarno holiday apartments list, which includes a few Maggio and Verzasca properties.

Enete Turistico di Locarno e valli
Largo Zorzi
Casella Postale 372
CH-6601 Locarno
Switzerland.
Tel: (093) 310333; fax: (093) 319070.

Accommodation in Locarno

The same apartment list applies to the town, and most of the apartments are in the central area. It is a lengthy list, so there is plenty around. The alternative is to use Interhome (Twickenham, Britain); they have properties to rent, both rustic and modern, although few of them are in the remote places.

Hotels

There are plenty of good hotels in Locarno. Some of them follow the big, modern style, with balconies overlooking the lake. These are generally on the promenades, and a good example of such a hotel is the Hotel Reber Au Lac, a four-star place, which offers everything including its own swimming pool. This sort of accommodation is very acceptable, but I like to use the older, more traditional hotels. Only a 20-minute walk from the centre of town is such a hotel. It has a lakeside position, a very good restaurant, and the family who runs it could not be friendlier. This is the two-star Hotel Nevegna. For really inexpensive accommodation, you will find no better than the Pension Citta Vecchia, where a room will cost about 26 SFr per person.

Camping

Camping is very good in **Locarno**, with a site at either end of the town. None of the sites are that far from the town centre, so if arriving by rail, it is possible to walk to the sites.

Locarno Delta Camping: a superb five-star site, right on the lakeside, with its own beach area. There are also

T he farming life is simple in the Ticino, without any of the modern techniques found in larger farms in Switzerland.

Locarno's flower displays on the promenade last from early March through to late summer.

bungalows and caravans for hire.
Open: 17 March–21 October.

Ascona Segnale: a three-star site, at the other end of the bay, near the small town of Ascona. This is the site near the lido and the airfield.
Open: 1 April–31 October.

Towards the mountains and the **Maggio** valley there are three sites:

it will have most of the amenities needed. Some way into the Maggio valley, it has its own pool, and is close to the river.
Open: 1 April–31 October.

Cavigliano has just two sites at Losone:

Losone Riposo: a very simple one-star site, in a wooded area.
Open throughout the year.

Losone Zandone: a good camping area in a wooded region, this is a two-star site.
Open: 15 March–31 October.

Transport

Visitors who are intent on some serious walking, and who are using the public transport system, may think there would be difficulties in reaching the smaller villages in the valleys. Not so, for there are regular PTT buses to the end of each road. It is good to use these services to take you to, or bring you back from your walk. The services leave from Locarno.

To Verzasca, bus route 630.55, marked for Sonogno. The buses start at 7.35a.m., and then run at 10.15a.m. (Locarno FFS), 12.05p.m., 1.50p.m. (FFS), 4.05p.m., 4.55pm., 6.10p.m. and 6.35pm. This journey takes an hour and a half, but stops at all the small villages on the way.

To Maggio, bus route 10, marked Bignasco/Cavergno. This service then connects with a bus up to **Fusio**, and these leave every three hours from 5.40a.m. onwards. The full trip to Cavergno takes two hours and it's an extra 45 minutes to Fusio, so it is quite a long

Avegno Piccolo Paradiso: set in woodland, but close to the River Maggio, this is a three-star site.
Open: 17 March–21 October.

Gordevia Da Renato: a simple one-star site, which unusually has its own swimming pool.
Open: 15 March–31 October.

Gordevio Bellariva: a four-star site, so

*T*he Centovalli, en route *to Domodossola, is a less-visited region of the Ticino, but is none the less an interesting area full of deep ravines.*

way. The first bus leaves at 5.20a.m. and then 7.18a.m., 7.55a.m., 9.10a.m., 10.20a.m., 11.55a.m., 12.20p.m., 2.15p.m., 3.55p.m., 4.55p.m., 6.15p.m., 6.50p.m., and 11.30p.m..

These are the main services, and the ones most likely to interest visitors to the region, but there is a very extensive network of routes into all the nooks and crannies of this region.

For the longer distance bus traveller, there is a service across to **Domodossola** from Locarno, which is very useful if you want an alternative to the train, or would like to see some of the other parts of this region, including those in Italy. The express bus takes just under an hour and a half and leaves at 7.20a.m., 8.50a.m., 10.00a.m., 12.06p.m., 1.23p.m. and 2.53p.m.

Information to Help You Have a Good Trip

Switzerland has a system whereby no single department or organization holds all the information, at least not in any great detail. The national tourist offices are very helpful in giving general details, but if you want to know anything specific about a place, then you usually have to contact the more local people. This is good in some ways, but frustrating in others, and it is very rare for one office to give you information about a nearby attraction, if it does not fall within their "patch". After all, the idea is to encourage you to stay in their town, not pop off to some other location. Bear in mind also that, because of this competition, all the resorts claim to be better than the next—be it in height, sunshine hours, snowfall or whatever. The glossy brochures produced in Switzerland must make up a minor industry on their own as resort after resort tries to attract a greater number of tourists each year. Fortunately, most of the claims are justified, and in this sense, you could almost pick a brochure at random and not be disappointed when you get there.

To make life slightly easier, and to help you to reach the right offices quickly, here is a list of useful numbers and addresses:

National Tourist Offices

London
SNTO
Swiss Centre
New Coventry Street
London W1V 8EE.
Tel: (071) 7341921, fax: (071) 4374577.

New York
SNTO
Swiss Centre
608 Fifth Avenue
New York
NY 10020.
Tel: (212) 7575944, fax: (212) 2626116.

*P*ractically the whole of Switzerland can be seen from the central position held by Mt Pilatus, near Lucerne.

Sydney
SNTO
203–233 New South Head Road
PO Box 193
Edgecliff
Sydney
New South Wales 2027.
Tel: (02) 3261799, fax: (02) 3624032.

City Tourist Offices in Switzerland

Basel Tourist Office
Blumenrain 2
Schifflande
CH-4001.
Tel: (061) 2615050.

Bern Tourist Office
Railway Station
Bahnhofplatz
PO Box 3001
Bern.
Tel: (031) 227676, fax: (031) 210820.

Fribourg Tourist Office
Square des Places 1
CH-1700
Fribourg.
Tel: (037) 813175, fax: (037) 223527.

Geneva Tourist Office
Gare Cornavin
CH-1201
Geneva.
Tel: (022) 7385200.

Lausanne Tourist Office
2 Avenue de Rhodenie
Case Postale 248
CH-1000
Lausanne 6.
Tel: (021) 6171427,
fax: (021) 268847.

Lucerne Tourist Office
Frankenstrasse 1
CH-6003
Lucerne.
Tel: (041) 517171, fax: (041) 517334.

St Gallen Tourist Office
Bahnhofplatz 1a
CH-9001
St Gallen.
Tel: (071) 226262.

Schaffhausen Tourist Office
Vorstadt 12
CH-8201
Schaffhausen.
Tel: (053) 55141.

Zurich Tourist Office
Bahnhofplatz 15
CH-8023
Zurich.
Tel: (01) 2114000, fax: (01) 2120141.

The Bern and Zurich offices are particularly good; both are at the railway stations. You can collect information not only about their own city, but also basic details on most resorts in the country—it may only be a hotel list, but this can help if you hope to book a room in advance. Other large offices, which can help for their area are:

Appenzell Tourist Office
Hauptgasse
CH-9050
Appenzell.
Tel: (071) 874111, fax: (071) 871366.

Biel Tourist Office
CH-2501
Biel/Bienne.
Tel: (032) 227575.

Bernois Jura Tourist Office
Avenue de la Poste 26
Case Postale 127
CH-2740
Moutier.
Tel: (032) 936466, fax: (032) 936156.

Château d'Oex Tourist Office
CH-1837
Château d'Oex.
Tel: (029) 47788, fax: (029) 47789.

Interlaken Tourist Office
Hoheweg 37
CH-3800
Interlaken.
Tel: (036) 222121, fax: (036) 225221.

Liechtenstein National Tourist
  Office
PO Box 139
FL-9490
Vaduz
Liechtenstein.
Tel: (075) 21443, fax: (075) 20806.

Lugano Tourist Office
Riva Albertolli 5
CH-6901
Lugano.
Tel: (091) 214664, fax: (091) 227653.

Morat/Murten Tourist Office
Schlossgasse 5
CH-3280
Murten.
Tel: (037) 715112.

Neuchâtel Tourist Office
Rue de la Place d'Arnes 7
CH-2001
Neuchâtel.
Tel: (038) 254242, fax: (038) 242852.

St Moritz Tourist Office
CH-7500
St Moritz.
Tel: (082) 33147, fax: (082) 32952.

Yverdon-les-Bains Tourist Office
Place Pestalozzi
CH-1400
Yverdon-les-Bains.
Tel: (024) 210121.

Most of these offices will have information on nearby attractions, so Lugano will be able to help with Locarno and vice versa, but you will probably have to ask. There is strong competition between areas. However, some places are so "out on their own" that information would have to come from them directly. They are:

Crans Montana Tourist Office
CH-3962
Montana.
Tel: (027) 413041, fax: (027) 417460.

Leysin Tourist Office
Case Postale 100
CH-1854
Leysin.
Tel: (025) 342244, fax: (025) 341616.

Saas Fee Tourist Office
CH-3906
Saas Fee.
Tel: (028) 571457, fax: (028) 571860.

Verbier Tourist Office
CH-1936
Verbier.
Tel: (026) 316222, fax: (026) 313272.

Youth Hostels, Campsites and Student Accommodation

These are important places to know about if you are on a low-cost trip, and although each individual office will have lists, it is useful to have the information put out by the national organizers.

Swiss Camping Association
Im Sydefadeli 40
CH-8037
Zurich.
Tel: (01) 445713.

Swiss Camping and Caravanning Federation
Habsburgerstrasse 35
CH-6004
Lucerne.
Tel: (041) 234822.

Youth Hostel Association
Engestrasse 9
CH-3012
Bern.
Tel: (031) 245503.

Farmhouse Accommodation

Swiss Farmers Association
CH-5200
Brigg.
Tel: (056) 423277.

Motoring Organizations

Automobile Club der Schweiz
Wasserwerkgasse 39
CH-3001
Bern 13.
Tel: (031) 224722.

Touring Club der Schweiz
Rue Pierre Fatio 9
CH-1211
Geneva.
Tel: (022) 371212.

Shipping Companies

The lakes of Switzerland offer a good alternative transport system in the country, so the following is a list of the shipping companies on the major lakes:

Geneva
Compagnie Générale de Navigation
  sur le Lac Léman
17 avenue de Rhodenie
Case Postale 252
CH-1000
Lausanne 6.
Tel: (021) 6170666, fax: (021) 6170465.

Locarno
Navigazione Lago Maggiore
Ch-6600
Locarno.
Tel: (093) 311865, fax: (093) 313024.

Lugano
Société Navigazione del Lago di
  Lugano
Casella Postale 56
CH-6906
Lugano 6.
Tel: (091) 515223.

Neuchâtel/Morat/Biel
Société de Navigation sur les Lacs
  de Neuchâtel et Morat SA
Case Postale 1460
CH-2001
Neuchâtel.
Tel: (038) 254012, fax: (038) 247961.

Zurichsee
Zurichsee Schiffartegesellschaft
CH-8038
Zurich.
Tel: (01) 4821033.

The Right Place at the Right Price

Hotels

To help you choose a hotel, the following is a selection based on the criteria of price, attraction and location.

The star rating of each hotel is indicated by 1*, 2*, 3*, 4* and 5*. The cost of staying at each hotel is indicated by reference to one of three scale bands, with **E** (expensive) for 200–800 SFr, **M** (medium) for 75–200 SFr and **I** (inexpensive) for 30–75 SFr. In Switzerland, prices are usually given per room except in some city hotels where they are given per person.

Appenzell

Hotel Lowen　　　3*　E
Appenzell
Tel: (071) 872187
Very much in the centre of things, the hotel also has its own shop, hairdresser and sauna. Restaurant.

Hotel Adler　　　2*　M
CH-9050
Appenzell
Tel: (071) 871389 and 872377
Central position.

Basel

Drie Konige am Rhein　5*　E
Blumrein 8
CH-4001
Basel
Tel: (061) 255252,
fax: (061) 255153
One of Europe's finest (and oldest) inns, with an historic guest book. Expensive, but you may be staying in the same room as Napoleon did. Restaurant

Merian am Rhein　　4*　E
Rheingasse 2
CH-4058
Basel
Tel: (061) 681 0000,
fax: (061) 681 1101
On the opposite bank of the river to the Drie Konige, a superb building with an elegant air. Sixty-three rooms and suites.

Krafft am Rhein　　3*　M
Rheingasse 12
CH-4058
Basel
Tel: (061) 6918877
A good traditional hostelry with plenty of character, right on the river. A lively restaurant and bar on street level.

Bristol　　　　　2*　I
Central Bahnstrasse 15
CH-4051
Basel
Tel: (061) 223822,
fax: (061) 223845
A good hotel for a quick getaway from the rail station. Not particularly exciting but reasonably priced.

Bern

Bellevue Palace　　5*　E
Kochergasse 3–5
Bern
Tel: (031) 224581,
fax: (031) 224743
Next door to the federal building, and one of the grandest hotels in the country.

Kruez　　　　　3*　M
Zeuhausgasse 41
Bern
Tel: (031) 221162,
fax: (031) 223747
Situated in a good position, in the old section of town.

Goldener Schlussel　2*　I
Rathausgasse 72
Bern
Tel: (031) 220216,
fax: (031) 225688
A fairly central position, but not in the centre of the town.

Biel/Bienne

Hotel Schloss
Hauptstrasse
Biel
One of the more traditional hotels of the town.

Hotel Elite　　　4*　E
14 Rue de la Gare
CH-2501
Biel/Bienne
Tel: (032) 225441,
fax: (032) 221383
A typically modern hotel of which there are many in Biel.

Château d'Oex

Hotel la Rocaille　　4*　E
Château d'Oex
Tel: (029) 46215, fax (029) 45249
One of the smarter hotels of the village, with plenty of room.

Hotel Ermitage　　3*　M
Château d'Oex
Tel: (029) 46003, fax: (029) 45076
A favourite with the balloonists, and a good atmosphere in its café/bar.

Hotel Richemont 3* M–E
Château d'Oex
Tel: (029) 45252/3/4
Central, medium-grade hotel.

Hotel de la Gare I
Château d'Oex
Tel: (029) 47717
At the rail station, the cheaper alternative.

Chur

Hotel Freieck 3* M
Reichsgasse 50
Chur
Tel: (081) 221792

Hotel Stern 3* M
Reichsgasse 11
Chur
Tel: (081) 223555,
fax (081) 221915
Located at the entrance to the ancient part of the city. Restaurant.

Crans-Montana

Du Golf and Des Sports 5* E
Avenue le Bonvin
Crans
Tel: (027) 414242,
fax: (027) 419758
At the edge of the golf courses, or th bottom of the ski slope, depending on the season. Big, modern complex, with all facilities. Restaurants.

Hotel Elite 3* M
Crans
Tel: (029) 414301,
fax: (029) 412421
A small hotel in the quieter part of the town.

Pension Monte-Sano 1* I
Avenue Mt Bovin
Montana
Tel: (029) 412427

Elm

Sardonna 4* E
Elm
Tel: (058) 861886
At the end of the village, a new hotel with plenty of rooms and a small swimming pool. Restaurant.

Elmer 3* M
Elm
Tel: (058) 861786
Situated in the centre of the village this hotel offers more traditional comforts.

Fribourg

Au Parc 4* E
Fribourg
Tel: (037) 821111,
fax: (037) 242526
The largest hotel in Fribourg, with 140 beds.

Elite 3* M
Fribourg
Tel: (037) 223836,
fax: (037) 224036
Reasonable rates, with restaurant/bar.

Rose 3* M
Fribourg
Tel: (037) 224607,
fax: (037) 223566
Another mid-range hotel with good rates.

Jura 1* I
Fribourg
Tel: (037) 263228
A small, but cheap hotel with basic facilities.

Geneva

Bristol 5* E
8 rue du Mt Blanc
1201 Geneva
Tel: (022) 7323800,
fax: (022) 7321989
In the main street of the city. You are likely to meet a few diplomats here.

Mon Repos 3* M
131 rue de Lausanne
1202 Geneve
Tel: (022) 7328010,
fax: (022) 7328595
A good-looking hotel in a central position, with prices reasonable for Geneva.

Strasbourg-Univers 3* M
10 rue Pradier
1201 Geneva
Tel: (022) 7322562,
fax (022) 7384208
One-hundred-bed hotel in a very central position.

Etoile 2* I
17 Vieux-Grenadiers
1205 Geneva
Tel: (022) 287208
In the quieter part of the city, but with only 40 beds. Good prices.

Pax 2* I
68 rue du 31 Decembre
1207 Geneva

Tel: (022) 7354440
In the best shopping area of the city, not far from the fountain. Seventy beds at reasonable rates.

Giswil

Hotel Bahnhof Giswil I
CH-6074
Giswil
Tel: (041) 681161
Just opposite the railway station, big, clean victorian rooms and a lively restaurant/bar. Also at rear of hotel are a group of apartments for rent.

Glarus (Glarnerland)

Glarnerhof 3* M
Glarus
Tel: (058) 631191
Restaurant and centrally situated hotel. Caters largely for business users.

Rossli 2* I
Glarus
Tel: (058) 611646
A cheaper alternative if accommodation is difficult during the Landsgemeinde.

Gottlieben (Nr. Konstanz)

Drachenburg Hotel M-E
CH-8274
Gottlieben
Tel: (072) 691414
An historic inn, featuring domed oriel windows. The hotel and restaurant is just by the Rhine.

Grindelwald

Hotel Belvedere 4* E
Tel: (036) 545434
A quality hotel with excellent views.

Eiger-Hostellerie 4* E
Tel: (036) 532121
A fairly expensive hotel in the centre of the village.

Interlaken

Grand Hotel Beau Rivage 5* E
CH-3800
Interlaken
Tel: (036) 216272,
fax: (036) 232847
The other top-class hotel, although only 170 beds. Swimming pool, fitness room.

Grand-Hotel
Victoria–Jungfrau 5* E
CH-3800
Interlaken
Tel: (036) 222671,
fax: (036) 222671
Magnificent building near the
casino. 400 beds with its own pool.

Beau-Site 3* M
CH-3800
Interlaken
Tel: (036) 228181,
fax: (036) 232926
A traditional Alpine hotel in a
good position. Eighty beds.

Splendid 3* M
CH-3800
Interlaken
Tel: (036) 227612,
fax: (036) 227679
A true tourist hotel in the centre,
but with some inexpensive rooms.
Sixty beds.

Waldhotel Unspunnen 1* I
CH-3800
Interlaken
Tel: (036) 223491,
fax: (036) 232260
Surprisingly big for a 1-star hotel
with 56 beds. On the edge of
town, near the Rugen woods.

Balmers Herberge I
CH-3800
Interlaken
Tel: (036) 221961,
fax: (036) 233261
In the area called Matten this
hostelry offers good-quality
dormitory accommodation. Take
the bus to the ice rink.

Leysin
Leysin-Parc 4* E
Leysin
Tel: (025) 342034,
fax: (025) 342011
A good high position for this 96-
room hotel. Block-like in
appearance, but has very good
amenities.

La Tour d'Ai 3* M
Leysin
Tel: (025) 341120,
fax: (025) 342132
A rather severe hotel; more of the
traditional style. Forty rooms with
most of the usual facilities.

Locarno
Reber au Lac 4* E
Burbaglio
Locarno
Tel: (093) 330202,
fax: (093) 337981
A lovely setting on the lake, with
its own jetty. Swimming, tennis.
140 rooms. Restaurant.

Beau-Rivage 3* M
Via Viale Verbno
Locarno
Tel: (093) 331355,
fax: (093) 315308
A 90-room hotel on the lake
promenade. Terrace restaurant.

Navegna 2* M
Via Navegna
Locarno
Tel: (093) 332222,
fax: (093) 333150
Quiet hotel, about 10-minute walk
from centre. Good restaurant and
managed by friendly owner. Lake
position. Thirty rooms.
Restaurant.

Campagna 1* I
Via Rivaplana
Locarno
Tel: (093) 332054
On a quiet road between Navegna
and the centre. A 20-room hotel,
about 5 minutes from the lake.

Lausanne
Beau-Rivage Palace 5* E
Quai d'Ouchy
Lausanne
Tel: (021) 6171717,
fax: (021) 6177878
A top-class hotel situated right on
the promenade at Ouchy. 204
rooms plus gardens, swimming
pool, fitness etc. Restaurant.

Hotel de la Paix 4* E
5 avenue Benjamin-Constant
CH-3013
Lausanne
Tel: (021) 207171,
fax: (021) 230207
Another grand hotel dating back
to 1910 with 116 rooms, in the
town centre. Restaurant.

Belle Rive 3* E
Avenue de Cour
Lausanne
Tel: (021) 269633,
fax: (021) 6173129
Eighty rooms in a quiet position
just on the edge of town.

Prés-Lac 2* M
Avenue Général Guisan
Lausanne
Tel: (021) 284901,
fax: (021) 260661
At the Pully side of town, near the
lake. Seventy rooms with good
amenities for a two-star hotel.

Hotel du Marché 1* I
Rue Pre du Marché
Lausanne
Tel: (021) 379900,
fax: (021) 364723
A good cheaper hotel to the back
of the town. Thirty-five rooms
with televisions.

Lucerne
Schweizerhof 5* E
Schweizerhof Quai 3
Lucerne
Tel: (041) 502211,
fax: (041) 512971
The best position in Lucerne and
one of the finest hotels in the
country. 214 beds with most
facilities.

Des Alpes 3* M
Rathausquai 5
Lucerne
Tel: (04)1 515825,
fax: (041) 517451
An average three-star hotel in
amongst the centre of the old
town. Eighty beds.

Park 3* M
Morgartenstrasse 13
Lucerne
Tel: (041) 239232,
fax: (041) 233069
Close to the station and the
information office, and around the
corner from some good shops.

Hammer 2* I
Eigenthal
6013 Lucerne
Tel: (041) 971287,
fax: (041) 971387
Some way out of town towards
Interlaken but lower costs at this
small two-star hotel.

Lugano
Villa Castagnola au Lac 5* E
Viale Castagnola
Lugano
Tel: (091) 512213,
fax: (091) 527271
Just outside the town, in a lovely
position; a 120-bed quality hotel.

Conca d'Oro au Lac 3* M
Riva Paradiso 7
6902 Paradiso
Lugano
Tel: (091) 543131
In a great position on the lake, near one of the Lido's. Seventy-two beds.

Dischma 3* M
6 Via G Cattori
Lugano
Tel: (091) 542131
A cheaper hotel in the Paradiso area of town.

Lugano–Castagnola

Aniro 3* M
Via Violetta
Lugano 6976
Tel: (091) 525031
Once the home of a Russian Duke, the hotel has terrific views. Sixty rooms.

Rosa 2* I
2/4 Via Landriani
Lugano
Tel: (091) 229286
Central position, with 57 inexpensive rooms.

Montreux

Hotel Eden au Lac 4* E
Rue de Théâtre 11
Montreux
Tel: (021) 9635551
Typical swish Montreux hotel with terrace restaurant.

Murten/Morat

Le Vieux Manor 4* E
Lausanne Strasse
Mayriez
Nr Murten/Morat
Tel: (037) 711283,
fax: (037) 713188
A superb-looking hotel in its own gardens, on the lake shore. All rooms beautifully decorated. Restaurant.

Hotel Krone 3* M
Rathausgasse
Murten/Morat
Tel: (037) 715252,
fax: (037) 713610
In the town centre, a well-kept hotel with 65 beds. Terrace restaurant looks out to the lake.

Murtenhof 3* M
Rathausgasse
Murten/Morat
Tel: (037) 715656,
fax: (037) 715059
Next door to the castle, so within the old city walls. Apartments are also available in this good hotel.

Bahnhof I
Bahnhofstrasse
Murten/Morat
Tel: (037) 712256
At the railway station, a less expensive place to stay in Murten, but not many rooms (13 beds). Restaurant.

Neuchâtel

Beaulac 4* E
Quai Leopold-Robert
Neuchâtel
Tel: (038) 258822,
fax: (038) 256035
Possibly the best in Neuchâtel, boasting views over the lake to the Alps. Ninety-two beds. On the lake side.

Beaux-Arts 2* M
Rue Pourtales
Neuchâtel
Tel: (038) 240151
Just a few minutes from the harbour area, a smaller hotel of about 30 rooms.

Marché I
Place des Halles 4
Neuchâtel
Tel: (038) 245800
Situated in the real heart of the city, at the place des Halles. Not star rated but plenty of atmosphere. Twenty rooms. Closed on Sundays. Restaurant.

St Gallen

Einstein 4* E
Bernegstrasse 2
9001 St Gallen
Tel: (071) 200033,
fax: (071) 235474
On the perimeter of the old town, near the cathedral. An elegant hotel, but quite pricey.

Hecht 3* M
Bohl 1
St Gallen
At the corner of the Markplatz so a good position to see the nearby old town and cathedral.

St Johan

Rossli 3* M
CH-9656
St Johan
Tel: (074) 52460
An older imposing building in the centre of the village, with 36 beds.

St Moritz

Hotel Corvatsch 3* M
Via Tegiatscha 1
St Moritz
Tel: (082) 37475
A good hotel, but as with all hotels here prices are high. Down by the lake, which in winter attracts the racing fraternity. Good big restaurant/café.

Soldanella 3* M
Via Somplatz 17
CH-7500
St Moritz
Tel: (082) 33651, fax: (082) 32337
A good hotel, with a superb restaurant. Quite expensive but all these hotels are.

Saas Fee

Ambassador 4* E
CH-3906
Saas Fee
Tel: (028) 571420,
fax: (028) 573420
Forty-room chalet-style hotel with swimming pool. Next to ski-lifts and sports area.

Au Chalet Cairn 3* M
CH-3906
Saas Fee
Tel: (028) 571550,
fax: (028) 573380
Good position for winter sports, with good restaurant. 32 beds.

Hotel Sonnehof 3* M
CH-3906
Saas Fee
Tel: (028) 572393,
fax: (028) 571370
Family hotel with good views of the mountains. Forty beds. Restaurant.

Waldesruh 2* I
CH-3906
Saas Fee
Tel: (0280) 572295,
fax: (028) 571447
Very close to the sports centre on the edge of the village. Fifty rooms at reasonable rates.

Schaffhausen

Rheinhotel Fischerzunft 3* E
Rheinquai 8
Schaffhausen 8200
Tel: (053) 253281,
fax: (053) 243285
Just 8 rooms in this river-side hotel, but also 3 apartments. Oriental cuisine.

Kronenhof 3* M
Vordergasse
Schaffhausen
Tel: (053) 256631
In the centre of the city, amongst the old section. Fifty-four beds.

Schweizerbund I
Hallau
Nr Schaffhausen
Tel: (053) 612044
Low-cost accommodation in this wine-producing village. Hotel/inn. Sixteen beds.

Steinbock I
Webergasse
Schaffhausen
Tel: (053) 254260
Quite close to the railway station, this small 10-room hotel has inexpensive rates, which do not include breakfast.

Solothurn

Hotel Krone 4* M
Hauptgasse 64
Tel: (065) 224412
Well situated in the centre of town, and convenient for the sights. Restaurant.

Stein am Rhein

Hotel Adler 3* M
Rathausplatz
Tel: (054) 426161
Historic inn, with some of the finest frescoes on its walls. Plenty of rooms, but some are in modern extension to rear.

Unterwasser

Santis 3* M
CH-9657
Unterwasser
Tel: (074) 52424, fax: (074) 53474
Alpine-style hotel with 64 beds. Situated between Wildhaus and Unterwasser.

Vaduz (Liechtenstein)

Parkhotel Sonnenhof 4* E
Mareestrasse 29
FL-9490
Vaduz
Tel: (075) 21192, fax: (075) 20053
One of Liechtenstein's smartest hotels, this is also the largest in Vaduz with 29 rooms. Indoor pool and all facilities.

Hotel Au Premiea 3* M
Staedtle 21
FL-9490
Vaduz
Tel: (075) 22222, fax: (075) 20891
Just 11 rooms, but a good range of facilities.

Verbier

Rosalp 4* E
Medran
Verbier
Tel: (026) 316323,
fax: (026) 311059
One of the better hotels, with a fine restaurant. Fifty beds and on the road up to the lifts.

Au Vieux-Valais 3* M
Route de Verbier
Verbier
Tel: (026) 316955,
fax: (026) 315115
A small hotel on the lower part of the village. Good for the sports centre. Twenty beds.

Rosa Blanche 2* I
Rue Barmettaz
Verbier
Tel: (026) 311472,
fax: (026) 312712
Quite large, but reasonable prices, with some basic rooms. Close to the village centre.

Wildhaus

Hotel Sonne 3* M
CH-9658
Wildhaus
Tel: (074) 52333,
fax: (074) 52357
A family hotel near the church. Good facilities at reasonable rates.

Zermatt

Mont Cervin 5* E
Zermatt
Tel: (028) 661100,
fax: (028) 674842
One of the grandest hotels in the country, with all facilities.

Parnass 3* M
Zermatt
Tel: (028) 672496,
fax: (028) 674557
A smaller 50-bed hotel next to the river.

Alpina 2* M
Zermatt
Tel: (028) 671050,
fax: (028) 672865
Very reasonably priced. Hotel with cheaper 'no shower' rooms.

Mischabel 1* I
Zermatt
Tel: (028) 671131
Close to the centre of town, but in a quiet position. Fifty-five beds.

Zuoz

Hotel Crusch Alva 3* M
CH-7524
Zuoz
Tel: (082) 71319, fax: (082) 72459
In the village square, cannot be missed with the crests on the facade. A 300-year-old inn with 23 beds.

Hotel Klarer 3* M
CH-7524
Zuoz
Tel: (082) 71321, fax: (082) 71214
An old Engadine farmhouse, beautifully decorated. Some simple rooms at reasonable prices. Café/ delicatessen and restaurant.

Zurich

Eden au Lac 5* E
Utoquai 45
8023 Zurich
Tel: (01) 2619404,
fax: (01) 2619409
Stylish, grand hotel near the lake, but one of the smaller of this type. 75 beds.

Franzikaner 3* M
Niederdorfstrasse
8001 Zurich
Tel: (01) 2520121,
fax: (01) 816431
A popular hotel in the centre of old Zurich. Good prices for this expensive city.

Schifflande 3* M
Schifflande 18
CH-8001 Zurich
Tel: (01) 2624050,
fax: (01) 2624367
Forty-bed hotel in a quiet area.

Grape I
Dorf 20
Herlliberg
Nr. Zurich
Tel: (01) 9152611
In the village (directions from the shore road); a family hotel with a good restaurant. 30 minutes from the city.

Restaurants Specializing in Swiss Cuisine

Appenzell
Restaurant Baumli
Tel: (071) 871249
Specializing in cheese fondue. Closed Mondays and Tuesdays.

Hotel Hecht
Tel: (071) 871025
Fondue/steak.

Basel
Restaurant Schlussel Zunft
Freistrasse 25
Tel: (061) 252046
Fondue. Closed Sundays.

Restaurant Steinbock
19 Centralbahn Strasse
Tel: (061) 2715846
Cheese fondue. Closed Sundays.

Bern
Restaurant Börse
Barenplatz
Tel: (031) 226945
Fondue.

Restaurant Schmeidstube
Zeughausgasse 5
Tel: (031) 223461
Steak.

Taverne Valaisanne
Genfergasse 1
Tel: (031) 227766
Fondue/raclette.

Chur
Restaurant Zum Acten Zollhaus
Malixerstrasse 1
Tel: (081) 221656
Fondue.

Davos Platz
Bistro Gentiana
Promenade 53
Tel: (083) 35649

Disentis
Hotel Bellavista
Tel: (086) 75273
Fondue.

Erlach
Hotel Erle
Tel: (032) 881108
Fondue/raclette.

Fribourg
Restaurant de l'Aigle Noir
Rue des Alpes
Tel: (037) 224977
Gruyère cheese quiche. Closed Sunday evenings and all day Mondays.

Café du Midi
Rue de Romont 25
Tel: (037) 223133
Fondue and truffles.Closed Mondays.

Geneva
Restaurant la Cave
Valaisanne et Chalet Suisse
Place du Cirque
Tel: (022) 281236
Steaks/cheese/raclette.

Restaurant du Platane
91 Boulevard de la Cluse
Tel: (022) 297198
Steak/cheese. Closed Saturday evenings and Sundays.

Café du Soleil
Place Petit Saconnex
Tel: (022) 7333417
Malakoff. Closed Sunday evenings.

Glarus
Hotel Rössli
Glarnischstrasse 12
Tel: (058) 611646
Fondue. Closed Wednesdays.

Grandson
Hotel du Lac
Rue Basse 36
Tel: (024) 243870
Cheese croûtes. Closed Thursday.

Grindelwald
Hotel Kirchbühl
Tel: (036) 53355
Raclette.

Gasthaus Marmorbruch
Tel: (036) 531318
Fondue, toast "marmorbruch". Closed Mondays.

Gruyères
Restaurant le Châlet
Tel: (029) 62154
Fondue/raclette.

Hotel Fleur de Lys
Tel: (029) 62108
Gruyère quiche, fondue.

Gstaad
Hotel Bernerhof
Beim Bahnhof
Tel: (030) 83366
Raclette.

Restaurant Chesery
Lauenenstrasse
Tel: (030) 42451
Cheese.

Interlaken
Hotel Bahnhof
Bahnhofstrasse 37
Tel: (036) 227041
Käseschnitten.

Restaurant le Petit-Casino
Höheweg
Tel: (036) 222521
Winter fondue.

Trattoria Toscana
Jungfraustrasse 19
Tel: (036) 222551
Italian/Swiss.

Klosters
Hotel Piz Buin
Tel: (083) 48111
Raclette.

Lausanne
Restaurant Cave Valaisanne
9 rue St Laurent
Tel: (021) 3122312
Cheese, croûte.

Café Lyrique
29 rue Beau-Séjour
Tel: (021) 206192
Fondue, cheese, croûte. Closed Sundays.

Restaurant Pinte Besson
4 Rue de l'Ale
Tel: (021) 3127227
Fondue. Closed Sundays.

Leukerbad
Hotel Ghrichting and Badnerhof
Tel: (027) 611227
Raclette.

Locarno
Albergo Reber au Lac
Viale Verbano 55
Tel: (093) 330202
Soufflé.

Lugano
Ristorante Gambrinus
Piazza Riforma
Tel: (091) 231955
Italian/Swiss cuisine.

Ristorante Orologio
Via Nizzola 2
Tel: (091) 232338
Italian/Swiss cuisine.

Lucerne
Restaurant Fritschi
Sternenplatz 5
Tel: (041) 511615
Raclette and fondue.

Restaurant Walliser Kanne
Burgerstrasse 3
Tel: (041) 231666
Crêpes. Closed Sunday mornings.

Montreux
Café du Grill "Chez Stella"
Grand-Chêne 8
Tel: (021) 9634265
*Croûtes. Closed Saturday evenings
and Sundays.*

Restaurant Caveau du Museum
Rue de la Gare 40
Tel: (021) 9631662
*Fondue. Open evenings only.
Closed Sundays.*

Murten/Morat
Restaurant Eintracht
Hauptgasse
Tel: (037) 712240
Fondue. Closed Wednesdays.

Hotel Schiff
Schiffstation
General Swiss cuisine.
Tel: (037) 712701

Neuchâtel
Buffet de la Gare CFF
Place de la Gare
General Swiss cuisine.
Tel: (038) 254853

Restaurant Pinte de Pierre-à-Bot
Route de Pierre à Bot 106
Tel: (038) 253380
*Fondue. Closed Saturday evenings
and Sundays.*

Payerne
Café du Marché "Chez Josy"
Place du Marché 20
Tel: (037) 616289
Fribourg fondue. Closed Sundays.

St Gallen
Fondue-Beizli Neveck
Bruhlgasse 26
Tel: (071) 224344
Fondue/raclette.

Saas Fee
Restaurant Arvu-Stuba
Tel: (028) 572747
Fondue/raclette.

Restaurant de la Gorge
Tel: (028) 572641
Raclette/omelette.

Schaffhausen
Hotel Hirschen Herblingen
Schlossstrasse 20
Tel: (053) 332323
*Kasewagen. Closed Sundays and
Mondays.*

Stein am Rhein
Restaurant Klosterstübli
Rhigass
Tel: (054) 412292
*Fondue. Closed Wednesday
evenings and Thursday mornings.*

Restaurant Sonne
Rathausplatz
Tel: (054) 412128
Fondue. Closed Thursdays.

Thun
Gasthof zur Lauenen
Goldiwilstrasse 30
Tel: (033) 222635
*Fondue. Closed Tuesdays and
Wednesdays.*

Restaurant Walliserkanne
Marktgasse 3
Tel: (033) 229414
*Fondue. Closed Sundays and
Monday mornings.*

Unterwasser
Hotel Wäldli
Tel: (074) 51214
Fondue, kaseschnitte "Wäldli".

Verbier
Restaurant le Caveau
Tel: (026) 312266
Fondue/raclette.

Weggis
Restaurant "Chez André"
Friedheimstrasse
Tel: (041) 931341

Post Hotel
Seestrasse
Tel: (041) 932323
Fondue.

Wildhaus
Hotel Alpenrose
Schwendi
Tel: (074) 52121
Fondue/pork.

Zermatt

Hotel Butterfly
Tel: (028) 673721
Crêpes/fondue.

Restaurant Otto Furrer-Stube
(Hotel Seilerhaus)
Tel: (028) 673520
Fondue/raclette. Open evenings only.

Zug

Gasthaus Linde
Aegeristrasse 1
Tel: (042) 210941
Fondue. Closed Saturdays and Sundays.

Zuoz

Hotel Crusch Alva
Tel: (082) 71319
Varied meals.

Restaurant Klarer
Tel: (082) 71321
Varied meals.

Zurich

Restaurant Belvoirpark
Seestrasse 125
Tel: (01) 2021054
Closed Sundays and Mondays.

Restaurant Chalet
Gasometer Strasse 36
Tel: (01) 2712390
Fondue. Closed Saturdays.

Restaurant Chez Max
Seestrasse 53
Zollikon (Nr Zurich)
Tel: (01) 3918877
Fish and seasonal specialities.

Restaurant Fribourger-Stubli
Rotwand Strasse 38
Tel: (01) 2419076
Fondue.

Restaurant Klosbachli
Klosbach Strasse 39
Tel: (01) 2512958
Raclette.

Index

INDEX